A New Leaf
3

Also by Jim Gold

Books
Songs and Stories for Open Ears

Handfuls of Air: A Book of Modern Folk Tales

*Mad Shoes: The Adventures of Sylvan Woods:
From Bronx Violinist to Bulgarian Folk Dancer*

Crusader Tours and Other Stories

Recordings
World of Guitar

American Folk Ballads

A New Leaf

3

Adventures in the Creative Life

Jim Gold

Full Court Press
Englewood Cliffs, New Jersey

First Edition

Copyright © 2003 by Jim Gold

All rights reserved. No part of this book may be reproduced or transmitted in any form or by any means electronic or mechanical, including by photocopying, by recording, or by any information storage and retrieval system, without the express permission of the author, except where permitted by law.

Published in the United States of America
by Full Court Press, 601 Palisade Avenue,
Englewood Cliffs, NJ 07632
fullcourtpress.com

ISBN 978-0-9709477-2-7
Library of Congress Control Number: 2020904310

Editing and book design by Barry Sheinkopf

Table Of Contents

January–March 1997

Life, *1*
Money And Its Brethren, *5*
Performance, *8*
Business, *12*
Inventions, *17*
God, *18*

April–June 1997

Writing, *25*
Languages, *29*
Life, *31*
Performance, *47*
Business, *50*
God, *74*

July–September 1997

Writing, *77*
Languages, *81*
Life, *82*
Performance, *93*
Business, *94*
Inventions, *120*

October–December 1997

Writing, *127*
Languages, *130*
Life, *130*
Money And Its Brethren, *155*
Performance, *155*
Business, *160*
Inventions, *162*
God, *167*

January–June 1998

Writing, *173*
Languages, *176*
Life, *178*
Performance, *192*
Business, *195*
Inventions, *205*

July–September 1998

Writing, *213*
Life, *214*
Performance, *223*
Business, *227*
Inventions, *231*
God, *232*

October–December 1998

Writing, *239*
Languages, *240*
Life, *241*
Performance, *251*
Business, *253*
Inventions, *256*
God, *265*

January–March 1997

LIFE

New Yoga Warm-Up Method

I am inventing a new way of doing yoga and guitar playing warm-ups. I start right away with a slow-to-very-slow exercise to the sun (maybe even doing it only once!). I focus intensely on every muscle I use. In this manner, I use my mind to help my body "warm-up" more quickly.

My mind does not have to get warmed up. I don't have to worry about pulling, overstretching, or injuring any mind muscles by using them at full capacity right away.

Body follows mind. I can "warm up" my body by focusing on each part and creating heat through mental concentration. Basically, I am learning to instant focus and concentration.

I have also decided to incorporate push-ups, sit-ups, and squats into my exercise to the sun. I'm focusing on the number nine—actually three times nine, which equals twenty-seven push-ups, twenty-seven sit-ups, and twenty-seven squats. I am sandwiching between the stretches in exercise to the sun. After I do one or two rounds of these, I move on to the other yoga postures.

Joining The Devil

The devil is taking over my house. He arrived this morning disguised as a cleaning woman. He promised to give my house a thorough cleansing.

Should I let him in? Or should I fight him, bar the door, shut my windows, plug up every hole, and open wound in a vain attempt to prevent this diabolical force from entering? Speak about Zoroastrian dualism! Ahura Mazda on the brain. I'm part of the endless struggle between the forces of light and darkness, good and evil.

Why fight the devil? Why not simply let him into my house? Let him break up the furniture, piss on the rugs, smash the windows, stamp on the pottery, tear out the light fixtures and sockets, and destroy hope of future light. Let him step on the radio, smash the tape and record player, and destroy hope of future sound.

I've decided to give up my fight. Why? First of all, he's much stronger than I. I can stave him off for a few hours, days, weeks, months, or even years. But I've only got a limited amount of time on earth, whereas he has eternity. Eventually, he'll roll over me. A few hours or years don't matter to the devil. This morning he's standing at my door, laughing at me, ridiculing my puny attempts to keep him out.

It's fruitless to resist. Besides, he may have something to teach me. True, he comes in negative form; that's the form I'll have to deal with: pain, suffering, hardship, frustrating and apparently fruitless struggle, hopelessness, and all the downdraft forces of the universe.

I'm letting him in. Now we're crawling on the living room floor together. You can't get much lower than crawling on your belly with the devil. But he may teach me a thing or two about the world.

And maybe, hidden in his back yard, is the ladder to heaven.

Temporary Permanence Is All I Can Expect

I've never fully recovered from leaving the womb.

The first day out was such a shock!

I've made progress since then, but not much.

This morning I am still in recovery mode.

I have stopped studying languages, reading the bible, metaphysical philosophies of reincarnation, oneness, transcendence, and divine union; I have stopped all attempts to improve myself.

Instead I am editing my journal. It offers incredible life directions and pathways. It is my personal bible, self-transformation, reincarnation, and oneness Torah.

Nothing is new. Yet everything appears as new. My journal reminds me of past despairs, financial worries, morning depressions, late afternoon joys, fears of victory and defeat. Every emotion is laid out. The low I feel this morning I have felt countless times; yet it feels like the first time. I've gone through the elation high jump countless times, too; also the hopelessness when my phone stays dead, the mail stops bringing registration checks, business stops, the bottom-line crashing-into-the-abyss feeling that no one will ever register again overwhelms me, that my tours are finished, that I'll be crippled and unable to teach folk dancing, that the weekend market is collapsing, that I'll end up poor, broken, homeless, and cast among the Bowery bums. . . I've felt it all countless times before. I've even chronicled all these passing clouds in my journal.

And yet, each time these illusions flood my being, it feels like the first time. "It's never been this bad before," I say. "This is the end." I first wrote about this sense of impending doom almost forty years ago. It is still with me. It always feels new, fresh, and frightening as hell.

Will I ever learn these emotions are not stakes in the permafrost but clouds passing overhead? Is it possible to get perspective on cycles? I've been trying for forty years. Can I ever conquer my wild horse of feeling?

The Jews spent forty years in the desert before reaching the Promised Land. Is forty years a short or long time to gain perspective and truly recognize the illusory quality of emotional life?

Do I need forty years to reach the Promised Land?

Will I ever reach a Promised Land?

What is a Promised Land?

Even when the Jews entered Canaan they had to fight. Building a kingdom there did not take place without a struggle. Their kingdom lasted about a thousand years. . . not too long in geological terms.

Is the Promised Land an illusion?

Perhaps one cannot remain there but only visit it short-term.

If the Jews couldn't stay too long in the Promised Land, what chance do I have?

Pain, suffering, and emotional cycles create the search for permanent residence. But the best I can hope for are temporary visits to the Promised Land. That's not too bad. Why be greedy? That means I can expect the roller coaster emotional life. Since each roller coster is different, every emotional situation and cycle unique, perhaps I will "never learn." I am imprisoned behind emotional bars. Meditative and artistic techniques may free me, but only temporarily.

Its the up-down cycle for me. I can expect it forever—or until something better comes along in the next life.

Yesterday my computer monitor broke. I bought a new one from Frank Carbone. Its resolution is much clearer, a pleasure to work on.

It seems that, every time something breaks down on my computer and I am forced to buy a new part, there is an improvement. This is a good philosophy for life. Although breakdowns are a pain in the ass, they often lead to improvements.

I am also organizing my *New Leaf Journal* into several books. It will take me several more years. Meanwhile, I'll keep adding pages. The journal is turning into my life's writing work. The writing style is the easiest for me, the quickest, most honest, open, exploratory, creative, freeing, and meaningful. It also puts me in touch with the higher forces.

Speaking of higher forces, last night at the Darien folk dance group a terrible rainstorm caused all the light to go out an hour before class started. I hung around in shock and anger, hoping local electricians would fix the lights before our eight o'clock starting time. Finally, at twenty to eight, I "knew" what to do. I realized that, if I packed up all my folk dance equipment, put it in the car, and prepared to leave, at the very moment I got in my car to drive away, the lights would go on. So I packed up. I was about to go out the door when, sure enough, all the lights went on. I unpacked, set up again, and ran the class.

How did I "cause" this miracle? Luck? Perhaps. But part of me also "sensed" such a change might happen. One of those mysterious "coincidences" that make you wonder whether you have any control over "coincidences."

Stage Fright

Yesterday I spoke to Lynn Kramer about the entrepreneur's life. I said that life is an extended form of stage fright. Instead of having it only on stage, you have it from the moment you get out of bed in the morning until bedtime. Stage fright is always with you. The entrepreneurial life only highlights it.

Stage fright frightens and energizes me. I have been fighting it for years. But it is a useless struggle. It's not a disease but a human condition. I also experience a version of it in social situations, parties, meetings, sales calls to customers, and even social obligations like calls to family and friends.

It is time to factor social obligations into daily life.

MONEY AND ITS BRETHREN

Fire And Debt: A Crisis Of Faith

As an eight-year-old boy, I loved to set fires. I was a firebug bordering on delinquent. I set fires in the Johnson woods near our Riverdale home. I thrilled at the leaping hot creation of my matches. After months of such excitement, my friend John Mayer and I finally ended up lighting a big autumn leaf bonfire along the Hudson River. We roasted some potatoes just for fun. That fire soon consumed all the surrounding leaves. A wind started blowing it up the hill. Soon it was out of control and threatened to engulf the Arturo Toscanini mansion. Someone called the fire department. Sirens wailed. As the firemen sprayed water and put out the fire, we stood around feigning innocence and saying, quite loudly for the surrounding bystanders to hear, " I wonder who set this fire?" and "How awful. What irresponsible people! In autumn leaves, too!"

The cops came. I realized I could have been arrested and carted off to jail.

I had reached the limits of my daring and experimentation. Fire-setting was thrilling and daring while it lasted, but it was too dangerous to continue. Then and there I ended my fire-setting career.

In later life, I discovered the thrill of acquiring large sums of money through borrowing. I read a book called *How To Borrow Your Way To Wealth*. It influenced my financial life style for almost twenty years. I soon learned how to borrow from various banks. In the beginning, debts were small. I got used to them. As my credit limit increased, I, in order to increase my thrills, borrowed even more. My debts grew as my dreams of wealth grew. True, there were times when I paid off all my debts. But I quickly felt an emptiness and lack of motivation. I missed the excitement of borrowing all that money. I was addicted to living on the financial edge, so I borrowed again. I kept up this debt lifestyle for years.

I shielded myself from worry by telling myself that I only needed one successful tour to pay everything off. But for years no tours were so successful. Finally, on our 1995 Bulgarian Koprivshtitsa Folk Festival tour, we got forty people. After that I paid off all my debts.

I was debt free, clean again. But it didn't last. I didn't want it to. I borrowed again to finance more tour growth through advertising. However, 1996 was a terrible year. Registrations fell to a historic low. Not only did I not pay off my debts, but I sank further into debt.

Then, in January of 1997, I realized this had all gone too far. My tours, contrary to my hopes, were not bringing in the big bucks. In fact, I was paying big bucks to stay in the tour business. When Miki called so say the farm account needed more money for taxes, and the dentist said I needed a thousand dollars' worth of dental work, and I had to prepay fifteen hundred dollars in social security payments to the government, I borrowed to pay it. I looked at my debts again. I was really over my head. Something had to give. I could no longer wait for my tours to materialize or live on the hope they would be successful. I had to fall back on Plan B, which meant selling stock in my personal account.

This really hurt. Imagine, delving into savings to pay off debt: I was in a cold sweat for days. My body trembled; my knees felt weak. Surges of fear poisoned my body. The same kind of terror had consumed me when I led my first trip to Hungary in 1984. I rarely experience it, but when I do, I remember it forever. It signified a new life stage, a change of direction.

I had reached the end of Debt Road. My lifestyle had to change.

In a sense, this was similar to my fire-setting experience. When my "potato fire" almost torched the Toscanini house, "playing with fire" had gotten too dangerous. I stopped.

Now the same thing was happening. By "playing with debt" I was "playing with fire." It had gotten too dangerous. I had to stop.

I kept my terror in mind for days, focusing on the mortification and humiliation of selling my stocks. I saw my financial life as a failure for the previous twenty years. I imagined every negative thing, financial and otherwise, I could, so that I would drill the lesson of no more debt deep into my brain. A new goal finally emerged: Get out and stay out of debt forever. The glory and excitement of a borderline life lived in debt had ended. The challenge and thrill were over. It had become an annoyance, a hindrance to a clear mind.

A body in debt creates a mind in debt. It also creates endless worry. In the past, part of me had enjoyed the worry; it'd energized me. But that chapter had finally come to a close. Why just then? I don't know. I was just ready for it.

The despair of my debt created a crisis of faith. In the process, I temporarily gave up everything I loved doing—my studies, writing, yoga, and running. I even gave up my tour business, deciding I should return to giving school assembly programs. No more dreams, I said, until I am debt free.

I sold stock and paid of half of my debt. I used tour monies to pay off more for the next few months. If my tours didn't work, I told myself, I might have to sell off even more stock.

But I have changed—not my financial situation, but my attitude. I have traveled down the debt road as far as I can go. It no longer holds an allure for me. I will somehow get debt free even if it takes months years.

Survival Pains

I have been completely lost since January, when I gave up on my former debt-ridden life. On the way, I realized how addicted I had become. Debt served as a stimulus, even an "inspiration." It pushed, drove, and excited me, took my mind off depression. But all my hopes for happiness and security through wealth crashed that day in January, along with my hopes of building a money-making tour business.

When that illusion fell, I sold some stocks and paid off debts—definitely a new road.

But I gave up hope, too. I considered my tour business a financial failure even though, on all other levels, it was a success. Certainly, it served as an inspiration to study languages and history, to contact agents and guides in foreign countries; it taught me about business, folk dancing, leadership, and many intangibles. Creating my tour business, along with writing, has been one of the great adventures of the last fifteen years.

The business downturn of the past six weeks reached its culmination yesterday. Overwhelming black clouds: By mid-morning I hit bottom. Then suddenly, things turned around. I got a registrant for my Greek tour, my stocks went up, and the day culminated with a large Monday night folk dance turnout. Marcia Kolman asked me to give an assembly program in her school; I planned a mini-week at the Fallsview Hotel in June. New ideas were filtering in. By late evening I felt totally whipsawed, torn between the incredible business down I had experienced in the morning and the upturn that seemed imminent.

This whipsaw is reflected in my body. I have a left foot pain in my metatarsal, which started in January when I taught the *schioapa*. This Romanian dance has lots of leaping onto the left foot. I must have leaped too much. Yesterday, I added back pain. Then I knew something psychological was affecting me. My back pains go away immediately once I turn the psychological key. Could I cure my left metatarsal if I turned the proper one? I know the pain had started with *schiopa*. But I also know that I was giving up on my tour business and considering making a living solely as a folk dance teacher. Since folk dance teachers make so little money, I would have to change to a cutting-back-on-all-expenses lifestyle. Economic survival would now depend totally on my feet. The pressure on my feet therefore increased. Perhaps that is why I developed left foot metatarsal pain.

Pain is a teacher. Once I learn her lesson, my pain goes away.

Is financial pain reflected in my foot?

PERFORMANCE

Hoping to Give A Concert.... No, Giving It

I'm at the Fallsview, running a Health Festival Weekend.

I spoke with Marcia and Phil yesterday after breakfast. Marcia said, Use humor, a Victor Borge approach. Phil said, Tell the audience about yourself and how you feel.

I thought about how these "new" approaches might work. Maybe there was hope of giving a concert after all.

This morning I decided to practice next Friday night's coffee shop performance in tonight's concert. I would start with a reading, then follow with three guitar pieces. Readings would solve the problem of humor and telling the audience about myself. They might put me more at ease.

Ultimately, there is no answer to concert nervousness but to take the plunge. Do it! Face the nervousness, accept it as part of your being, and hopefully, move beyond it. Denying or trying to conquer it does not work. Evidently, pre-concert nervousness will always be with me. Many years of unsuccessful attempts to conquer it have shown me this.

The Man and the Tiger

I came out of "retirement" last night. I gave a concert. I learned that nervousness and stage fright will never go away. They are part of the show. They exist because the audience exists.

The audience is the great imponderable, the Great Unknown, the mysterious, new, and frightening energy entering the concert equation.

Technical self-improvement will never change the fact that I must conquer and win over the audience anew with each performance.

Rajam told me a great story about stage fright. I must use it at the beginning of each program.

A man goes into the forest. He meets a tiger. The tiger is panting; his mouth is open and dripping saliva.

The man tremble with fear. Then he notices the tiger is also trembling.

"Why are you trembling?" the man asks.

The tiger answers, "Because, after I eat you, I have to give a speech."

Visits

Nervousness will never go away.

Depression will never go away.

They are two sides of the same coin.

Yet they can cancel out; they can "cure" each other.

Depression can't bother me when I'm nervous. Nervousness can't bother me when I'm depressed.

Nervousness and depression are therefore interlocked. They walk arm and arm down the street. They are married to each other.

Though I know them intimately for years I have always resented them. They often visit me. When they emerge, I try to get rid of them. Who wants such a miserable couple dominating my house? One of them is hard enough to handle, but two! Yet I can't get rid of them. Their visits multiply or diminish but never disappear. They're renting space in my brain.

"Happily," I have made peace with them. I remember when I decided to root out Nervousness twenty years ago. I said, No more concerts until I vanquish you. If I practiced and became technically excellent, I thought Nervousness would simply walk out of my life. I practiced twenty years under this illusion, giving fewer and fewer concerts, diminishing to none during the past two years. The few times I did perform, Nervousness still stood by my side, whispering fears into my ear. His strength and gusto had not diminished. He'd only disappeared temporarily when I gave up concerts.

Finally, this Washington's Birthday Weekend, I "made peace" with him. How? I realized he will never go away. Welcome or unwelcome, he's a permanent resident in my house.

What about his sidekick Depression? Since the two are inseparable, if I accept one I have to accept the other. I can hold off my morning visits from Depression if I take my writing medicine. But she always returns.

The best I seem to be able to do with this noxious couple is to send them on short vacations. When they return, they take a bath, dress up in new clothing, and start bothering me again.

Since they will never leave and are even an integral part of my identity, I might as well call them friends. Enemies can reside within, but why insult them by calling them enemies? I pride myself on being polite and a good host. Besides, friends can be enemies, and enemies can be friends. Witness the word *ra* in Hebrew, spelled *resh, ayin*: It means "bad" or "evil", *and* "friend".

Two New Folk Dance Teaching Methods

I'm starting a new leaf.

I'm at an ending and a beginning even though it doesn't feel like any of the old endings or beginnings. It's so calm, easy, uneventful. Nothing feels new. Yet I know it is. I don't quite understand why. I'll go with it and see where it leads.

I saw these seeds of tomorrow planted again yesterday when I went to Oscar Appel's post-Tamburitzan concert party and spoke with Garry Karner about Romanian dancing. He said it is dying. When he asks other groups to do Mihai David's old Romanian dances, the leaders say, either "We don't know them" or "We stopped doing them."

This year I find I'm teaching many old, forgotten dances. We haven't done them for years. New dancers don't know them.

What does this return to the past mean?

I've always taken these old dances for granted. They are like family members. I treat them like family, too. Perhaps it is time to reexamine this approach.

I've seen my job as a dance teacher as introducing new dances into our repertoire. Teaching old dances was boring. Why put effort in when I knew them already? True, my *students* didn't know them, but my job was to inspire myself first, then let the students follow. The result is, I lead old dances with minimal-to-no teaching. "Just follow me!" I say. Perhaps stumbling along is not satisfying for my students, but my attitude has been, So what? *Let* them stumble. It's good for them. They get a feeling for the music, choreography, and have a modicum of enjoyment.

Perhaps it's time to teach the old dances. The next question is: How do I stay enthusiastic while walking old paths and treading in known waters?

The answer may be in a creative improvisational approach to teaching old dances. First, I can use new "training" music to teach them. I'll teach old steps, old forms, old choreographies, to new music. Once the students know the steps of the "training" dance, I can simple insert the old dance in its place.

Thus, in a sense, I will be constantly "choreographing" new dances using the old forms. I did it with Reka the other night. I can teach many other dances in the same way.

Another "new" technique may be using verbal innovations and improvisations while reviewing the steps to an old dance. I can use journal writing skills, humor, spontaneity, inventive language and phrases drawing in history, current events, languages, stock market, etc., to make my teaching more interesting. I've already done it teaching *Ghunega*: While dancing, everyone counts in Armenian *Meg, yergu, yerek, chorz*, says "good"—*barev*, and "Thank you"—*shnoorhagalutzion*.

BUSINESS

Connecting Sales and Money to Spiritual Life

I have developed a new sales letter, complete with commissions and free trips, in order to include others in my profits. They make money, I make money.

I cut down my mailing list to five hundred; second, I plan to personally call most of the people on my list; third, as I speak to them, if they feel and sound right, I will include them in my sales plan. They will be part of my sales team. We will all work together.

In other words, my customers will also become my sales agents.

Sounds good. It *is* good. Will it work? No one knows for sure. However, what is for sure is that this sales plan motivates me. I'll do the calling, selling, and pushing. Even though I can't speak for others, I can speak for myself. Thus, in terms of my own personal commitment, the sales plan is an unquestionable winner.

Sales and Inner Vision

Sales focuses the mind outward. That's fine. But it can also distract the mind from the inward journey. In doing so one risks a deterioration of the inner vision. Slowly your passion diminishes; you forget why you're doing things in the first place.

Inner vision is the source for outer action. It is the invisible electricity that lights the bulb. Without it there is only darkness.

During the past two months, sales have distracted me from my inner vision. Leading a debtless life, along with a renewed focus on selling my tours, have drawn my mind so far outward that I have lost sight of my center. This is manifested by lack of desire to read, study, or do anything to push myself up the ladder of growth. My inner core has been pummelled, squeezed, forgotten, and lost.

I have given birth to An Evening with Jim Gold concert appearances. Businesswise, I have developed a tour sales letter, the idea of teaching a Wednesday night folk dance in Montclair, organized a mini-week at the Fallsview Hotel, and even made the first hour of Tuesday night a beginner's folk dance hour. I have introduced the radical lifestyle idea of "making a minimal living" teaching folk dancing.

Teaching folk dancing for a minimal living, coupled with the idea of careful attention to cutting back expenses, will free my mind for other purposes.

What purposes? That is the question.

But before I find new purposes, I must refocus my mind backwards. I must tread the inner path and return home to my inner vision.

Starting Over

Yesterday I visited Ganas, a cooperative living venture on Staten Island. They have about eighty members and run four stores. They also bought a Catskill Mountain hotel they call GROW II. I had driven there to look it over before our Washington's Birthday Weekend. The place was blanketed with snow and in disarray. I still wasn't sure our group could use it. I decided to meet with the cooperative members themselves in Staten Island to see what kind of people I would be dealing with.

I took the Jersey Turnpike from Teaneck, crossed the Goethals Bridge, and entered Staten Island. George of Ganas, who gave me driving directions, said to get off at Richmond Road. I got off at Richmond Avenue instead, got completely lost, returned to Route 287, drove to the end of Staten Island, and got off at Richmond Road. I twisted and turned through Clove Road and Victory Boulevard, made a left turn on Jersey Street, into a slum, got lost, asked a local for directions. Finally, I pulled up at 135 Corson Street, the "headquarters" of the Gana Cooperative.

What a dump! I felt like turning my car around and going home. Nevertheless, I parked on Corson Avenue, hoped my car wouldn't get stolen, and climbed the steep steps to Ganas.

I entered the house. Wow! Paintings on walls, books piled everywhere, antique furniture, soft brown interior decorating. I loved the place!

I met one of the directors, Mildred Gordon. She asked one of the members to give me a tour of the eight Ganas Cooperative houses. Then, another member, Richard from California, took me to visited their four stores, all well organized, well run, and profitable. The Gana members who worked there were extremely friendly. So was everyone I met the Mildred's house. Evidently, this community is known all over the world. Originally started in the '60s by a group of six from San Francisco, they now have members from all over the world, including, Spain, Bulgaria, Slovakia, and Russia. Mildred said the only country not yet represented is China.

I ended up booking a June Folk Dance Weekend in their Catskill mountain GROW II hotel. This means that, in June, I'll have a mini-week and weekend at the Fallsview, followed by another weekend at GROW; one week later, I'll be running a tour of the Czech Republic and Slovakia. Mucho work.

I drove back from my full day on Staten Island totally exhausted. My body, bones, and muscles all ached, and I had a headache. Totally drained, I fell into bed and slept for nine hours!

I awoke next morning with the words "starting over" echoing in my mind. Having visited Ganas, I set up another folk dance weekend. Starting over means running more weekends.

Starting over also means returning to my miracle schedule.

Until today the fact I was "doing nothing new" depressed me. Maybe it shouldn't. I had wanted to return to the spirit of adventure, daring, newness, dynamism, and challenge that had occasioned the birth of my businesses and miracle schedule. But evidently, whatever newness I create will not be horizontal but vertical, not lateral expansion but expansion in depth. I'll build something new on old foundations.

Bereshit—in the beginning—is my favorite biblical word. By reaching the end, I'm just beginning.

Learning to Live Peacefully in the Whirlwind

I'm very excited this morning—too excited. Yesterday was my best business day in over a year. Paul Kerlee registered for the Romanian tour—a quality guy. He can do a video of the tour. Fred and Mary Bender called from Santa Fe. They also want to go to Romania. Suddenly, the Romanian tour has tripled its registration! In the evening, when I came home from teaching, I found a call from Joy Seskin: She wants to come on the Czech Republic and Slovakia tour! This followed a great night of folk dancing. A big crowd. Plus three registrants for my June 20th Weekend! All in all, a great day.

I woke in the morning to read that all my stocks had gone down. But still. . .

I am back to daily journal writing. Witness my *New Leaf*. But I do not want to return to the overwhelming feeling I used to have when I piled up hundreds of pages of unedited *New Leaves*. Now I want to combine daily journal writing with daily journal editing. This means almost doubling my writing work and output. However, it must be done. It is part of my vow-of-poverty commitment, no-more-debt commitment, and no-more-overwhelmed commitment. I never want to go down those three paths again. Never again!

My vow of poverty means accepting less, doing less, thinking smaller; my vow of no debt means exactly that—no more debt; my vow of no more overwhelmed combines the first two vows. It also adds a wider mental state: no more being controlled by my conflicting and contrary desires. This is a very difficult state to achieve. It means constant vigilance, watching, and monitoring of the erratic movements of my mind. I'll have to do it on a daily, hourly, even minute-to-minute basis. I can start right now! Excitement about yesterday's successful tour registration day is unbalancing me. Just as I dropped into a deep pit with low-to-no registrations, I am now scaling the wall, banging on the ceiling, and jumping for joy with higher registrations. My mind is scattering down many directions of new hopes, plans, and desires. A vision of mucho people, money, and excitement is returning to haunt my brain. I am, in a sense, trapped on an upward path. Sure, I'd rather be trapped on an upward path than a downward one; reaching for the stars is better than plummeting down the abyss, falling into the molten center of the Earth. But does heaven really have more benefits than hell? Do we truly know what's good for us? Is there much difference between being trapped on an upward path and being trapped on a downward one? Isn't freedom better than living chained to the opposites?

Balance is best. So is inner peace. I like the term *dynamic inner peace*. It means living quietly, calmly, peacefully in the whirlwind. I am in a whirlwind of registration. I want the power and strength to remain passionate yet calm, fired with enthusiasm, yet balanced.

Is it possible to live in these two worlds at once?

Sounds like a wonderful goal for me.

Beginnings and Endings

Endings excite and depress me. I want to reach the end, yet I know once I do, I'll be disappointed.

Endings let me down and lift me up.

Endings are resting places where new beginnings occur.

What then is the big deal about them? This ending is similar to my high school graduation. After that, I took a brief summer vacation, then went to college. Surely, after I finish editing my journal, I'll graduate to something else—probably new writing and more editing.

So why get upset?

It's time for a new approach.

First let me clear the air.

My "improvement and perfection" guitar practice started almost twenty years ago; it ended this year. That's a twenty-year cycle. Nevertheless, it boils down to simply another kind of beginning and ending. My tour business begins and ends; so does my weekend and folk dance business. Such cycles begin when I wake up every morning and continue in smaller cycles as the day progresses.

I hardly notice them. But when a long-term cycle ends, I am often in shock. I've built a lifestyle around it, which style usually ends when my goal is accomplished. Long-term endings have a more powerful effect on me than short-term ones. Nevertheless, they are merely another form of the same thing.

How does one approach beginnings and endings with more equanimity, learn to accept the ceaseless nature and repetition of cycles?

Simply accept them. Then move on.

The Essence of Business

Business is meditation in action.

Focus on the customer is a most powerful form of concentration. It can free you from the bonds of ego.

INVENTIONS

Despair

Black clouds move across the sky—chased by carcasses of ancient hyperion cows, bulls masked in concrete, and wild geese flying though the fecal-infested skies, whirling and bombing their downward bladders towards a Babylonian ziggurats washed by Euphratic waters.

Can answers be far away when questions rise so easily?

Why is the des-pair cloud rising?

A cycle has cycled full swing. Debt had laden my virgin wings with negative weights of gold and silver. Pearls strewn from black-steel cross a range of mountain chains. Darkness of obliteration. Only resilience with baby-skinned warts so difficult to assess in times of revolt, can crack the castle wall of Despair-Fog Creator.

The Despair Fog rolls in, poisoning the stock market swings inhabiting the American Exchange of my brain.

Why was I in despair?

The rolling blackness of a desert sand storm strewn with bills and debts covers the landscape. Revolution took place. Cosmic worms crawled beneath illusory top soil, ancient caterpillars, topped, christened, and hardened by Bethlehem Steel. Cycles have ended, returned, and metamorphosed into new cycles. Cycles arrive in twos, threes, and fours; as bicycles, tricycles, and quatrocycles. But no matter how they ride in, they soon ride away. Surfaces change but the infinite and eternal nature of the rolling wheel never does. Why pay much attention to it? But if you suffer from humaneness you cannot avoid it. Nevertheless, a small corner of verdant mind can gaze, glance, watch, and witness. So does one free oneself from the cyclic grip.

I had given up.

Debt had crunched me into the nauseating arms of the cyclopean chest squeezer. Everything fell down; hopes crashes in the down cycle; despair kicked in. I crawled at the bottom of Give-Up Cavern, wet, frozen, and worked in stone; straightened, bent, and misshapen by worry. I was a stalactite in the making—or was it a stalagmite? But whether ceiling or floor, I crawled on stone at the bottom. Tours, weekends, folk dance classes, guitar playing, writing, yoga, running, publishing, languages, history, studies, all the dear, important, and good crashed around me.

Caught in the vise-like grip of two-ment, I needed one-ment.
Trapped in des-pair, I needed re-pair.
I needed at-one-ment but two-ment kept knocking at my door.
What could I do but stay the course,
And let the course run its course.
I had given up.
Well, I'm moving on now.
Here are two good names: Jupiter Harvard and Brother Jumbo.

GOD

Writing a Letter To God in the Great Upstairs

I just feel like sitting at this computer and writing and writing until the soggy, miserable, monstrous, clammy, balloon-shaped, foggy black cloud burdening the skies above my brain starts to disintegrate. The end of an era is in sight, nay a millennium.

The golden age of financial chaos has bottomed out. I see the stars in sight. A black lining of underhanded upheavals, strutting clouds covered with rash-infested sores, is clambering for a change of diapers. I see them rising, crying, scampering, and blabbering on the horizon. Oh, how I need such a bath in the hemispheres, this deep sinking in the words of the spheres, and of spheres beyond spheres, universes whirling among breached branches of bygone celebrants, leaping Furies gone awry at Saturday night parties, potted plants lost in the equilibria of star-studded planets, intergalactic in scope and twisting towards their star-busted, leaden, and explosive doom.

There's lots of shit in the bucket, and I mean to fry it.

This is a clean-up operation. I'm sweeping my Augustean stables, looking beyond the Italian peninsula, that fertile boot of poetic minds; I'm reaming my ass-wiped pen towards the Syracuse of Sicily ,where Herculean Pythagoras reigned, or was it Corona? I've forgot tenthe city where Pythagoras lived his mystical, musical, fairyland, god-oriented life, the distant city in which his fertile brain created the Pythagorean School. It was the rage throughout the ancient Greek world, a world I'll be visiting in a few months.

Can I excuse myself for such a lapse? Does it really matter? Indeed it does, but not for the reason I am thinking. Pythagoras, or Python or Mercury or the aerial war-god Ares, even Mars-upon-Satan, a mixed salad of nomenclatures make no difference in this fertile, fervid fervent, phrenetic cleansing process, sweeping my stables with Herculean broom, unclogging the flowing Tiber River of my clogged, besotted, snail-infested, luke-warm mind where tyrants dwell in infant garb.

I had all but forgotten how to call up language from my home source, how to tap the subtle unconscious solar energy dwelling in the forefront of my backside. These stellar haunts had all but disappeared in my quest for financial security, balance, and oneness. First, I needed to balance my budget and balance my brain filled with its unbalanced financial ideas. These hanging cliffs created constant turmoil and situations needing frantic adjustments. The rolls and bagels falling off them, the Rolls-Royces and Mercedeses clambering up their jutting mammary-gland hills, needed periodic oiling and cleansing. Can one really visit Brest and survive without mother's milk? Can an infant suck at the tit of succulence and survive in a world of ever-polluting galaxies? Isn't the brain merely an organ of the finger, a structure built within a suture whose strange fruit and forbidden cantaloupes reside only in the wonderland of Central Asian shamanic knowledge? These questions remain unanswered even by Dr. Grossman von Himmelfarber, Head Lice Hunter for the University of Worms.

God was right when I spoke to Him last night. "You'd better write me a letter," he said. "If not, I'll use Zeus Express and send you a thunderbolt and lightning flash message to electrocute your brain into action. On second thought, why should I bother with you at all? You're not worth an iota of solar energy or inclement weather reading of my time. I'll let you lie alone in your bed, to stew and be stewed, to wrestle with your demons in basketball-fulfilling splendor, shooting hoops with the devils of your choice. Then, after you're tired of these hard-court press babblements, you'll realize the importance of a phone call and letter-writing program to your shut-in heavenly father sitting besides your heavenly mother, waiting to hear from you. Why don't you ever write or call? We never hear from you anymore. Do you have a girlfriend? What is taking up your time? Are you too busy to write? Or have you just forgotten about your parents? Do you really thing all we're good for is paying your electric bills?

"My son, we're mad as hell! You'd better pay us a visit, or else! No more delays. I'm sending down Heavy Depression as a warning."

I answered this morning. "I hear you calling, Pop. Here's my letter. Once I clean the pipes, empty the garbage, and freshen up my house, I'm planning to visit you with my new girlfriend. We're getting married, but I don't know when. She's good for me, a stabilizing force. In fact, she's the one who suggested I call you this morning."

Mix with the Thunder, Ride on the Lighting

I'm trying to find a way of writing without cramping my shoulders and neck. How about holding down my shoulders? I'm concentrating on my body rather than my mind. Is that so bad?

It's a technical morning. How to write without hurting myself, with good posture, is the question. Forcing my shoulders down, stretching my neck upwards, coupled with periodic head turnings, may be an answer.

Lost and alone, biting and turgid, the cry of the lonely fowl. Can't you see the painful bowl of cherries rising on the horizontal, the false horizon created by the Hand of God, falling, blaspheming, rising again, swelling, diametrically opposing the sinking, broad-backed neck-infested waters of cerebral hemispheres bedecked by medulla oblongata, where words walk backwards through spheres of longing?

A new step is being taken. It's a passive-tense world. "Being, being!" Is that a cry for an active person? Indeed, not. Action verbs would be better. But I am beyond action. I am lost and whimpering in the wilderness.

A weakness in my lower neck bends me low. I want an epiphany, but all I get is an epoohphany. A puff, a light wind, a breeze, but no burst of light from the horizon, no booming thunderclaps from above. I sit in a Placid Land, waiting for placid events to float me upstate towards Lake Placid.

I'm ready to organize *New Leaf Journal*. But I have no idea how. When the title *Mix with the Thunder* came to mind, categories come to an end. I need flashes, cacophonies of fire, rising bells rinsed in song. Where is the beauty, loftiness, and bell-ringing in *categories*? But *Mix with the Thunder*, or its sequel, *Ride on the Lighting*, is an apocalyptic title. In a flash, *New Leaves* merge around one trunk of the eternal flaming tree. I like it.

Can a title be an "organizing principle" for *New Leaf*? It means there is no order to anything I've written; there is only one large soup, one great ocean. It means yesterday's entry can be followed by one written three years ago. "Falluca" can precede "Power and Strength." Is this the way to go? It feels right, yet it is so chaotic.

I have found an order by rejecting all order. Is this possible? Am I fooling myself by taking a back road? Or perhaps there is more to my title than I thought. *Mix with the Thunder* and *Ride on the Lightning* were born of intuition. A sudden leap out of the primordial slag of my unconscious. They must signal some kind of emerging reality, one I am preparing to perceive but cannot yet perceive. Can I trust the deeper meaning of *Mix with the Thunder?* Is there a deeper meaning?

Trust my intuition. What does the title say? Is says God is speaking to me, intuition is blasting through concrete material reality, epiphanies are everywhere, transcendence dresses in daily clothing, miraculous sparks are everywhere, the fire of enlightenment can burn up your ego at any moment, and surprise is the order of the day—as is serendipity.

My title speaks to my deepest values, if epiphanies can be called values. Actually, they can't. Rather they are experiences, enlightenments, meetings with God, clothing the flesh in a flash of transcendence, the thunder clap from Mt. Sinai, Moses seeing the lightning flash in the burning bush.

Mix with the Thunder and *Ride on the Lightning* are poetic organizations of *New Leaf.*

Is poetic organization the way to go?

They create a central themes: meetings with God, angry fiery visions mixed with beatific violin and Cheerios experiences.

April–June 1997

WRITING

Mitzvahs in The Flesh

I read today that mitzvah is exerting oneself on behalf of others. That sounded good: Giving a concert is exerting oneself for others. If I in fact thought about others, even stage fright might go away. I wouldn't have to concern myself with self-improvement. I liked this mitzvah idea for a few minutes; I thought it might point out a new direction for me. But soon the illusion faded away. Whenever I focus on thinking of others, exerting myself in their behalf, I lose my direction, spark, center, and sense of self.

Perhaps I should redefine "other." Who says I am only one person? I know I have many selves. Therefore, when I am exerting myself on behalf of others, I am, in reality, exerting myself on behalf of myself and my other selves. Myself, my other selves, and all my subselves, are a family. We work together. Serving others is really serving yourself. In the bigger picture, people, animals, things, and surrounding places are all part of a cosmic whole, one universe, one Oneness subsumed under the oft-mentioned, or, in Judaism, purposely unmentioned, unspoken name of God. All is one. Endeavors to unite my many selves into others, attempts by others to unite my selves into their selves, attempts at kindness, mitzvahs, illuminations, and unity, are attempts to achieve a spiritual realization deep in the bowels of your spirit center.

It is a question of intention and attitude. It is often hard to know what will help someone else. Even when you're almost certain, you still wonder if your energies cannot be more helpful elsewhere. Nevertheless, helping you will do. But the most important self-help project is to realize that all is one, and that, since you are part of it, by helping others you are helping yourself. Thus, on a deeper level, there is no difference between helping yourself and helping others. Only the style changes. Superficial differences. Help is help. But judgement intercedes, deciding which help is better at which time.

Celebration

I sure hit pay day yesterday in my "Goals Speech." Everything came together again. Thank God for writing. Once again it cleared my mind and pointed out new directions.

What happened? On an emotional level, I'm just thankful I'm back on the path. But I also want to know how the negative aspects of my mind work. I don't want to make the same "mistakes" again. Pain is supposed to make me wiser. If I don't learn its lessons, I'm bound to repeat myself.

After "finishing" my gigantic projects of editing New Leaf, relaxing my right guitar hand, and polishing off my debts, monumental movements and growth projects really, I needed to celebrate. I took off two weeks as part of an extended celebration. I remember the day I finished editing New Leaf. I felt like celebrating. How do I celebrate? I don't know. Oh sure, for a day I whoop-dee-dood down the street; then I added another day. Truly, my celebrations were over after that. Yet I strung them out for almost three weeks. Finally I descended to old, familiar borders of depression. Then I knew it was time to stop, assess, and analyze my errant mind.

I returned to writing. In the process I rediscovered my miracle schedule.

How should I celebrate after a victory? Good question. I have no "celebration forms" that I know of to fall back or forward on. Oh sure, I like having a celebratory meal in a restaurant, running full speed around the block, or whooping, hollering, and jumping up and down in my the living room. My short-term celebrations are wonderful, but they are precisely that—short-term. Perhaps they are all I need.

While celebrating, I dropped the rituals of my miracle schedule.

Should I celebrate by dropping the rituals I love? Is that a good idea? Is even taking a short break from them? If the rituals of my miracle schedule cement me to sanity, if through them I express my feeling, fulfill my promise to this world, and make myself happy, why should I drop them when I celebrate? Wouldn't it be better to do them with even more intensity?

Logically, I should stick to my rituals "in spite of" happiness or sadness. Celebrating by falling apart doesn't seem like a good idea.

However, during moments of victory I want to kick off all restraints and shout, "Wahoo!" Fine. Do it. But realize it is a momentary shout, a short visit to a higher plane similar to the moments I break down in tears listening to the majesty of a Beethoven symphony; then, as my ego disintegrates, I realize once again with absolute certainty that a higher force exists within me and without me. Soon after my revelation, I return to "normal" life and its routines.

Perhaps celebration is the same thing. Kick off my shoes, shout hallelujahs, burst free for a quick epiphany, then return to "normal" life and the routines of my miracle schedule, which in itself a form of daily celebration.

If I don't need to read books from the beginning anymore why should I write them that way?

If I don't care about order or plot anymore, only style and content, I can now start reading a book anywhere: at the beginning, in the middle, at the end, or somewhere else.

A result of this thinking is: what difference does the order of my New Leaf Journal make? There is no plot in the ordinary sense but only the development of an individual in chronological order. Actually, that is a kind of plot in itself, something in the order of Finnegan's Wake or Ulysses. What a style that is!

Style and content are what count for me now. I can be happy reading and thinking about one sentence.

If order does not matter anymore, then the organization of New Leaf takes on a whole new light. See Way Of The Ascetics; think Way of the New Leaf.

On Not Publishing Ever Again

Writing is has always been my private form of prayer. Must my prayers be published? What do they have to do with the outside world, anyway? Prayers are simply talks and communications with the Creator. If this is the case, why bother publishing any of my New Leaves?

Such an attitude would certainly free my mind.

But can I think this way? Isn't it a sin not to "share" my thoughts with others? And what about ego stroking? Don't I need publishing to put the final cap on self-satisfaction and on the completion feeling of my labors? Can my cake be complete without icing? Isn't publishing the icing?

This would be the Mount Athos monks' writing approach: writing as prayer; writing as service and communication with the Higher Power; writing as submission to God and the Voice within.

It is the approach Paul Brunton used during the last thirty years of his life. He published his "final" book in his fifties. Then he simply wrote notes to himself for thirty years, in the process filling over seven thousand pages. If not for the editing of his son, his writings would have been lost to the world forever. Because of his son's work, I own the complete journals of Paul Brunton and am inspired to create my own. However, I am also "inspired" to think about never publishing again, of adopting the Paul Brunton attitude: "What for?"

By the end of his life, Brunton was completely forgotten by the public. It didn't bother him.

Would it bother me?

It would be a major step forward in my prayer forms. Not only writing, but guitar, and exercise could be included making a clear delineation between public and private forms.

It would be another step towards freedom. But can I stand the aloneness, and do I want it?

Completion, Revelation, and the Moment

Why write? Write for the glory! Whether others read it or not is a secondary. The process of laying down word after word, of sweeping out my brain and cleansing the filth that has accumulated in those back woods, the attics, rooms, halls, and closets of my mind, provides a cleansing directional effect; it straightens me out and puts me on the road to somewhere; it pricks and forces me out of tired, stagnant molds and puts me on Light Highway. Yes, it's all part of the glory of writing.

This means living the rest of my live with a focus on revelation rather than improvement, living under the protection of God's immediate hand, gathering the incredible ions together, creating an atmospheric moment where the universal forces of revelation collect, and, with my brain as a lighting rod, focusing their cosmic light through the narrow fissures of my individual self, shooting strengths and pockets of glory through my wiry body. In so doing, they connect me in electrifying fashion to the earth beneath my feet. This is podiatric medicine at its best. Let hammer toes hammer out universal messages; let bunions sing not of wider feet spreading through galaxies beyond the known universe.

Yes, I am on a new road, the glory road. Thank God! Born today in twenty minutes of writing, this road leads first to hell, then to heaven. As I walk along the edge of a cliff staring into the abyss, I focus on revelation and a lifestyle of sparks and dynamite.

This revelation lifestyle thrives in a world of completion. Living in the moment means driving wedges in opposites, unifying each experience, and completing every moment. This must happen in both long term and short-term projects, for long-term projects are but reflections of short-term projects that, in turn, reflect the completed moment.

Thus, my *New Leaf Journal* must reach publishable form even if it is never published. I need such a completion project.

LANGUAGES

Hand-Written Journal

I'm back to handwriting in a hand-written journal.

It's so pleasant and relaxing combining words with drawing. It gives you a free-flowing hand to change the letter shapes if you like, draw new letters, write in foreign scripts like Greek, Cyrillic, and Hebrew, and even add calligraphy.

"Intuitive Czech": My New Linguistic Approach

We're leaving for South Bohemia this morning at 9:00 a.m. I got up at 5:30 to read my Contemporary Czech book. I glanced through it quickly from beginning to end, basically wanting to look up how to conjugate that most important irregular verb: chtit, to want. Along with adverbs such as kde—where, I want is probably the most used word.

As I read, I realized I may be, must be, want to be ready to, move to the next linguistic level.

What does that mean? It has something to do with an "intuitive" approach to Czech.

What does that mean? It has something to do with the fact that I have been studying languages—the Slavic linguistic family as well as the Latin, Germanic, and Semitic language families– for many years. It is time for the next qualitative leap. I am ready to make the virtual reality assumption that, at this point in my linguistic development, instead of needing to learn languages, the old direct intellectual-memorize them approach, I should instead assume I know them. From there I leap into idea that all I need is short refresher and review in order to remember them.

Let's take the Contemporary Czech book as an example. I semi-studied it pretty thoroughly last year. And I've semi-studied other Czech language books over the years. The result of years of semi-study is that I still can't speak Czech. It's true of the other languages I have semi-studied; I can babble and blunder through but still have no fluency in them. True, I'm not in the countries long enough to really learn the languages, and the purpose of learning them, which was to survive running my tours, has long been realized. I am now fairly relaxed and confident as a tour leader. I hardly need to know languages at all to run a good tour.

Thus, at this point, the question arises, why bother studying the languages anymore? Why not just fall back on the guides I hire or on the elaborate sign language I have developed to communicate? Somehow my need to function and perform and speak in the contemporary languages has been satisfied. Linguistically, I have gone as far as it can go.

And yet I still bring my Czech book with me.

Perhaps, at this point, I have studied languages long enough to initiate a new "intuitive" language approach. This is based on the assumption I know the language already: I have gone over most important verb forms, memorized most important adverbs, adjectives, and nouns. Now I simply have to now bring them up from my unconscious.

I may be fooling myself with this approach.

Or I may be on to something new.

I believe the latter.

I'll move ahead with it. From now on, my new intuitive linguistic approach will be my approach. We'll see where it leads.

LIFE

Go Right Past It

When someone attacks you, must you fight back?

Is fighting back the best way to fight back?

Thus if someone calls you a racist, bigot, right-wing weirdo, conservative, depressive, instead of answering and getting into an argument that will only heat you up, leading to more arguments and ultimately getting you absolutely nowhere, answer the accusation only once. If it continues, then go right past it. Hold your tongue. Restrain your anger and annoyance in favor of the upcoming higher state of unity that will slowly be achieved by "going right past" your accusers. They need an opponent to play their game. If you take away the opposition by "not fighting back," eventually you win and they lose. But the good part is, both parties thinks they've won; it feels like a win-win situation.

This strategy is so utterly brilliant, I wonder why others don't use it all the time. I didn't use it for many years. The result was we fought most of the time. Then I initiated my "retreat" strategy. I backed off whenever hot political topics or the accusation "You don't care about my feelings" came up. I held counsel with myself and held my temper in check. I made progress. Our fights ended almost immediately. Now we hardly fight at all. I am perfecting the technique, improving upon it.

I usually handle "hot" subjects with a strategic retreat. I back off, move away from the fire. My instinctual self realizes the threat of a fight, the hopelessness of its entanglement, of its endless descending cyclical trap of fight-and-fight-back with predictable results of opposites endlessly colliding and no future conciliation of any sort. Direct fighting rarely brings peace. More important, it rarely brings inner peace.

Direct fighting engenders more fighting. It doesn't solve anything. True, sometimes there is no choice. But it is better to fight indirectly. You're driving down the road, and another car drives straight at you from the opposite direction. The best way to avoid a crash is to pass it by. If you cannot, the best you can do is hope you will survive the crash. A direct hit, a direct confrontation, is the last choice. It should be taken only when all other options fail. The result will invariably be a win-lose situation.

Political questions are questions of power. They exist on the level of power over the external world. But power over the external world is an illusion. The only power we truly have is power over our internal world, the power of attitude.

Because external power needs opposition, it can never achieve unity. Unity, harmony, oneness—the higher and highest spiritual states—cannot be reached through manipulation of the material world, or the Marxist mechanism of dialetectical materialism. Nor can it be achieved through implementation of a socialist dream that forces all people to be "equal" and "unified" in the future socialist paradise state. It can only be achieved attitudinally, through a spiritual state where one "sees" *fsitchko e edno*—all is one.

I Need Renewal

Perhaps it is renewal time.

"Perhaps" is the maybe state of groping, not sure, repeating myself, wondering, surmising, feeling my way. "Perhaps" is the where-am-I-who-am-I word.

Everything feels like it's falling apart. My left metatarsal has been hurting since January. I haven't paid much attention to it. Now suddenly, it's making me panic as I see myself turning into a cripple and my whole folk dance career disappearing. New pains keep appearing first in my right metatarsal, then in my ankles, toes, and knees. All my motions are slowly being restricted. Soon I won't be able to walk at all; I won't even be able to move. I am in the process of becoming paralyzed.

My physical condition is a reflection of my mental state. Mentally I feel paralyzed. I've finished many projects, some having taken years to complete. Guitar tremolo, editing of New Leaf Journal, tours programs, even my finances are in order. Taking myself out of debt has taken the financial pressure off me. Instead of worrying about finance, I worry about health. Indeed, my physical condition reflects my mental state.

I am in need of true renewal.

What does renewal mean? How do I do it?

A new project, a new direction, something to take my mind off my foot.

Something Is Wrong

The dates don't work anymore on this fucking computer program. Something is going wrong but I don't know what it is.

One thing I do know, those fucking words better flow—or else! Knock the skyline over the wall, pilfer white lighting behind the barn, enter sky-blue rhinoceros under mud-walled, aproned skies. The rational masonry rips away. Through the cracks dawn sucks effervescent splendor from the cosmic worm of light. I'm panting at the gate, dripping to open, waiting to pour through my purging purgation. Will white lilies ever cease their ritual time scheduling?

I will revise: First thing in the morning will be guitar followed by yoga, breakfast, then desk work. After lunch is bottom time, down and dumping. Then around three p.m. I'll write, then run. It may not be quality slow-thinking meditative morning rolling time, where jewels bubble up across empty hairpin turns of sizzling mountain roads, but it will at least keep the old brain oiled. Then I can end my day accomplishing something useful in this world.

I am lolling through limbo land. My guitar, writing, tour, and financial endings have yet to bear new beginnings. Wallowing in the shit farm of the here and now, I dribble through books and contemporary power house libraries.

Shall I go back to the unedited life, pile up new pages of manuscripts? No. Back is not where I want to go. I want forward. . . but to where? Too early to cock the crow, drift the juice, or sift and plough in the anthills of cyclopean Mycenae where the Lion's Gate nests. With my upcoming trip to Greece on the horizon I am caught between an occidental rainbow filtered by Gothic sun, and an oriental sun dripping light across Ephesian ruins of a broken coliseum.

Images, images, perhaps you will float my walrus teeth above the nightmare of somnabulance. Empire is lost; African states lie in ruins. The doldrums have long ago visited Siam and Timbuctu.

Three weeks to play with my schedule before I leave for Greece. Where I am now I do not know. Keep flobbering. See where it leads.

Goals Along the Infinite Route of the Miracle Schedule

Amazing how my goals have dribbled away.

I used to have them. They filled me up, filled my day. Although, on one level, there were a pain in the ass, on another, they gave me purpose and direction.

I had a guitar goal: to play "Alhambra," and "Leyenda," and have a perfect tremolo. That goal is "fulfilled"—and gone. I had a writing goal: four pages a day, publication, improvement. That goal is "fulfilled"—and gone. I used to have a physical body goal: train for a marathon, do 150 push-ups, sit-ups, squats, improve yoga postures. Those goals have not been fulfilled. Nevertheless, they too have dribbled away. I had a language goal: learn the languages of each country I tour—gone. I had a business goal: make lots of money; it has also vanished away with my vow of poverty.

The juice have been drained out of my miracle schedule. It stands dry and dusty. Yet it is irreplaceable. By downsizing my desires and goals, I have also downsized the meat, juice, fire, and fuel that constituted the core of my spiritual life. Thus I am feeling quite low but don't know what to do about it. Well, I do know intellectually—return to my miracle schedule. But I can't do it. Without emotion to blow my sail, my boat will not move.

Why do I feel this way? Is it simply a resting state? Am I sitting around waiting to get so depressed that I am forced to get on my horse, ride into action, charge across the field of my miracle schedule? The very term itself feels dry and empty, a puff of smoke, an empty phrase.

If I take a good look at my former goals, I must admit, on a deeper level, none of them have been accomplished. This is the most profound aspect of their nature: They can never be totally achieved. Short-term goals along their path can be, but the overall aim of improvement and "perfection" can't. What, after all, does mastering the guitar, learning a language, improving my writing, running a marathon, expanding a yoga posture, reaching for the 150s, actually mean? Treading a path towards the impossible. I will never master any of my disciplines. That is both their frustration and their beauty. My need is in the trying. Effort gives them life and makes them sing.

By getting out of debt, I have removed so much anxiety that I see hardly any reason to work at all. Why bother with my goals, since I am now "economically secure?" Surely, this is the most materialistic of views: Economic security can create relief but not joy, happiness, and fulfillment. Only hard work can do that.

It is a question of juice. Better yet, it is a question of having fooled myself once again. I fell into the economic-security-equals-happiness trap. A stable economy is necessary: it is my base. On it I must build my pyramid of quests. But then I must climb, climb, climb.

My miracle schedule is the daily ritual of my life. It is forever a good-in-itself, eternity in verbal form. Although it needs economic security to thrive and flower, its existence and survival do not depend on economics.

Editing New Leaf Journal, finishing guitar right-hand relaxation, paying off my debts, although all positive deeds, nevertheless threw me off balance. I saw their accomplishment as final goals rather than temporary stages along the endless ritual path of my miracle schedule.

It is time to return—today.

"Laying Tfillin"

Yesterday was a good day. I implemented everything on my miracle schedule.

My ritual went like this: I rose a 5:45 a.m.—excellent beginning—had coffee while stretching my Achilles tendons and reading the New York Times, and followed this with a half-hour of journal writing. I only wrote a first draft. Then, instead of editing right away, which is my wont, I walked away from it in amazed and thoughtful contemplation about the ideas and directions I had discovered. Why kill my enthusiasm by editing right away? I thought. Instead I'll follow my feelings, take a break, and move on to another aspect of my miracle schedule. I practiced guitar for about fifteen minutes, did an hour of yoga, took a five-minute break, returned to edit my morning journal writing, and concluded the morning's ritual with a half-hour run followed by a half hour yoga warm-down. I ate breakfast. By noon I had successfully completed my rituals.

The main difference in how I handled my miracle schedule lay in how quickly I moved from one ritual to another. I didn't linger long between courses, didn't allow myself to "think" and slow-fall into the nebulous arms of transient depression. I kept the rituals at the forefront of my mind; I remembered they were a "permanent" cause of satisfaction, happiness, and fulfillment. And I practiced what I remembered. This is good.

I must continue on the road. The miracle schedule is my "laying tfillin." I put the crown jewel with its tiny parchment of biblical injunctions on my head, focus on it, and try to remember its primal ego-blasting importance. My tfillin say: Keep up the good work. Don't waver.

The Philosophic Advantages of Slower Memory

Purpose, purpose, purpose. I keep coming back to purpose.

Would I want to write my autobiography? What purpose would it serve?

Very scattered this morning. Many stray thoughts filtering through my brain. I thank the writing process for keeping me alive and functioning. Why I need this process is beyond me. But as the rabbi said, "I don't need explanations. I believe in miracles."

Is my memory going? I don't remember people's names the way I used to. Is this also true of facts? My brain seems to be moving more slowly. Is this simply part of the aging process? Perhaps there a deeper reason for it. I know part of my brain doesn't want to be bothered remembering facts and people. Why put effort into remembering such a transient phenomena? Besides,

I have always been more interested in the beauty of flow rather than memory.

These are good explanations for the "slowing" of my memory. I need certain people and certain facts less and less. As I grow older I am becoming stronger and more independent. Are such new powers mirrored in my slowing memory? I want to remember the big things, the fundamental truths like oneness, holiness, transcendence, and eternal life beyond the transient cycles of existence. Specifics like names, places, dates, and facts are less significant. Spiritual truths are general truths. They are discovered through the higher faculties of intuition. I don't need a specific memory power to tap into it; in fact, I wonder if too much focus on specifics inhibits intuition, blocking it with factual "trivia."

For a searcher, a slower memory may be prelude to new growth on the path to higher learning.

As your life develops, it may be natural to move from specific to general. It is a preparation for death, when everything is forgotten in preparation for the next life.

Stray Thoughts

Always carry a piece of miracle schedule on my person. When leaving the house, going for a walk, visiting the city, socializing, eating out, carry a notebook to jot down a sentence, a history book to check a fact, a language book to memorize a word or sentence. Do a push-up en route, or a stretch.

My miracle schedule is based on the art of stressing yourself slightly. Keep your mind actively moving its path.

The miracle schedule ritual is similar to the rituals of Judaism. Both are ways of remembering the God on a daily, even hourly, basis.

Instead of technical prowess—relaxed right hand, speed, slow, etc.—think of guitar playing as a path of discovery.

Perfecting My Miracle Schedule: Adding Sleep

Yesterday after waking at 5:30 I did everything right. I wrote, played guitar, did yoga, edited, then ran. I could tell I was tired when my running collapsed after ten minutes. I decided to move my running, with its yoga warm-downs, to the late afternoon. I ate breakfast at about 11:30.

Then I slept for an hour. That's my new miracle schedule addition.

The one-hour noon sleep was deep and beautiful. I woke really wonderfully refreshed. I was able to study an hour of Greek, do some errands, bring my car to Quirk to find out I needed a new transmission, then return home to my running and yoga warm-downs. I finished at 6:00 p.m., ate supper, read a few pages of The Mystery Of Light: The Life and Teachings of Omraam Mikhael Aivanov, by Georg Feuerstein (a book about the life and philosophy of Mikhael Aivanhov, the saintly celibate with his perfected Bogomil/Cathar philosophy of life), then slept for a half hour. After waking, I studied Hebrew, read Bereshit for about an hour, did calligraphy, letting the Hebrew letters fly, played guitar again, and made some business phone calls. I even got a new customer for Romania! At 9:30 Bernice came home, and we called David in Santa Fe.

All in all, it was a long and excellent day of perfecting my miracle schedule.

The purpose of the schedule is simply to fulfill dictates. In doing so, I keep my mind focused on a higher plane. By focusing on process, not product, by concentrating on fulfilling the commandments rather than hoping for accomplishments in this world, I put myself on the path beyond depression. It is a very healthy binding, and good for me.

A few other things happened on the path. Carefully and slowly I followed my feelings. I watched my mind. When I tired of one ritual, I "jumped" to another.

Adding sleep to the miracle schedule ritual is so refreshing. It commands me to relax. This fulfills the stress and relaxation dictates of the discovery path.

By making it part of my miracle schedule I can get less sleep at night, wake up at 5:30 a.m., and use the fruitful early morning time.

After lunch has always been dead down time. Why fight it? Use it to sleep.

An End To Business?

What is the role of fear in motivation?

Shouldn't I scare myself a little every day?

Does scaring myself make sense if my goal is happiness?

Is happiness a good goal to strive for? If it is, how does one get there?

By alternating slight stress with rest, I'm making a good first step. The slight stresses of language study, yoga, guitar, etc., lift me up. Following these with a short sleep feels ideal. Yet, something is missing. What could it be?

On the surface, I have everything. Financial stability and lack of worry fill my horizon. This frees my mind for other things. But for what?

Yesterday I did yoga three times: one hour in the morning, half an hour after my run in the early afternoon, and a half hour in the evening. During the evening session I was incredibly loose! What a wonderful feeling of progress.

Perhaps that feeling is my reward. Much work and self-discipline go into it. Yet the payoff, even if just a few seconds of satisfaction, is well worth it. It may be the only reward I can expect in this life.

But I am avoiding the subject: Fear and self-scaring. Yesterday morning, a wave of nausea overcame me. I had to pack for Greece. My mini-vacation was over. I had to reenter the world of tours.

It was a familiar anxiety. And yet what do I have to be anxious about? I need some fear in my tours, something to worry about, something to promote awe, wonder, and focus, to make them even more successful. But I can't even find one worry. Everything is in place and in order.

How can I strive without worry?

Good question. I must learn to do it regardless of worry. But for what?

Today I can't think of one business challenge. Ninety percent of my motivation used to come from financial worry. By paying off my debts, taking my mind off the stock market, and assuming a vow of poverty, I have put the financial worry lifestyle behind me. Sure there will be tough upcoming periods when business cycles slow down, but that is not the subject. Today's question is: Can I find business motivation beyond financial worry? In other words, is there any reason besides money to engage in business? If I had lots of money, would I still want to be in it?

I love studying, the physical exhilaration of exercise, and the arts. Can I also love business? Did I ever? Was I simply forced into it to make a living? With my improved financial situation, do I even want to bother with it? What reason can I find?

Business has never been part of my miracle schedule.

Will I be traveling the road of student, scholar, and artist? Should I give up my business and devote myself to fulfilling my miracle schedule? That is a daring thought.

Another option is to do as little business as possible.

In the past, I had goals. I wanted to expand my tours, get more customers, more folk dancers for classes and weekends. I wanted to learn to be an entrepreneur, build up a big organization, run tours to lots of countries, make lots of money. That dream has run its course. At the moment, I have no interest in building my business. For now I'll just have to traipse along on my old business trail with no future goals in sight.

Is this the end of it? Will I become a hermit-scholar? Can my future direction, based on the dictates of my miracle schedule, ever include business? Should it?

Do I have a need for it that I am not recognizing?

Is this an end or the beginning of a new definition?

Accepting Cycles, or Happiness and its Cycles

Although we all strive for happiness, it is an impossible stage to reach on a permanent basis. Perhaps the only permanently happy people are dead people.

I had it all last week. All my work and vacation "events" were going beautifully. I had the perfect balance between stress and relaxation. This "perfect state" lasted about a week. Then, even though I "knew" the answer to how to be happy, knew the philosophy of stressing yourself slightly, followed by rest, knew the techniques for happiness, knew the spirit must enter the body of the happy person and fuse with the flesh, knew everything there is to know about being happy and what it takes to be happy, I ended up with the same descent into the downs, sadness, depression, demise of enthusiasm, loss of spirit, that always follows an up period. Reading The Mystery Of Light didn't help me either. Sure, I once again found a perfect philosophy and attitude to create happiness and oneness with the Spirit, if only I could follow it. But once again, my attempted ascent into sainthood failed.

There is no escaping the downs. They come even when I have everything I want. True, they don't last long, maybe a few days. But neither do my ups. No matter what I do, how I think, how I twist and change my attitudes, how I try to find just the right philosophy, just the right mix to reach a perfect happy state, I cannot hold on to the up I experience. I think, "Ah, finally I've got it. The elixir, the magic potion. At last I own it. It is mine, all mine, and forever! Happiness will never depart." And almost as soon as I start thinking this way, sure enough, happiness dribbles away. Soon it has vanished down the drain, and I'm back to where I started.

This cyclical state is particularly noticeable to me today, because I've "solved" so many of my long-term problems. I am at a good place mentally, and I've got much less to worry about. My tours run easier, my finances have improved, my guitar playing is improving. Basically, although problems will come up, I imagine I've finally got much of my life together and in order. What a surprise then to see my mood fall apart, descend from the glories of personal happiness with its growth through the slight stress philosophy to the depths of na-na land. They're not even depths, but rather flat lands, a semi-desert, with enough water so I won't die, but not enough spiritual nutrients to fill life with passion and enthusiasm either.

Perhaps I should simply accept this situation and move on— simply admit I was wrong, that I will never find a solution to personal happiness, that I'll have to be satisfied with momentary jumps into the stratosphere. My happiness will spike upwards for awhile, then descend into the pits. Such is my nature. Perhaps I can never change it.

I like what Feurstein said about knowing the difference between pleasure and happiness. Pleasures are transient; happiness puts you in touch with the permanent transcendent forces. Yes, I know this, and it's nice to read it again. But big deal: I know it but can't do it, at least not for long.

Such is life; such is me. Perhaps the best thing I can do is go along with my changing moods, expect them, expect they'll simply move round and round in endless cycles with an occasional spike upward. It's the artistic approach to life, and like it or not, it seems to be the only thing I am capable of doing.

Accept my nature. Try not to be fooled by the ups and downs of my cycle. Try to remember that during the up times, the downs are right around the corner, and that, during the down times, the ups are right around the other corner.

Well, Jump!

Suppose the negatives I keep thinking are all excuses to prevent my jumping into the Ocean of Being?

I've been standing on the shore for many years, trying to perfect my skills so one day I could "jump safely" into the Unknown, that vast, mysterious, awesome Ocean, and lose my ego in its timelessness. I have practiced guitar, perfected my writing style, tried to find financial security. For years I used the excuse "I am not yet ready. When I achieve financial stability and am safe and rich, then I'll be secure enough to let myself go; then I'll be ready to jump. If I could only perfect my guitar technique, get a perfect tremolo, then I'll be able to jump."

This year I did the latter by perfecting a relaxed right hand and tremolo. I also got out of debt. These two achievements colored my entire year. I have removed all impediments. I have no excuses left. What is left but to jump?

Yet I am still afraid. I now stand at the edge of the Ocean, trembling, waiting, frantically looking for another excuse. I know I have run out of excuses. There is only one direction left: Jump! Not only in guitar, writing, business, miracle schedule, but all events, moments, activities, parts, and aspects of life.

This jump is for good.

Why was I down after last night's Balkan Bash folk dance? I didn't take the plunge; I didn't jump. Instead, I stood on the sidelines talking, or, when I danced, I thought about how to get the beginners involved. It was the "thinking of others" excuse, noble but an excuse nevertheless.

I'm at the end of Excuse Road, hovering at the edge of the Ocean of Being, my fears disguised as depression, hesitation, ennui, and limbo.

Do I want to find awe, mystery, enthusiasm, and reverence in my tours? Well, jump!

Do I want them in my guitar playing? Well, jump!

Do I want them in folk dance classes, bookings, or anything else I do? Well, jump!

Do I want to move to the next level? Well. . . .

Greed and Desire

Are my greed and desire related?

I gave up greed when I retired my debt. But with it I also gave up my desire and motivation.

Something is wrong here. Perhaps the Buddhist state of nirvana is not what I want. Perhaps desirelessness is not a worthy life goal but only a short-term reward, a sparkling reminder of the higher world, a by-product of work, struggle, push, and attainment.

Are greed and desire wedded to each other?

Greed is desire unbalanced.

Desire is greed set straight.

What about enthusiasm? Do desire and enthusiasm go together? Where does greed fit in? What exactly is the relationship between desire and enthusiasm?

Desire rides on the worldly road of wants; enthusiasm is a visit from the divine en route.

Thus desire breeds enthusiasm.

We can break through to the world of nirvanic light, briefly touching the divine essence, but we cannot stand in the holy fire too long. Soon we must "withdraw" to our human condition, encasing ourselves in the worldly grays of fleshy desire, greed, and enthusiasm.

On the Well-Springs of Motivation

Fears are motivations in disguise.

I can either scare myself or get depressed. There are three basic states of mind: fright, depression, or the resting state between the two.

How to scare myself to new heights.
1. Run a tour to Eastern Turkey
2. Run a tour to Israel, including visiting Petra in Jordan, climbing Mount Sinai, and visiting Saint Catherine's monastery in Egypt.
3. Run and dance with metatarsal pain.
4. Perform, give a concert, play, and practice fast.
5. Overwhelm myself with work.
6. Do the 150s.
7. Face embarrassments; live in the embarrassment.

This fear, this desire to scare myself to new heights, is related to the cosmic fear, the awe and trembling before God.

The overwhelmed feeling—and the fear of being overwhelmed—is related to the awe and trembling before the burdens which the Creator has placed upon me.

There is the pain of being overwhelmed, and there is the fear of pain. What and how do they differ?

God reveals Himself through His gifts. By acknowledging and honoring the gift of my talents, I am acknowledging and honoring HaShem and His revelations.

A revelation a day keeps the doctor away.

Falling Apart

"Falling Apart" is a chapter I'm reading by Pema Chodron from her new book, *Falling Apart*.

Falling apart is certainly the way to go, the way to think, the way to be. Besides, whether I like it or not, it always happens. Falling apart is at the root of all my fears; it is death in transient disguise.

If I can handle the fear of falling apart, I'll do just fine. But how?

Maybe I don't have to practice; I only have to recognize it. Falling apart is with me every day. Only I'll do almost anything to avoid facing it.

How does falling apart manifest itself? Through a fear, bordering on panic, of forgetting my pieces during a concert. Yesterday, while I played my Bach "Fugue and Gigue," I imagined an audience before me. I panicked and forgot the notes. Now, I have been playing these pieces over thirty years. If I don't know them by now, I'll never know them. The problem was not in knowing all the notes, but rather in being afraid of falling apart in public. Beyond the humiliation that would entail, there were the deeper fears of falling apart like fear of death, vulnerability, weakness, and my lack of control over the great forces of life. Those have never left me and probably never will. Public humiliation in the form of falling apart on stage is only one of them.

What other falling-aparts do I fear? How about worries that my tours will fall apart? That fear haunts me almost every waking moment when I run my tours. How about falling apart physically? When I hurt my foot, heel, metatarsal, back, or knee, I imagine my folk dance teaching career falling apart; then when I add my neck, shoulder, or upper back, I see my entire physical system crumbling as I head for cripplehood, weakness, disability, nursing home, and finally death.

Yes, there is almost no end to these falling apart fears. They are almost my foundation. What does that say about my foundation? As I struggle to hold on, to find mental, emotional, and financial security, I see that the foundation of my foundation is truly without foundation, that my ground is groundless, that the center and core of my being are constantly perched on the razor's edge, tottering on the abyss between somethingness and nothingness.

Perhaps falling apart can lead me to an essence I am always searching for, an essence that is essentially ungraspable: the heart of Big Truth. I want to cling to the "little truths" I invent, to live in safety and security. But there are none in the transient forms I cling to. Paradoxically, they only exist in falling apart.

I would do well to face this fear and even "practice" it. I could start with a guitar concert, then move to daily meditations on body and business falling apart, and then to the grand finale of death. For what is the fear of death but the daily experienced fear of falling apart?

New Directions and Idea for 1997–98

New ideas and directions resulting from my farm experience:

1. Running. I ran an exhausting hour and a half. While running, I realized that, during the year, I had slowly "given up" my running in favor of yoga. No good. Change it. Now, a short warm-up, followed by a run, then a longer "yoga" warm-down.

2. Jewish Education. Buy Dershowitz's book The Vanishing American Jew. Inspirational passages on pages 299. Start and restart my Jewish education.

3. Buy the Oxford Universal Dictionary (first published in 1933), with its Greek roots written in Greek.

4. Writing: Based on the "Falling Apart" and "Love and Compassion for Self" idea: Editing and organizing New Leaf.

Suppose I consider each New Leaf journal entry with love and compassion. I know, after I write a journal entry, I want to "throw it away." Out of me! Like a large shit, once it is out, I want to flush it down the toilet and forget about it. This is true of most of my creative efforts. Once they are over, I want to move on to the next. It feels as if, by writing or creating anything, I am purging myself of dirt, cleansing and healing my soul by sloughing off these lumps of creative dirt. This is hardly a loving and compassionate approach to my creations. Rather than loving these creative and created parts of myself, I am rejecting them; I never want to see them again, acknowledge or recognize that they were part of me, and that, even though they are now "in my past" they are nevertheless still a part of me.

A loving and compassionate approach to my writing—and all of my work—might be the key to editing and organizing my New Leaf. Self-love may well the answer and the doorway and the road to universal love. Why not? The universe is in the self and the self is in the universe. We cannot know the universe except through the self, and self-knowledge. It all makes mucho sense. Something to think about.

New Beginnings

Today is a day of beginnings.

Before I start, I must I must pack for the Czech tour, GROW weekend, put together my fall brochure, call Barbara Tapa about the internet etc., and do some minor mop-up details like calling Arlene and Batya. Then I can start my new beginnings.

Better yet, based on the desire to stay calm and follow my star even in the midst of chaos, disarray, and total disorder, I shall start my new beginnings today—now—no matter what!

What are my new beginnings? A running restart, a writing progression: starting the habit pattern of daily organizing and editing a bit of past New Leaves; I'll start thinking about my own personal Jewish education program as inspired by Dershowitz; and on guitar, I'll keep exploring the tyranny of speed and past forms.

That is all for this morning. But that is a lot.

PERFORMANCE

"You're Really Good!"

Yesterday I sat on the front lawn of the farm, playing Bach on the guitar. Miki heard me playing.

"You're good," she said.

"Thank you."

"No, I mean you're really good. There's okay, good, and really good."

"Thank you," I said again. "It's because I'm sixty."

As I said it, I realized it was the usual "put-down" answer. Imagine someone saying I am good. What does it mean? I have to face the internal "good guitar playing" part of myself.

Part of me still can't stand hearing I am good. It is that same critical voice which keeps speaking whenever I play guitar in public. Truth is, I don't even need a public; I don't need an audience listening to my playing. I create my own audience whenever I play; I create a critical public ready to pounce on every mistake I make, ready to criticize me, tear me apart, and destroy any attempt at creativity. My audience is my own creation; my audience is the various factions and part of me fighting for survival, leadership, and dominance in my mind. I create them all. Many are negative thinking ghosts, probably the same ones that I am afraid might come out of the farm walls at night.

My new "falling apart" and "beyond good and bad" project is to look at these aspects of myself, keep my eye on them, watch the negative thought patterns relentlessly, and accept them with a compassion and love for my miserable self, knowing that these selves, parts, and the problems they create will change but never go away. They are part of my human flaws, the pebbles, rocks, and boulders on my spiritual path. If and when I remove them, others will appear. Life is one transient obstacle after another. My only hope for a more sympathetic survival is compassion, and love for my poor tired struggling heroic self as it fights for breath under the Niagara Falls of never-ending problems each day threatening to overwhelm me.

I took a run two mornings ago; that afternoon, my left knee started to hurt. Yesterday I could hardly walk. It's true my left knee pain has distracted me from my left foot metatarsal pain. But I'm the guy who is doing the 150s squat program; I've even added some one-legged squats. I haven't had knee pain for years. Why now? Partly it could be because I've upped my exercises by adding one-legged squats. But it could also be psychological, some kind of new fear expressed through knee pain. Such a psychosomatic ailment would certainly not be new. As a creative person, I generate, not only my own pleasure, but my own pains as well. The knee pain came the day after two folk dance teaching jobs: first, for the folk dance dysfunctional crowd at the Westfield bar mitzvah, then the enthusiastic Shavuot Reform Temple group in Franklin Lakes. The latter was such a fantastic evening. I left high and inspired and happy. Such a youthful, dynamic bunch of dancers. But I left thinking how my body is no longer youthful, that I could be many of these dancers' father, that my physical and mental components are part of another generation, that soon I will be passed over, passed on, and passed out, if not today or tomorrow, then soon enough. The future in front of me reads "Exit." So a sadness, alienation, even ostracism, softened the ecstasy of the folk dance evening. Added to this, my tours, weekends, and next year's folk dance teaching schedule were completed. All in all, it was an ending, a death in disguise. Next day my knee pain began.

If my knee pain mirrors death in disguise, it also signals rebirth up the road. The ups and downs of the flow never end. There are as many positives to sixty as there are negatives. I'm still in shock over the "meaning" of such an age. It sounds so venerable, vulnerable, wise, and archaic. Could this really be me? What does it mean? Certainly I play the guitar better.

And I get credit for practicing. The "You're really good!" is another part of myself, of the never-ending progression of problems that I want to learn to accept with love, compassion, and humor.

Learn To Be Yourself in Public

I arrived at GROW II last night. Very impressed: Clean to spotless, good people, good future here if Mildred, the supreme director and center of the community, doesn't get sick and die.

Last night while I was playing guitar in the living room, the staff invited me to play for them. I "serenaded" them from the dining room while they washed dishes in the kitchen. The clanging of the pots and pans was pretty noisy; nevertheless, they loved it. I'm surprised I did it. I guess I wanted to practice playing in public.

I don't have to guess. I know. Playing in public is an excellent way to practice focus and concentration. I must put myself in public more. To be myself in public, to play "for myself," to focus and concentrate on my playing while the eyes of the public are on me and the ears of the public are listening, all subtly pressuring me to please them and distract myself from my inner voice, is a supreme learning challenge for me. That is last night's long-range lesson. It also creates a future vow: play in public as much as possible; place myself under the scrutiny of the public eye. Learn to be yourself in public. A difficult but worthy task. It is a marvelous exercise in focus, concentration, and "meditation in the lion's mouth."

BUSINESS

Enthusiasm

I need a few people to go on tour with me—for enthusiasm—but not many. I need a few people to dance with me, or go on weekends—for enthusiasm—but not many.

Can there be business without money?

Business is service to others. But service is secondary, a by-product of enthusiasm.

I believe in enthusiasm. Service comes out of enthusiasm.

"Make your problems your pleasures"—Barbara Goldschmidt

No New Tour Attitude in Sight

I read about northern Spain in the travel section of the New York Times. An idea grazed my head. I can't call it a business idea yet; I can't call it an inspiration. It's only a bubble on the calm Lake-of-No-Ideas that washes my business brain these days. The bubble of running tours to new destinations. There wasn't much of a thrill in it. I hoped for a return to the old thrills, chills, fears, and excitements of travel. I wanted to be inspired; I wanted new enthusiasms and interest to suffuse my soul and fill my empty brain with longing, learning, and higher visions.

Running trips next year to Sicily in February, Iceland (and perhaps Norway) in July, and even Spain won't envelope me the way my first trip to Hungary did. Deep down, I must admit, I've lost the glory of tour adventure. Tours have become "just a job." My only thrill comes when new customers register. The trip itself, the adventure, has lost its luster. I'd rather stay home and study.

This is too bad, but it's true. With such a miserable attitude, why should I run tours in the first place? Well, they make good money. That's about it. As for adventure, new directions, daring jumps into the unknown, I'll have to look elsewhere.

Where should I look? I can only see my miracle schedule.

I am so sorry I can't find thrills and glory in travel to strange, exotic foreign lands. How can I get back my luster?

I don't know. I need a fundamental change in my attitude but I don't know what it is or where to find it. Perfecting my tours is one way to go. That would be using the guitar improvement model.

But what's to improve? The tours itineraries I have are fine already. Yes, they can be changed, but improved? Perhaps by trying to "improve" them, I'll make them worse. Besides, after the itinerary, hotels, program—the basics—are in place, my tours can only "improve" by having good tourists on them. And that is something I have little to no control over.

I can only find my pleasures, fulfillments, growth, and tour happiness in myself and my own touristic vision. And at the moment, I can't find any. Adding a new country is fine. But such quantitative changes will not bring back the thrill of newness. Only a new attitude will do that. And, at the moment, that attitude is lost and far away.

End of Tourism As I Know It

Let's face it: my tours are dead. Tourism as I know it is over. There's no way I can put new life in them, no way to resurrect the old thrills, fears, excitements of former tour days. I can't return to the past but only move forward. The future tells me I've done it all before. I've solved my "tour problem," answered the tour questions I started out with.

I've learned the fundamentals: how to be an entrepreneur, how to organize, run, and lead a tour, how people folk dance in foreign countries. I've learned how to become a leader. Even the goal of making money, although not fulfilled in terms of wealth—I still don't have much money—has been fulfilled in psychological terms. I've stabilized my financial environment through my vow of poverty and freedom from debt.

If all the goals and purposes of tourism have been accomplished, why beat the dead horse of tourism? Why keep pushing it? Running tours to new destinations will not inspire me. Just more of the same with a slight twist.

I'm not going to drop them. First thing, though, is to realize their place. They will no longer rank at the top or even middle of my list but sink near the bottom along with weekends and folk dancing classes. I'll keep doing them with a modicum of pleasure, but I won't put much mental effort into them.

If tourism is over, I'll have to look elsewhere for thrills and chills. Where? I don't know but at least I do know it isn't tourism.

If this is true, why bother searching out new itineraries and destinations? Why not just keep doing what I'm doing, running tours to the same countries? It's easier and will take much less effort on my part. My brain can be free to focus on the new chill-thrill activities, even though I don't know what they are. I may add a new country just for my amusement. This year it's Romania, next year Sicily. Iceland is also on the horizon.

Where will new thrills and chills come from if not from tours, weekends, or folk dance classes?

Concerts?

Good question.

Hoping For Metatarsal Revelations

We had a wonderful Romanian dance workshop with Mihai David last night. Great crowd, exciting dances. I even made money.

Why am I still low? Well, one ostensible reason is my left metatarsal problem. During my week off from dancing the pain stopped; I thought I could return to a normal life. But when I danced last night the pain returned. How discouraging. Mihai taught dances I love, with lots of leaps, off-beat stamps, shouts, quick moves to the right, left, and center. But I could hardly dance. Every time I jumped, I felt intense left metatarsal pain. Then I anticipated the pain and held back. Soon any dancing pleasure I hoped to receive from Mihai's dances disappeared.

No wonder I feel low and hopeless. But I wonder if there is more to this pain than I think. Let's look at the history of my metatarsal problem in the light of the "as above so below" philosophy. Perhaps the Higher Force has prepared a lesson for me in metatarsal form. I'm hoping that, when I learn it, my pain will go away and I'll be able to dance with full gusto again.

I'm suffering from "schioapa overuse"—limping Romanian dance syndrome. (*Schioapa* means "limping" in Romanian. It is one of Mihai's great leaping Romanian dances.) In January when I taught schioapa to our Tuesday night group, I kept leaping onto my left foot. By the end of several weeks my metatarsal hurt. But I didn't pay attention to it. I figuring such temporary pain would soon go away. Our Tuesday night dancing was so good I thought I should make it an advanced dancing night. The best dancing in Jersey! We were taking off! It was the superman complex in dance form. Superman usually comes at the top of the cycle, when I'm flying with all barriers down. I'm heading upwards. Nothing can stop me. Spirit runs my ship. Body has vanished, along with all earthly limitations. This kind of thinking, where both feet are firmly planted in mid-air, usually initiates some kind of downfall. The law of gravity states that, when one leaps, one falls. I've fallen into a metatarsal hell.

The seeds of this attitude were planted in January at the top of my cycle. Entrapment in repetition may be the psychological basis for my metatarsal condition. I am trapped— but in what, I am not sure. Successes in guitar, finance, and vow of poverty have put the mark of peace and satisfaction on my agenda; they have ripped away any hopes for joy through anxiety. I should be happy. Yet a gnawing dissatisfaction never leaves. Perhaps it will when I solve my metatarsal pain.

I am in a slow descent. I see no freshness, no new visions or directions in the future. I am in repetition mode. Everything I am doing I have done before. The joy of beginning a new venture or adventure has disappeared. Yet, these thoughts of stagnation are a result of long-range successes. My metatarsal pain may fill the emptiness born of success.

I can't jump or leap. I can't release myself into the full enthusiasm of a new adventure. Could this depressing static state be reflected in my metatarsal? I hope I'm onto something. if I am right, it will affirm my belief that, just as ideas begin in the ethereal heavens above and are reflected in matter on earth below, so disease begins above and is reflected below, so metatarsal pain began in my mind and is reflected in my foot. Once my conflict is resolved, my metatarsal will follow.

If this is true, it means looking at my metatarsal problem as one of direction and attitude.

My outer life is as good as it's going to get. It's my inner life that needs fixing.

I finished lunch with Mihai David, and Ginny and Hal. Mihai may design folk dance meetings, workshops, and events for our Romanian tour in August. He may even join us in person. This would be excellent news.

While talking to him I forgot Fred and Mary Bender's name. I am forgetting many names lately, along with geographical facts. Is this the prelude to Alzheimer's or a reflection of the lack of interest and enthusiasm I am experiencing in just about everything I am doing? Is it the prelude to a life change where, in order to move on, I must forget the old to make room for the new?

Is it the prelude to starting a new business?

Glimmer of Hope

I need to build something in the real material outside world; I need to do it both for my physical and mental health.

I'm inching back to the path. It's the first glimmer of hope.

Last night I watched a program on entrepreneurship on TV. It said teaching entrepreneurship was helping kids and communities in the inner cities, that colleges and high schools were teaching it, and that ninety percent of new jobs in America were now being created by entrepreneurs. No government involvement. Just private enterprise teaching people to work for themselves and realize their dreams. That they put such a positive program about business on TV amazed me; they showed entrepreneurship in a positive light. I remember when it was a dirty word.

I watched the program and started to cry.

Why was I crying? It was the same crying I did when, because of an injury, I couldn't run. I saw a runner in shorts and T-shirt running down the street on his way to the runner's high. My injury had put me out of the loop. How I missed the joys of running! It made me cry.

Now I was crying about entrepreneurship. Why? Obviously I missed my entrepreneurial days. Somehow setting myself straight financially, getting out of debt, having a few dollars in the bank, and taking my vow of poverty had driven me away from the dynamic anxieties of the entrepreneurial life. The "security" I had achieved felt so boring; it filled me with heart-breaking ennui. Part of me used to think such security was a "goal" and would "free" me for the higher, peaceful pursuits of scholarship, learning, art, bible study, and the private growth adventures embedded in my miracle schedule.

I must have been wrong. Since this attitudinal "success," I have been on a downward path. Joy, wearing shorts and T-shirt, has been draining from my brain, "running" out of me. Evidently, I need entrepreneurship for my physical and psychological health. If the dream of making lots of money is no longer enough to motivate me then I'd better find another reason. Without a dream, a goal of building something concrete, real, material, and substantial in the outside world, the dynamic spirit simply withers away.

Evidently, entrepreneurship is a bottom-line gut-wrenching need.

I wonder if it is partially the psychological cause of my left metatarsal problem.

Taking the Easy Way: The Easy Way Is Death

New ideas are starting to come. Fundamentally, I've got to return to hard.

I took the easy way when I taught folk dancing at the Jaguar Motor Plant yesterday. I had a rank beginner group. Nevertheless, I tried no experiments, did nothing new. I only taught what I knew.

Taking the easy way is death.

I need hard. I need challenge, risk, daring, and the mystery and excitement it creates. Without it I dry up and return to Pruneland. Hard is probably the best—maybe the only way—to wake myself from the sluggish, semi-depressed, state of mental torpor I've been living in for the past few weeks.

I'm developing some new ideas, directions and paths. Aerobic yoga, aerobic guitar, cataloguing my New Leaf Journal, and dumping most of my old folk dance repertoire in favor of learning, choreographing, and teaching new dances. In a visceral way, I torture myself to remember: Take the hard, challenging, creative path. The easy way is death.

I'm thinking about other challenges, too. My Greek travel challenge can be to think, write, and speak "only" in Greek. I might also try remembering names of folk dancers I keep forgetting. It's a habit I got into many years ago when my "in-group" deserted me. I developed the habit of thinking: Why bothering remembering their names—or anyone else's? It's too painful. Why put in the effort if eventually they will abandon me? So I consciously—and unconsciously—tried forgetting them. Now it is becoming a habit to forget people's names almost immediately.

But I see a change of attitude up ahead. Now I have another reason to remember names. Why should I? Because it's hard, that's why.

The act and effort of trying to remember is a good-in-itself.

Jumping into Greece, *New Leaf*, and Eternity

I'm leaving for Greece today. I'm so sad and frustrated. I can't get started or inspired about anything. Resistance, indeed. It's not because I'm leaving today either but something more basic.

What is my direction? Where am I going? My gut tells me my next step is to organize *New Leaf*. No choice. I am trapped in a corner. What else is there to do? A sense of incompleteness hangs over me.

Beyond the organization of *New Leaf* looms the question: what will I do with the books that come out of it? Publish them? Why bother? But if I follow the "Why bother?" route I'll have to ask, "Why organizing them in the first place?" The "Why bother?" question always leads to the same dead end.

I always ask the "Why bother?" question when I'm standing at the edge of the ocean afraid to jump in. Ah, what wisdom! Afraid to jump in—a lifetime fear revisiting me in its newest form. On a lower level, it's the same fear with my upcoming Greek tour. Why did I wake up with a headache this morning? Afraid to jump in, of course.

Two immediate upcoming goals are forming: first, jump into my Greek tour; second, jump into organizing New Leaf.

On the upper level, I'll also add: jump into everything else. Make "jumping into" my newest project, my newest skill development. Make jumping a habit. Of course, it is the most difficult thing to do, the biggest challenge. I am asking myself to dump my ego in favor of swimming naked and egoless in the deep dark unfathomable mystery of the ocean; to take off my protective clothing, and jump, nude and unprotected, into the loose-fitting waters of awe, wonder, and reverence.

What other choice do have I? I've walked the path of self-improvement, of hopes for financial security hopes, of waiting and working for the skills of self-fulfillment. I stand at the end of paths. There is nothing left to do but jump.

Thus, on my lower level, jump into my Greek tour, and organize my New Leaf; on a higher level, jump into everything I do. A life time project, a discipline, a path of spiritual practice and form of meditation. It is my only path to eternity.

Arrival in Thessalonika

We flew into Athens, then took a domestic flight to Thessaloniki where I met our guide, Eleni Gogas, at the airport. She wore blue jeans, looked disheveled and lively. I liked her right away. Her father collects folk songs and plays the Cretan lyre. She's pushy, smart, lively, funny, an ex-art historian, and she knows how to dance. She feels like just the right guide for us. I think we're in for some good guideship. Indeed, the Lord puts angels along my travel path.

I'm glad I brought my computer along. Thank you, Mr. Lord, and Bernice, for pushing me to bring it. Two days without sleep can rot the mind. Although I woke up this morning feeling absolutely awful, my morning coffee, combined with writing, is slowly bringing me back to life.

On the plane flight to Greece I wrote some thoughts in my journal about the relationship between greed, desire, and enthusiasm. I should consider and remember them not only for this tour, but for my life.

Barbara Gorbet, the Grain of Sand

Yesterday my illusion of having a wonderful tour group cracked. It is a wonderful group except for Barbara Gorbet. She is my grain of sand. Hopefully, the friction of rubbing against her miserable personality will help turn me into a pearl.

Yesterday, early in the morning, we headed for Philippi and Kavala by bus. En route, our wonderful, dynamic, opinionated, assertive, up-front guide, Eleni, told me we were near the Chalkidikian towns of Stagira, birth place of Aristotle, and Stratoni, where Heracleitus of "you never put your foot in the same stream twice" fame was born. I thought about what a great Greek Philosopher Pilgrimage it would be to visit Aristotle's and Heraclitus's home towns. I could put them at the end of our Mount Athos cruise next year.

Meanwhile, after visiting the ruins of Philippi and viewing the jail cell where St. Paul wrote his epistle to the Philippians, Barbara Gorbet complained—along with a few others—that Eleni talked too long and in too much detail about the historical sites and museums we were visiting. When I told Eleni about it, she said, "No problem, I'll change my talks. I'm still trying to get the feel of this group." She took the "criticism" beautifully, very professionally. On the bus, she told our group if they had any questions or problems, they should speak up. She told us her father had told her as a child: Speak up, girl! What's the matter? Haven't you had enough to eat? "Be direct," Eleni said. "It's our Greek way. Say what's on your mind."

Later, before lunch in Kavalla, Eleni and Barbara had a confrontation. Barbara said she was unapproachable. They argued it out.

How should I handle Barbara? Is there anything I can do to make the trip better for her? Perhaps I should ask her to go home and I take her off my mailing list. It's hubris to believe I'll ever change her. What makes me maddest is how naive I was, even with all my tour experience, to think this was the best tour group I ever had. Any tour is a work in progress. There is no way to ever predict how it will turn out. You handle it day by day, hour by hour. You never really know how the people will react, even those you've known for years. Some rise to the occasion, others sink. No matter what, it's always a surprise. My mistake, my hubris and problem, was expecting my tour group to blend together without difficulty. Yes, I expected it; worse, I predicted it.

Expectations and predictions are just about the worst mental constructs I can have, not only running a tour, but in life. It is almost impossible to cut them back to zero—even though that would be wonderful. But certainly I should guard against them. Actually, expectations and predictions are really projections of hopes, wishes, and dreams. It goes back to greed, desire, and enthusiasm. Wishes and hopes are desires in disguise.

I must return to a day-by-day, hour-by-hour handling approach. The fight for tour success is won and lost on a daily basis. Live in the moment and fight for my vision.

A unified tour is part of my vision. However, that is often close to impossible. I'll up my vision to fulfilling the kind of program I like with lots of dancing, meetings with local groups, people-to-people contacts etc.

How do I handle Barbara? I still don't know. But at least I can fight for my vision, and to understand my instincts and intuitions when I deal with her. In the process, I can also aim to cut my expectations of success back to zero.

Pearls

Barbara Gorbet may turn out to be the grain of sand in my oyster. The irritations are making me wiser. All my predictions, expectations, and plans must be reviewed and altered. I've learned that I cannot predict how tour participants will react. I could not have predicted Barbara would be such a pain in the ass. She sounded so easy on the phone. Her voice tone was soft and understanding, with that good psychologist "I understand" tone. My only hint of future misery was that she was a psychologist.

Why was she put on my tour in the first place? God sent her to punish me for my hubris of predicting this would be a wonderful tour. I didn't live "in the moment" or let my intuition over-ride my intellect. Instead of realizing wishes and dreams are hopes in disguise, I turned them into "concrete realities"; I predicted their future existence. Thus I broke the biblical injunction of Thou shalt not worship graven images. Instead of praying for guidance from above, I worshiped the false idol called Future.

That's what I did wrong.

Now, what can I do right? Is there any way to improve the situation? Last night Barbara called my room at eleven o'clock and asked if she, Jane, and I could have a conference. We met in the hall lobby. I listened to an hour of her complaints, softly supported, to my surprise, by Janet. Along the way she said she had just ended a nine-year love relationship and that her daughter had gotten married and could no longer travel with her. I thought that explained part of her unhappiness and also showed the near impossibility of satisfying her. Finally, she broke down in tears. I felt sorry for her but even sorrier for me for having her on our tour. What could I do for her? She wants to rewrite our tour program to fit her needs, as well as reprogram our guide. She wants an outline and overview of every spot we visit, how much time we will spend there, what to do there, etc. Her demands are so vague, I don't know what to do with them.

I gave her two suggestions: first she could think about going home, and perhaps get her money back through her tour insurance; second, we could try working something out together. We opted for the latter suggestion. We'll see where it leads.

Greek Musings

I'm writing this St.Paulian epistle in Kalambaka's Edelweiss hotel at the foothills of the Meteora monastery complex.

Yesterday was an "improved Barbara day." Eleni and I worked hard to satisfy her. We succeeded to a certain degree but nevertheless, I doubt if she'll ever be happy even thought we're trying our best. It is impossible to satisfy some people. Somehow I think she'll sue me at this end of the tour—or at least ask for a portion of her money back.

Meanwhile, with Eleni as our guide, I'm reconsidering running tours to Greece without me. I'll use the "Adam Molnar Hungarian Tour" model. Now that our program is in order, the big question will be how to get customers. Marketing is a life time problem somewhat like the daily struggle between good and evil.

What else is new? Not much I can think of. I'm drained from yesterday's long day: we visited archeological ruins at Pella, folk museum at Naousa, the royal Macedonian tombs at Vergina, stopping for coffee in the village of Litchoro at the foothills of Mount Olympus, then drove all the way to Kalambaka.

I'm tired but at peace with myself; my urge to write has diminished. Perhaps I should read *The Falsification of Macedonian History* by Nicolaos Martis.

Running a Tour: (Unity) Oneness at Delphi; Achieving "Tour Mind"

We are staying at the beautiful Xenia Hotel in Delphi. Our view in back extends across a deep gorge; I can see all the way to the Gulf of Corinth. Last night's supper here was good; the rooms are quiet; we are away from the traffic noise of the Delphi streets. In the future, we should stay at the Xenia.

Yesterday we visited Meteora, had lunch in Kalambaka, then drove across the Thessalian plain to Delphi. I sat next to Barbara. She offered me a cookie stick she'd purchased in Kalambaka. That was step one: feed me, and I love you.

"How are we doing?" I asked.

"Much better," she answered with a smile.

"Good," I said. I raised my right arm and shouted, "Yes!"

Then as the bus rolled along the Thessalian Plain, I turned towards the window and started to cry. I had won! All my effort at putting this tour together, at uniting the people, at making oneness out of a conglomerate of diversities, at turning many directions, differences, and opposites towards one road, at harnessing the pearl-creating grain of sand strength of Barbara's miserable attitude, had succeeded. The two a.m. commitment I had made in my Thessalonika Phillipion Hotel room to turning Barbara's misery into something positive had worked. I was victorious—at least for today.

So why was I crying? I'll tell you: suddenly, I realized how running this tour had beaten up my ego, not only by Barbarian miseries but other embarrassments such as poor service and miserable food at the Phillipion. Running a tour is an exercise in humility, submission of the ego to inexorable forces, and dealing with events beyond your control while you fight for survival in strange unknown inhospitable climates with people whose minds are often on a loose string.

As Laura Perls said, "I have learned to live in the embarrassment." The first few days of every tour totter at the edge of the cliff, leaning over the abyss of humiliation.

I cried not only for my victory over the forces of lethargy and inertia, but also for the glory of my strength of determination to make this tour work at all costs.

Now I also know why I can't concentrate on learning Greek, reading, or any other intellectual endeavor on tour. All my mental energies go into creating unity and oneness. That is my ultimate tour goal. Everything else—guiding, itinerary, hotels, food, and program are secondary. With unity, our tour can survive minor and even major bumps and annoyances; without it—if everyone is lost in their own distant and divisive thoughts, our tour won't survive an overboiled breakfast egg.

What do I mean by unity? In the beginning, a tour consists of separate individuals focused on their own wants and needs. But, by the third, fourth, or even fifth day, a strange transformation begins to take place. By experiencing events together, tour members begin to coalesce. Individual minds, including my own, begin to melt and blend into a "group mind. " A new brain is created along with a new soul, a larger "individual" consisting of twelve separate tourists, which is now unique in this world.

When I run a tour, my mind is not free until this "group mind" is formed. It is the ultimate nature of my job. Tonight in Delphi, I feel our group has finally coalesced. Of course I still cannot rest. Each day has new challenges. Nevertheless, most of the torturous spade work I did during the first few days of this tour is beginning to bear fruit. We'll see where it leads.

Olympia

We arrived late and tired in Olympia, checked into our New Olympia Hotel, had supper, and discovered the Touris Club Folk Dance performance had been canceled. I announced it to our group: "I have bad news and good news. The bad news is the folk dance performance has been canceled; the good news is that the shops in town are open." To my surprise, not only did no one complain, but most were relieved. They were just too exhausted.

The American Exercise Plan

We arrived in Athens yesterday, checked into the Philippus Hotel—everyone liked it—and took a three hour afternoon break. In the evening, I led a walking tour of the Plaka; we ended up eating, dancing, and watching a fine folk dance performance at the Sissofus Taverna.

Our group loved the Plaka!

Once again I thought about how much fun it might be to guide my own tour. I could put all my knowledge of history to work. Will I ever do it? Something to consider.

All this by way of introduction. I still can't get hold of Concept Tours to find out about tomorrow's transfer arrangements to Pireus and our cruise. It's Sunday, and all agencies are closed. What a pain in the ass. I wanted to take today off. Now I have to worry about whether Concept Tours will contact me. My only hope is they will phone me.

I like my "personalized American exercise plan." Thanks to Eleni's sentence, "Yoga does not fit the Greek character," I'm applying the concept, "Yoga does not fit the American character," to myself. Although I call what I do yoga, I've always sensed it isn't quite yoga. I've also tried other names like calliyoga, callisthenic yoga, and calliyogathenics. I've never thought of it as "pure" yoga. Rather, I have incorporating callisthenics, yoga postures, chi kong exercises, and who knows what else along the way, and have welded a conglomerate of exercise systems into one. The best name I can think of for it is the American Exercise Plan.

Someone once said, "A tourist is one who learns about a country; a traveler is one who learns about himself." I've just learned something about myself.

Reality Is a Mess: Can I Tolerate Such Imperfection?

I walked the late afternoon streets of Athens in a state of total drainage. I thought about a cruise project of two hours of writing a day plus the American Exercise Program with ship gym and running.

Suddenly, as I crossed Syntagama Square I realized it was not drainage I suffer from but rather rage at Barbara. She is the poison on this tour. Irma also complains too much. Both complain about Eleni. Eleni's main problem is lateness; also her lectures are too long. I can live with the latter but the former drives me nuts.

Barbara is poison; Irma is a whiner; Eleni is late. They are all imperfect. So is this tour. In fact, I have been operating every day on various levels of imperfection. Reality is a mess.

Can I learn to tolerate imperfection?

If I accept it, will I try to perfect myself nevertheless?

My tours glide between messy reality and the perfection of sublime fantasy. Paradox Tours would be a good name for my company. It would specialize in subterranean tours of the underworld, travels through the unconscious with flashes of lighting and rolls of thunder along the way.

Physical Exhilaration

I'm in my cabin aboard the Olympia cruise line. After the chaos of getting on board and settling into our cabins, I had a great afternoon sleep followed by another seven hours at night, This morning I'm on the border of feeling rested.

Yesterday evening in my room before supper I began my American Plan exercise program. I did 150 push-ups sandwiched between various forward-bending yoga postures, then 150 sit-ups sandwiched between various back-bending yoga postures. It took about half an hour. By the time it was time for squats I was tired. Nevertheless, I did thirty in sets of threes sandwiched between a few standing yoga postures.

I tried explaining this American Plan philosophy of exercise to Charlie and completely failed. This new philosophy is important to me but somehow I can't convey it nuances to anyone, yet. I don't know why.

My American Exercise Program makes me feel more American, more in the tradition of my Riverdale upbringing, more in line with the exercises I did in high school and college. I discovered yoga after college, when I bought a book on it in Woodstock with a picture of a yogi standing on his head. I figured I would read it, learn yoga, and, as a joke, teach it to the guests at Chaits Hotel where I worked as a social director. I taught it in the afternoons, always reading up and staying a chapter ahead of my class. To my surprise, not only did the guests like it, but I did, too. I started practicing the postures. Soon they became a habit, part of my daily routine. I liked the yoga philosophy, too. But the philosophy had little to do with the way I practiced the exercises. I like the sensual erotic quality of the postures. They sure raised my kundalini! In the beginning, my kundalini was running wild and out of control. Now it's still running, but not as wild.

But I never felt I was doing true yoga. Maybe that's why I never looked for a yoga teacher. I didn't love yoga the way I love music. Language and writing have always been subservient to my love of music; yoga exercises have always been an off shoot of my love of movement, which, as a child, was expressed in the physical exhilaration I felt running wild around the park or on the farm before a storm or, as a teenager, by playing basketball.

My yoga is related to physical exhilaration, which is why I teach folk dancing and why I run. It's the musical high of a Beethoven symphony felt throughout my body. And it's totally American.

This morning I awoke with the sound of Erna Jayson's complaints ringing in my ears. Although her body was not in my bed, her brain certainly was. What a whiner! She's part of the negative forces.

Yesterday, we visited Patmos, my favorite spiritual island. Sadly and slowly, I walked through the streets of the town. I found a bookstore, bought two copies of Ted Petrides's Greek Folk Dances—one as a present for Sigrid and Charlie—then sat down in a coffee shop overlooking the harbor. I ordered coffee and had a long, slow, deep consultation with myself. I carried a small pocket notebook with me—I should always do this—and wrote down some thoughts. Here they are:

Where are my tours going? Where am I going?

I'm dropping language study and history; my boutique with all the fun of making purchases is also disappearing.

What is left? I've lost my way.

Dance and love of music started me on these tours. I have to get back to my roots, to the basics. But how?

While writing these meditations, suddenly I realized how much the negative forces had been pressing down on me during this trip and causing me to lose my way. In reality, this was a great tour! Our day in Thessalonika, where we met the dancers of Peristera practicing in front of the church, were invited to their village for a workshop, followed by a late evening in a taverna of more music and dance, followed the next evening by a performance of the village folk dance group of Peristera, who came all the way from their village to perform only for us in our hotel, were events I'll never forget. They rank with the major tour experiences of my life. They never would have happened without the inspired push of Eleni. In spite of the complaints about her, some of which I agree with, she must be credited and yes, loved, for making this experience possible.

Suddenly, after realizing this, I wanted to run another tour to Greece again. Eleni and I designed a beauty on the bus, which includes Thessaloniki for four days, Florina for one or two, Ioninna, one or two, and who knows what—Corfu, or an Ionian island cruise, or perhaps two nights in Kalambaka in a nice hotel with visits to Meteora and dancing the original Karagouna.

After that breath of fresh air and rebirth of energy and hope, I decided to analyze my tour into positive and negative forces. Barbara, and Erna—softly, are the negative forces; Sigrid, Charlie, and Helene are the positive forces; Ginny and Joe are quiet positive forces; Norma is a mezzo force slanting mostly towards the positive; Janet is probably a positive force although, because she is so quiet and has become friends with Barbara, she is harder to read. Thus, most of the people on my tour, excepting two, are in the positive camp. Reiterating, Barbara is the major negative force while Erna is the minor one. Two out of eleven isn't a bad percentage. Yet the negative forces are the ones I have been paying most attention to. Why is that?

At this point in my tour life, I don't need negative comments anymore to push me to improve my tours. Are negatives comments even useful? Most likely they reflect my own negative forces, my worries that things won't go right. It would be good for me to slant myself towards the positive, to constantly remind myself how great these tours are even though our bus may not be the best, our hotel rooms the newest, and our guides, drivers, and tourists might occasionally clash with each other. In spite of this, unforgettable adventures and serendipities pop up at every turn. Simply because some of pain-in-the-ass participants—or lack of participants, really—don't appreciate it and complain about it, doesn't mean I should focus so much on their troubles. After all, I cannot make them happy; only they can do that. Keeping my eye on the positive is the best thing I can do for myself—and for the majority of my tourists as well.

Forget about the Barbaras and Irmas. Consider them as flies buzzing around my head. As with a fly, I must make a small effort to either swat it or brush it away. A small recognition of the negative forces is all right. Just don't hand them the whole bus.

After all these meditations I returned to a bookstore on Patmos and bought about seventy dollars worth of books on orthodox Christianity. One of them, The Way of the Ascetics by Tito Colliander, I read on the toilet this morning. Beautiful quotes in the introduction by Kenneth Leech:

"The material world is the vehicle, not the enemy, of the spirit."

"All theology is mystical theology."

"The unity of the mystical and social is something we have largely lost in the West."

Indeed, I could focus on uniting the mystical and social on my tours. It is a good challenge to think about.

Sitting in a Rhodes Café

We're coming to the end of our tour. This morning we're docking at the port of Heraklion in Crete; in the afternoon, we'll visit Santorini; early tomorrow we'll disembark in Pireaus, spend the day in Athens, then fly back to New York. This is the last writing I'll be doing in Greece. Soon I'll pack, pay my bills, and pick up my passport from the ship's registration deck.

As I sat in the Rhodes cafe drinking Fanta and reading Hellas, A Portrait Of Greece by Nicholas Gage, I had an epiphany. I'll refer to the notes in my pocket notebook, which from now on I will always be carrying on my person. Here's what I wrote:

A surge of excitement and energy. Lifetime commitment. That was why I hesitated for so many months. Should I make one to Greece? Israel? Bulgaria, Hungary, and Turkey? Others? Greece means Byzantium and learning Greek; Israel means Jewish and learning Hebrew. Both are centers of civilization. I might add Sicily and Turkey but seeing them as an expansion through Greek eyes, since they were first settled by Greeks.

I am searching for a commitment. I need it. Should I just pick a country and go for it?

I looked back over the year. Since January, when I paid off my debts, I have been depressed, low, bottomed out; slowly I dropped my commitments to language, history, and even running. Questions of Why bother? and Why do anything? hung over my head. Why did these questions drag me down so long? I don't know. But I couldn't shake them. However, yesterday as I sat at the Rhodes cafe, the cloud lifted and I felt reborn. Ready to make new commitments. But commitments no longer based on making mucho money, but rather on the "pure" need to commit myself to something. One of the rationalizations I used during the past few months was, I'm getting older. I'll soon be sixty. How embarrassing. How could such a thing happen to me? What is left to do after sixty? The clock is running out. Then, as I read Way Of The Ascetics, I was reminded that Abraham didn't start his trek from Haran to Canaan until age seventy-five. Even Iron-Man Johnson didn't start his twenty-two-year marathon career until age seventy. Again I was reminded: It is never to late to start. I had used age as an excuse. But nevertheless, the gray cloud wouldn't lift.

It did yesterday. Thank you, tour! More proof that while a tourist learns about a country, a traveler learns about himself.

New Travel Ideas

1. Travel to new destinations, make new itineraries.
2. Become a travel consultant for the countries I know. This takes care of my "big tour company" problem.

Most important: I must excite myself! This means new countries, new itineraries, new ways of traveling in old lands. It means many folk dance meetings, too.

With this attitude, I can open up Sicily, Italy, Turkey, Iceland, Scandinavia, and Baltic countries.

New question: Why travel with me?

I am your leader, not your guide.

If this is the case, why should people pay me?

They pay for my leadership abilities, not form my specific knowledge of a country. We go on an adventure together often to destinations even I do not know. I hire guides and drivers for that. My job is to take responsibility, to organize, manage, watch over, and create the tour "in the moment." My tours are not finished products but works in progress.

Mine is the artistic approach: I excite myself; in the process, I excite you.

I'm leaving Greece tomorrow. So ends another *New Leaf.*

Tour criticisms—and my reaction to them—are reflections of the never-ending warfare in my soul.

The trials and tribulations of running tours help me find faith.

I'm just about finished with my month-long project of setting up next year's schedule. Next year's tours are almost in order; so are my classes and weekends. This month most of my time was spent setting up the February Sicily tour, less time on the May Greek tour, even less on the March tour of Hungary; I'm considering running Czech Republic and Slovakia again next summer, but without me. Also Romania, which I'll lead. We'll see. It's a little early to tell. I'm considering Turkey for September (again without me), and Israel, including three days in Jordan with a visit to Petra, and an extension to climb Mount Sinai and visit the Saint Catherine monastery. I might even add Cairo and an Egyptian cruise extension. I've wanted to climb Mount Sinai for a long time. I've got lots of questions for HaShem. St. Catherine's has also been on my list. I see it as one of those "end of the world" places.

The 1998 tour and business schedule chapter is almost complete. I'm coming to the end of a chapter. Time to fish around for new directions. I like new directions.

The Embarrassment of Breaking My Word

The Weekend at GROW was such a smashing success! That is the "hotel" for me. I booked three weekends there for the 1998 season. More important, I shone as I ran my Weekend there. I was "on" and hot. My concert was excellent. During the whole Weekend I put my discovery of how to transcend ego to work; I focused on ardor and passion as my bridge to transcendence. It worked every time. I must continue this practice in the future. I have "discovered" a most important truth, a personal approach to transcendence. Remember to practice it every day and every hour. It is the fundamental Fundamental of a joyous and fulfilling life.

How will I remember it? What will happen when my energy cycles hits bottom? Too early to tell. Meanwhile, I'll keep trying, trying to focus and concentrate on ardor and passion in every big and little thing I do.

I'm leaving for the Czech Republic and Slovakia tomorrow. Yesterday I put countless details in order. At about 5:00 p.m., when I finished packing, I received a fax from Teri at Europe at Cost, offering an incredible price for my Sicily tour next February. I'll call her this morning to see if it is based on four-star hotels. If it is, I'll have to cancel my "commitment" with Amelia Tours. I feel embarrassed doing it. After all, I gave Dawn, the owner, my word; I had "committed" myself to Amelia Tours. But Teri is making an offer I can't refuse. If four-star hotels are included then, for survival and the best deal, I'll have to cancel my Amelia Tours "commitment." What good is my "word" when I change it next morning, or next week or month? What can I learn from this embarrassing process?

First, my word is never permanently my word. It's like the instant decisions I make running my folk dance classes or "commitments" and "definite directions" I decide on tour. I myself do it, then, next moment, new information comes along and I often decide to reverse myself. This may be the nature of "commitments;" it may be the art of navigating through life. Why is this embarrassing? Is it an excess of ego? Am I so good, strong, and smart that when I, Jim Gold, make a commitment, I must stick to it no matter what? It is more important to keep my word than follow new realities that appear? Sticking to such "commitments" is not heroic, good, or strong, but stupid. In my little world, I often make decisions that turn out to be mistakes; higher powers have other things planned for me which I do not yet know. It is good and wise to keep my eyes open for new possibilities the higher powers offer, then, change my mind in order to gather those fruits; this is wiser than sticking bull-headedly to decisions based on the limited vision of my little mind and narrow ego. Yes, I'm embarrassed and feel false, stupid, and bad for giving Dawn my word which, in the end, turns out to be worthless. Perhaps my ego needs such a beating in order to be surmounted. In any case, I may have to call Dawn this morning and cancel out. We'll see where all this leads.

Travel Meditation

I'm leaving for Prague in a few hours. This morning I made some goals for my trip: Study Czech, practicing breathing, follow my "standing" exercise program, and write both on the computer and in my pocket notebook. Then, when I took a run this morning, I thought of the most incredible type of meditation and goal for this trip, one that would free me from travel anxiety: Focus on them!

Focus on the people in my group, my participants, my tourists. Serve them. Try filling their every need.

Why is this goal so good? Because it takes my mind off myself. If I do it with ardor and passion, it will free me from my fears and help me transcend my ego.

I need my tourists as much as they need me. We serve different purposes. Their job is to focus on the trip; my job is to focus on them. It is my form of travel meditation.

My Czech Republic and Slovakia tour is my gross vehicle; serving my tourists with ardor and passion is my subtle vehicle.

I'm now in Prague, settled into my lovely room at the Quality Hotel. Naturally, I'm drained after our all-night flight and sleeping two hours in the afternoon. It's hard to write without coffee or desire. But I've taken my first step.

This seems like an excellent tour so far. The tour members seem very compatible. Yet I shouldn't be so quick to judge. Look what happened in Greece with pain-in-the-ass Barbara. I wonder if there are any incipient Barbaras on this tour. Who could they be? So far, my only guess is Roger. He has a bad leg; so does Doris. But it's too early to tell. Let's see how things develop.

Meanwhile, both Jasan and Gabriela showed up at the airport; our flight was fine; the weather in Prague is pleasant. All smooth up to now.

Remember my truth of ardor and passion in the moment.

The "Bump" in the Vltava

Last night, as we were crossing the Charles Bridge, Roger asked me about a "bump," a water bridge, a tunnel, a pipe combustion engine, a dissecting frog, a bobbing asterisk, and a melon-upwards lying to our right across the Moldau River. (I can't figure out what the name of this bump is yet.)

I answered, "Better start calling it the 'Vltava'—that's the Czech name; 'Moldau' is the German name. Smetana used it when he wrote his famous 'The Moldau.' At that time Prague was under the Hapsburgs—the Austro-Hungarian empire, and German was the lingua franca." That was my easy intellectual answer based on former knowledge. Truth was, I had seen that "bump" in the Vltava for years but never paid much attention to it. I had not the slightest idea why it was there. Finally, I answered Roger with, " I don't know."

"You're supposed to know these things," he said. "You're the leader."

"But I'm not your guide," I answered. "Ask Gabriela. She's our guide." I paused, then said, "Answers such as 'I don't know' keep me humble."

Grace, the Tom Funk "beautiful one," was also walking with us. She commented: "You must be pretty humble by now."

I took her comment in my usual fashion—as an insult to my leadership. Old reactions came flooding back. I am the leader. I am supposed to know these things. I am supposed to know not only these things but all things. Otherwise how can you call yourself a leader? Why should people follow you if you don't know? In many cases, my customers who are in Prague for the first time, know more than I do. What kind of leader am I if my tourists know more than I? Shouldn't they be leading me? And, if they know nothing and ask you these questions and I answer that I also know nothing, aren't we equals? Can equals lead each other? Doesn't leadership put you above the others. And, if you can't qualify for the "above" state, the Hebrew al, then how can I call myself a leader?

These ancient self-doubt questions rose up in my mind. What were they based on? My old friend, Mr. Fear, of course. I meet with him almost every day; he is part of my past, present, and future. He 's always there. I might as well deal with him today, right now, seize the present while he's standing in front of me.

First, let me deal with the "arrogance of leadership." This is the arrogant assumption that as leader I should know everything. Since the other side of arrogance is humility, the other side of this assumption is humility; My leadership arrogance is based on the fear that I will fail as a leader, that I will lose the respect of my clients, that I will be embarrassed by my short-comings—everything from not knowing about the "bump" in the Vltava to losing a few tourists as our group wanders through the twisted streets of Prague.

I must look my monster in the eye and say, "Yes, Mr. Fear, you are my miserable, disgusting, unrelenting teacher. Even though I hate your guts and would love to live under the protective clouds of illusion whose break-through sunbeams tell me what a wonderful, wise, illustrious leader I am, you are forcing me once again into the humility of self-realization; you are pushing me to my knees, twisting my tired intellect into submission. Soon I will weep with compassion for my poor miserable self, tortured by unrealistic expectations, so weak and small before the impossible challenges of leadership I put upon myself to prove how powerful and important I am supposed to be. Yes, you are a fucking miserable lout, a pus ball on my face, a pimple in my eye, forcing me to see what I don't want to see. I suppose I should thank you for the self-knowledge you inflict on me, and perhaps someday I will. But this morning I can only curse your existence with one mouth as I welcome your assistance with the other.

Two mouths? Well, why not? I live in a two-eared, two-eyes, two armed-two-legged schizophrenic body. Why not two mouths? One to tell the truth, and one to tell the lies. It seems only natural.

I still don't know what that "bump" in the Vltava River is. But I'm curious. I'll try to find out.

The job of leadership is to have a vision, and, like a flag, keep it planted before the group. Knowing particulars, like the "bump" in the Vltava, is a plus, but not essential. The president leads the country and hires others to care for the particulars; Alexander the Great did the same when he conquered Asia, using used local guides all the way. Thus, the leader's job is to keep the vision planted high, reminding others, in case they've forgotten, why they are here in the first place.

They suffer the travails of the travel adventure in order to discover their higher good.

What about pain-in-the-ass clients? They are often my best teachers. The Minnies, the Barbaras, the couple from my 1995 Bulgarian tour whose names I have repressed, have all taught me a great deal. True, I've taken them all off my mailing list. Once I have learned my lesson I don't want to make the same mistake twice and that mistake was taking them in the first place. When you are ready to learn, your teacher will appear. But it is also true that once you've learned, your teacher will disappear. That is the deeper meanings of removing pain-in-the-ass clients from my mailing list. Ultimately, I thank them for coming, then say good-bye.

GOD

A New Torah Morning Habit

The big problem is remembering! Remembering, remembering. . . . But remembering what? Remember the spark that ignites, the stars that light my path: Remember fsitchko e edno, that God is One.

When I remember this fundamental truth I feel calm, peaceful, even blissful. But I forget it almost minute to minute.

How can I remember?

How about daily morning Torah readings as a reminder?

Instead of reading the New York Times with my morning coffee, suppose I read the Torah. A morning reminder; start my day right. I could read it after the New York Times—or before. Even just a line of Torah will do. This would be a big change of life style. A new habit. Something to think about.

Daily Reminders of the Existence and Closeness of HaShem

How do I remind myself of the existence of divinity? Through work, ardor, and passion. They are my daily, even hourly, meditation.

July–September 1997

WRITING

Writing and Meditation

This morning I'd like to once again acknowledge Pema's book as my Slovak Talmud of Kezmarok. I'm dripping with ideas from its fruits. For example, I woke up thinking about meditation and is relationship to my writing. At supper last night, I asked Val about her morning schedule. "I wake up, have coffee, then sit and meditate for twenty minutes, " she said. "I've been doing this for years. It has become a habit; now it is part of my life."

"Writing in the a.m. is my form of meditation," I answered. Soon we began a short discussion about the differences between active and passive meditation.

I went to bed, my mind agitated with questions: Do I really meditate? Can I? Is the whole form of it so foreign to me I'll never be able to do it?

As I sipped my morning coffee, I continued reading Pema's book. She was talking about "thinking," watching your thoughts pass like clouds across a clear sky. Don't try seizing the clouds; simply watch them, then let them go. Some are ugly and full of hate; others are beautiful and filled with love; some are restless, angry warriors, puss-filled nincompoops, blatant sexual perverts, horn-nosed pigs filled with snakes of unsatisfied desires, worm-eaten and rotten bellies filled with jealousies, black toads jumping through arctic hoops frozen in guilt; other clouds are positive princes' and princesses' treasure chests over flowing with blissful music, thrones of laughter, kingdoms of rich successes beyond compare, radiant caterpillars dancing on their way to the bank, perfect smiles and pearl-filled ocean waves. Whatever they are, in whatever form they travel, they are nevertheless clouds, thoughts; they are only "thinking ." Therefore, watch them, touch, feel, and squeeze them. Then, with whatever love and compassion you can muster, let them go.

That is the essence of meditation.

That is also the essence of my journal writing method.

Sitting in a corner quietly meditating, watching thoughts pass through my mind is too inactive for me. I have been writing for years. Before I started writing, I had been dreaming about writing for years. In the beginning, I wanted success and recognition for what I'd written. Now, although I'd still like some, it is no longer as important. But what is important and essential to me is the daily writing process. It clears my mind, brings me inner peace, starts my day with a lovely bang, and makes my existence feel worthy and worthwhile.

It is best to write first thing in the morning. After coffee and shits, of course.

Isn't writing my form of meditation? Can I admit and accept the fact, even after so many years, that I have developed my own personal form of meditation? Why is that so hard to accept? Doesn't everybody on this earth develop their own form of meditation? Aren't we all experiments of one? Doesn't each person develop their own religion, their own brand of worship even within the traditions of Jewish, Christian, Moslem, Hindu, or whatever religious labels?

I am revisiting old questions? Perhaps once again it is merely a matter of having faith in myself and my voices, realizing I must live beyond books, reading, and faint hopes that someone else knows more about me and how to live my life than I do.

Perhaps it is lack of confidence revisited. Isn't there a god out there to take care of me? Can't someone bring me a few sparks of divinity and direction? Isn't there someone traveling in human form who can bring me the message? Isn't there a god out there through whom I can work? Must I only depend on myself?

I know there is a God who lives in me. I know there are servants of God—gods, angels, or whatevers who also inhabit my being. They are my bridges to the divine; they humanize the divine, bring it down to earth so I can handle it, grab a few sparks, and stay reminded that the present carries both the future and past in its eternal moment. Only the i and the I can know this. Everything else is a cloud in the sky, part of the endless procession of cloudy thoughts passing across my firmament. I'll watch them, touch them, grab them if I must. But then I'll have to let them go.

Writing helps me send these birds on their way. Once again I realize: I'd better write—or else!

Momentary Calm on the Stormy Sea

Indeed writing is my meditation, especially if you look at it as my method of letting thoughts come and go. A cleansing, a purification.

It is so nice to put my mind back on Romania, work, guitar playing, exercises, running, and studying Hebrew. I'd like to free myself from the clutches of Mr. Thralldom, from the ever-present sinking, falling, and alone feelings. This morning I am sick of them. I wish I could get rid of them.

But most likely, I can't. Thoughts keep coming. Falling thoughts, helpless, lonely, wanting, and desirous thoughts flow steady on my river. This morning may simply be a temporary lull. What can you expect as 4:30 a.m.? In any case, I like the writing-meditation idea. Having thoughts but not judging them good or bad; seeing thoughts pass like a stream through my mind, strained by my sieve of brain cells, making new appearances at my pain centers, arriving, late and lonely, in the interstices of hidden patterns of wanting answers, wanting the certainty of the known road, the security and certainty of closure, completion, and unity.

But I'm no longer living a unity life. I'm in fragments and tatters. My mind moves left, right, forwards and back. A standard folk dance pattern. But instead of bodies dancing, it is thoughts flying through the barnyard, tapping on the rafters, injecting hot-blooded arguments into my heart chakra and the jumbled stock market of my cerebellum.

At least I can write about it. I like the steady flow of words leaving via the gateway of mind, traveling quickly and unencumbered through fingers tips and onto the keyboard. Yes, it is a relieve to finally flow again.

A new sun is rising—at least for today. We'll see how long this tranquility lasts. Meanwhile, I'd like to make plans: business plans, work plan, even study plans.

What's on schedule?

1. Finish up as much of Romania as I can? Address all letters, fill some with forms, call Mihai.

2. Make my Czech Republic/Slovakia 1998 tour flier.

3. Fulfill the chore details on my list like calling the electrician, bring sandals to Panetierri, etc.

Writing Saves: Back to Four Pages a Day

I haven't been so low for years. Well, at least months. Sure I feel that aching loneliness, the wanting, yearning, pain, and emptiness of unfulfilled wants. But then it hit me: haven't I been through down feelings before? Sure, this is stronger. Nevertheless, down is down, loneliness is loneliness, emptiness is emptiness, and loss of self in the wilderness of desire and lack of discipline is qualitatively always the same. Sure, the feelings may feel, seem, be more quantitatively intense, but they are not qualitatively different. Loneliness and emptiness remains the same; only the degree changes.

That means I've been through these feelings before.

What have I done about them?

Until a few years ago, I did nothing. I merely felt miserable and left it at that. Then I discovered journal writing. Since I started my *New Leaf* in 1994, I've found an antidote to loneliness, loss of self, depression, and emptiness, and all the other big sinkers into the abyss.

Look at my Journal entry dates and amounts. During the last month I've hardly written at all. Only twenty-eight pages. True, I've been "doing other things." Nevertheless, the loss of balance, disorientation, emptiness, and loneliness I've felt have been exacerbated by the fact I've hardly written at all.

I know writing is my life line to sanity in the stable clear world of fiction I live in. It is my only cure. Nothing else works. Nothing else clears my mind, frees me, purifies my soul, clears out the garbage, weeds, and sagebrush from the fast-growing forest of bushes, trees, and wilderness, of the illusions and dreams that seed and quickly grow in the vacuum of my mind. Mind, if not kept busy, will destroy me. Especially my mind. Simple as that.

There is no cure like writing. As the words flow out of my finger tips I'm starting to feel better. God bless it, God bless me for doing it, and God bless the revelation of its importance to my survival.

Something else is happening. As I cry my way through the reading of my New Leaves, taking steps backwards into the past, seeing and examining my talents laid out before me, as I appreciate, admire, and love the beauty I've produced, I am also sinking away from new creations. In other words, too much self-admiration, adoration, and love is causing me to drift away from the creative process. I am dwelling, lingering, falling, losing myself in past writings. I am also piercing and appealing to the rational aspect of my mind as I begin organizing New Leaf. It's fine to touch the rational but I must also stay in touch with my mystical creative aspects. This can only be done by writing fresh new entries every day.

And I must think in terms of quantity as well as quality. Why is that? Because the creation of quantity, turning out page after page no matter what, creates its own rhythm and flow, throwing me back into the stream of the creative process. Once again, I am flowing downstream on the backs of words. I love it.

With each new word I write, I am slowly regaining strength, regaining balance and structure. My feet are once more touching the earth even as my head touches heaven.

LANGUAGES

Why Study Hebrew?

Why am I breaking my head learning Hebrew? Why am I spending so much time and energy learning to read Torah and Tannach in the original?

I'm a mountain climber. Torah and Tannach are my personal Himalayas. I climb them because they are there.

My earthly benefit is found in the challenge itself. The challenge unleashes my energy.

Beams of energy carry me upwards. Riding in my chariot, my personal merkhaba, with Ezekiel at my side, I travel skyward, reaching for the great Within/Without.

I contact my energy in the moment and become one with the moment.

My goal is not mastering Hebrew or even reading Torah and Tannach in the original.

Rather it is connecting to energy, giving it birth and release in the here-and-now.

LIFE

On "Relaxation"

This morning my mind is dense and foggy and filled with uvular tracks and unending chasms of Slovak and Vah rivers. I simply open my gullet and let the words flow. What will come out? Who knows?

Isn't "Who knows?" the state I usually live in?

Will this question ever go away? I doubt it. I still love my separate self with its petty illusions; I still chase after pleasure and avoid pain.

I do not blame others anymore for my lot in life.

When did I start to think this way? Probably when I became a conscious entrepreneur.

I began my writing career in Greenwich Village; my guitar career, and marriage with its guitar-playing economic base followed. At the time I still thought outside forces controlled my life. I only started questioning that belief in my forties along with my belief in communism. Finally, when I gave up my guilt at becoming a capitalist and entrepreneur, belief in self-sufficiency, independence, an self-responsibility expanded until the concept of blaming others for my state is quite foreign. It took over twenty years to reach this state of mind. How long will it take to give up the concept of a separate identity, a separate self?

When will I join the world of oneness?

Well, it's a developing state. I'll have to wait until I am totally fed up with a separate self, disgusted with living and believing in the same illusions and repeating the same dead-ends patterns. Only then will I give them up. But meanwhile, I'll keep living my merry illusory life with its ups and downs, its hopes for improvement and progress. Perhaps someday I'll progress to the point beyond progress, improve the point beyond improvement. Someday I'll walking the road, enjoying my footsteps without looking back at my footprints and/or forward to the future.

I'm still throwing out words, doing anything I can, using every mental trick I know, to get my writing flow flowing. Truth is, I've lived much of Pema's book already. I know there is no place to hide from pain, suffering, pleasure, and the illusory concept of the separate self; I know about "relaxing with the ambiguity and uncertainty of the present moment."

I know about it, but I can't yet "relax" in it. Is that something to think about? Would it be an "improvement" of sorts? But I'm giving up the path of improvement.

Therefore, I'll have to accept the pain of the unrelaxed state. Learn to accept my worries.

I do! I love them! They are a source of pride and joy. Perhaps therein lies the problem. I not only accept my worries, but I consider them a motivating force! I cannot "relax with the ambiguity and uncertainty of the present moment." Nor do I want to. I want the ambiguity and uncertainty of the present moment to bite me, prick me, pin me against the wall, suffer me into a chaotic anxiety-producing state of fervor. I want the abyss. I want to hover over the chasm of creativity. Fuck this relaxing shit! An artist does not need to relax. More, an artist does not want to relax. Relaxation comes a few moments after the herculean labor. It is the short sweet fruit of great effort.

Maybe Pema's book is wrong for me. Maybe the Buddhist philosophy, although I agree with it, is not right for the artistic approach to life. Mine is the artistic approach to life. I grab the fire and the light; I with the pythons of darkness, and squeeze the juice out of descents into the maelstroms. Depressions bring me joy; back aches are mere pebbles along the learning path.

Who wants to relax? Not me. I'm an activist. My floating self does not rest easy on a river. It wants to live with one foot in the sky while the other sinks into the bottomless Noah's flood, endlessly searching for a firm foothold on the murky bottomless ocean bottom.

Artists burn their bridges as they walk across them. They are their own dharma. They don't concern themselves with appreciation of impermanence and change; their life-style with its twists and turns on the path into the chaotic darkness of creativity exemplifies it.

Relax? Why give it a thought? There are no brushes on the relaxation palette.

Artistic ecstasy will burn the bridge of impermanence.

Flowing with the Names

We arrived at 1:00 a.m. in Kezmarok after witnessing two incredible performances in Vychodna. The first, by a local Slovak folk dance groups in the intimacy of the Kultury Dom- Culture House, was televised by local TV stations; the second, a full concert in the outdoor amphitheater, was given by SLUK, one of the outstanding professional Slovak performing groups from Bratislava. Absolutely brilliant choreography and dancing! The "Moiseyev" of Slovakia.

We're staying at the clean and charming Hotel Club in Kezmarok. I slept until seven this morning, had two cups of excellent espresso coffee in the dining room, then returned to my writing and bedding chamber, and set up my computer to write.

Yesterday on the bus, Val, a former student of Martha Graham, was sitting behind me. She is a practical, Jewish-by-birth practitioner of the yoga and Buddhist arts. I showed her Pema Chodron's book, then asked: "After studying eastern philosophies and techniques for many years, do you ever reach a point where you've 'read everything' and there's nothing else to read?"

She answered, "Every time I read these books with their new languages, slants, and ways of putting things, it is a confirmation and a reminder of the life style I want to practice."

I know one needs constant reminders. Val made me feel better about seemingly reading the same ideas over and over again. They are variations on a theme—but a truly worthy theme. Besides, what is there better to do with my life?

So while drinking my morning coffee in the Kezmarok Club Hotel dining room, I once again glanced through Pema's book. I came across the chapter, "Relax As You Are" or something like that. (I don't remember the exact title, but, since I am "relaxing as I am," I won't bother looking it up.) Pema spoke about her teacher, Trigma Rinpoche. He found his students needed more technique in order to study meditation. He told them to focus only 25 percent of their attention on their out-breath, and leave the rest of their mind free to let events from the outside world pass through. If thoughts arise, call them "thinking."

I won't describe more; but I will read more. Needless to say, I am onto something useful and practical here: namely, "meditation while standing in place." Focusing 25 percent on the out-breath is something I can do. Then I can focus 50 percent on my tour and the remaining 50 percent on how I feel about myself, my tour, Slovakia, and everything else that is flowing around and through me. True, this adds up to 125 percent, but who's counting? And besides, I may, in this creative process, discovery a new way of looking at numbers.

In any case, by using this manner of "standing meditation" I can still function in the outside world as I meditate. It is "easy." To label my thoughts "thinking" is also a good idea. It is an excellent way to become aware of them, that they happen, take place, and are only what they are, namely, thoughts.

Something new to practice. It is another example of the tourist learns about the country but the traveler learns about himself. While I am away from the stiff challenges in Teaneck, I have a chance on tour to open my mind and explore new options.

I also like what just happened. I named Pema's "Relax" chapter without worrying about getting it right; I also wrote Tringma Rinpoche's name without getting that right either. It is a creative approach to naming which does not stop my writing flow. Plus I can tap the immediate effects of my unconscious.

In fact, it is a great new way to write, think, and even speak! Imagine no longer being held to saying the correct anything. A totally non-judgemental way of writing, thinking, and speaking. The stiffening, concretizing, and narrowing effects of "getting it right," of correct spelling, places, dates, etc. can come later—if it is even needed. Meanwhile I am free to forget whatever I want. Besides, what is a name but a label for the past. By forgetting about labels, I can put a fresh new slant on what was once old and worn. True, Trigma's name may have been spelt Trungma, Trigma, or Turngman Rinpoche in the past, but, in my hands, "born in the flow," it has been transformed into a new name and a new experience. What could be so bad about that?

What is the correct spelling of Trungma's name, anyway? I am getting interested. It's forcing me to look it up. I just did. The correct spelling is Trungpa. His full name is Chogyam Trungpa Rinpoche. And Pema's chapter is "Relax As It Is."

"For Others"

It started when I inadvertently hit upon the idea of fighting pre-tour fears by focusing on satisfying the needs of my customers. I called it "travel meditation." As soon as the idea hit me, I felt peaceful. Then I let it sink in for two weeks while I ran my tour with its usual and unusual twists and turns.

Now, although I am home, I find myself thinking of others again. "For Others." It is finding peace by thinking of others, doing for others, taking my creations, works, and forming them with the purpose of serving others. Certainly not a new idea in history, but definitely a new idea for me.

Could this be the larger meaning of love?

The idea is still too new for me to believe it. Yet I am certainly ready for it. It could be an incredible new motivating factor. It is the only reason I can see for organizing and editing my New Leaf Journal. I can see no personal reason for editing and organizing it for myself. Why bother putting effort to publish it, says my old mind. I've published enough already. I'm satisfied. The old urge, motivated by desire for recognition, is no longer strong enough. Without a new urge, a new reason and meaning, I'll just keep adding new pages to my New Leaf without organizing it. "For others" could give me that new meaning. Then the main question would be: will reading New Leaf Journal help anybody? Is it useful to anyone besides myself? Will it bring others some self-knowledge, inner peace, new motivation, and reason for existing? Can it be a service to them? Never mind me. I'm satisfied with my past publications. Yet I know satisfaction never accomplished anything. Without the spark of dissatisfaction, frustration, wanting, and desire, there will be no motivation to create something new. Therefore, I need a new tikkun, a new reason, spark, "frustration," and purpose to fulfill.

Could the "For Others" attitude be the service philosophy par excellence?

Isn't focusing on others the vehicle I need to attain inner balance and peace?

I need others as much as they need me.

By focusing on them as a form of meditation—the "travel meditation form" I developed in Book 5—I can forget myself. If I do it with ardor and passion, it will free me from fear and help me transcend ego.

"For Others" is the only new and valid reason to publish I can think of.

"For Others" is a long-term "permanent" travel meditation. If my New Leaf Journal is to be about travel in both physical and metaphysical realms, then I need a traveling meditation program to go with it.

"For Others" combines love making with a new way of thinking. It merges the flesh with the spirit. It gets my mind off me and helps transcend ego.

It seems only a "For Others" attitude will motivate me to Edit my New Leaf.

It's not just for myself anymore. It's for others as well. Will I be studying Romanian, Hebrew, and all my other languages for others?

Will I be reading the bible, turning over words, phrases, and ideas in classical Hebrew for others? How about Talmud? For others, too?

How about miracle schedule activities? For others, too? What does it all mean?

Can I connect the chills in my flesh, the classical music goose bumps, and even the "bump" in the Vltava River, to a larger "For Others" universal goose bump?

Do personal chills and thrills translate into a larger picture that includes others? Is the vibrational chill of joy, the teary-breakdown of the ego that opens the window to reveal the splendor of the Higher Forces, for me alone? Or does it open the door of my house for others to enter and be included in my family?

Is there such a thing as the family of self? Can I realize it in my mind, heart, and spirit? Can I expand ego to include others? If I did, would it expand to full length?

It I cover everything I do with a "For Others" attitude, if I pour all activities of mind and body into the "For Others" mold, how will it effect me?

At this point in my life is there even a choice? I've walked many new roads. Many of my explorations have been sated. What is left but to walk on the new "For Others" path?

A new door has opened. Perhaps that is the ultimate "meaning" behind all the events on the Czech Republic and Slovakia tour. An external qualitative change in my life may well mirror a qualitative change within.

There are two selves: the wise self and the stupid self. The stupid self thinks only of itself; thus it suffers perpetual frustration and pain. But the wise self, although just as selfish as the stupid self, realizes that the way out of frustration and pain is to focus on and adopt a "For Others" philosophy; it means serving others by "using" them as a travel meditation bridge out of the prison of ego.

Living In The Void

It's about falling into the void, having no reference point.

How can I stand in the middle of the circle without going left or right, forwards or backwards? How can I stand there without a goal, path, or direction? How can I lead or run my life while I dissolve and fall straight into the void?

Falling into the void is my Torah; commentary on it is my Talmud.

Can there be any peace, hope, security, and happiness in the void? Does it only consist of a sinking stomach, darkness, and death? Can stability ever come after you've fallen far enough? Do you ever fall far enough?

Or do we all live on cotton? Do we all float on misty clouds mistaken for reality? Why do we yearn for this concrete surface, this steady base, this solid foundation called home?

Do you want to meet another? To truly meet, face them directly, then, in front of their face, fall into the void. Each person is different if you face them while falling. To compare one to another is odious, false, and wrong. No comparisons. Each person is its own love soul, a constellation of starry, molten, wispy, space traveling, earth-bound traits unique in the universe. Each soul is filled with lessons for the physical and metaphysical traveler. I travel with my own shopping bag collecting jewels from one end of the earth to the other. My jewel bag is never full.

When my feet slip, I fall through the soft crust of illusion; I enter the molten center of hell's university to pick up nuggets of knowledge. Such learnings help soften my tred, lighten my steps along the hard earth surface.

But first I must fall.

And fall I do. More and more each day. I am almost "getting used" to falling. Instead of falling all the time I am now falling every other minute. That may be progress of sorts along the inner peace road. But let's not be too quick to jump on this soft log. The void is a huge place. It can, at a moment's notice, easily turn a rock of direction, fortitude, and certainty, into a laughing, screaming, crying fool. Watch out for hubris before the powers of nothingness.

A Life of Passion: Falling Through the Middle Harnessed to the Middle Way

This morning came my first twinge of self-disgust. Thank God! I may be getting my life back, my mind back, my energy back. There is nothing like self-disgust for motivation.

I'm so sick of that teary feeling, along with the inner loneliness, whining, and obsession. I want to get some focus back; I want to work again, to return to the focused energy of my former life.

But it's not so easy. That focused former life was lived on the right or left side of the ledger. It felt sure, secure, and energized. But now I have given up right and left. Now I'm falling through the middle with no handles. I'm living in the abyss. I doubt it will change. Nor do I want it to. Part of me welcomes that sinking feeling. It makes me feel alive, vulnerable, and passionate. But I hate it, too. The old road is so easy, known, safe, calm, and pleasant. But it is also dead. Yes, I'm making a choice between passion or death. Unfortunately, I've chosen passion over death. That means periodically falling into the abyss. In the life of passion I fall in on a daily basis, then pull myself out. It may not be pleasant but it certainly is alive.

And I have chosen the passion route over the easy and known. There is no turning back. Nor do I want to turn back. But I also want some stability, some focus and ability to concentrate and perform all the good things I used to do.

Is there a middle way?

Perhaps I can "get used to" falling into the abyss. Is that possible? Can someone "get used to" living on the edge, falling off the cliff, hurtling through space in terrifying descend towards the blackness and igneous molten earth centers of fire, lava, brimstone existing at the hidden bottom of the abyss? Can the unknown ever be known? Should it be? Should one even try to know it? And doesn't knowing the unknown cause it to lose its sting? Doesn't it take all passion out of the abyss, turning such a fall into a boring, habitual, dry, dull, suburban event? Isn't it the unknown that turns wood into fire and stone into lave?

Perhaps the middle road is to not only live with the abyss, but to fall daily into it. I don't know if this is possible. On the other hand, I've been on the old route of hand-held passion and ardor in chains too long: I've been looking over my shoulder, checking that all finances, schedules, economics, and rituals are in place. But now I'm at the border of giving it up. Nay, not the border. I am there! I have given it up. There is no turning back. It's forwards and downwards; it's over the cliff, jumping without parachute into the abyss. Maybe after doing it a million times I'll realize there is no other way. I may even get "comfortable" with it.

Fucker or Fuckee

The world is divided into two ethical categories: good and bad.
Judgements of good and bad rule most activities.
One of the goals of meditation is to move beyond judgements, to see the world beyond these primary judgements.

My established meditation forms are writing, guitar, etc. Thus, when I ask the question: can I get beyond the ethical questions of good or bad in my meditations, I am asking can I get beyond good or bad in my writing, guitar playing, and, here's a new one, even in my human relationships?

For example, when I am criticized, when my whole being is questioned, when the roof is falling down on my head, can I then start thinking about meditation and moving beyond good or bad? Sure, sometimes I have to answer their criticism and "waste my time" defending myself. I say, "waste my time" because I believe you never really succeed in defending yourself. Ultimately, there is little way to change the minds of others and arguing about your own goodness or badness, who is right or wrong in a given situation, usually leads only to more fighting, arguing, bad feelings, and distance.

So what am I to do when others criticize me? Should I answer them? Defend myself? Remain silence? Maintain my calm? Should I criticize them back even though it will only lead to more fighting?

What has been my technique up to now. For years I never fought. This approach to criticism ended around age forty when I decided to start standing up for myself. It resulted in ten years of fighting, arguing, and bad feelings. Did the fighting get me anywhere? Yes. It taught me how to fight and stand up for myself. That's it. The fighting didn't improve relationships. In fact, it usually made them worse. But at least I learned how to fight.

Now I am a fairly skilled fighter; I have more confidence in my ability to stand up. Recently, with my newfound strength, I decided on another approach to criticism. Instead of arguing and fighting back directly, I decided to soften and deflect the blows by fighting indirectly. When criticism came, I returned to silence, taking my anger inward and using it to hold the fort, building the walls of angry silence around me to divert the blows. I must say that, on the surface, this technique worked. My critics were silenced almost immediately. What could they say if their criticisms received no response, if their barbs and diatribes fell on so-called "deaf" ears? They could say nothing. Eventually, they did. Criticisms diminished.

However, my interpretation of this diminishment was incorrect. I thought I had not only deflected the criticism but caused it to stop. Wrong. It had only gone underground—and not that far underground. As soon as I stood up for myself in the old way, spoke up and said so and so is wrong, I view things differently, the old criticisms returned with a vengeance. Thus, my silent approach only worked to sooth and smooth out the surface waters. But the cauldrons and hot waves of rage seething beneath the calm surface didn't change at all.

What can I do about all this?

I think I will return to speaking up for myself even though I doubt it will change anybody's mind. The only good I can see coming is it will help me verbalize my own anger in "public."

Maybe my speaking skills will improve. Yes, speaking up will get me mad! But in a "hopeless" way. It will not divert or change the opinions of my critics. Or, it may. But whether it does or not is beyond my control; it is even besides the point. The real question is: what will a return to speaking up, defending myself, and even attacking others, do for me?

Look what I just said. "Even attacking others." Do I want to attack others? Or do I want to defend myself? Is there a difference?

There is a difference. One is passive, the other is active; one masculine, the other feminine, one you dish it out, the other you take it, one you fuck, the other you are being fucked.

Obviously, in life, you need both fucker and fuckee. I have been the fuckee for a long time. Isn't it about time I practiced being the fucker? I think so. It's a new approach and worth a try.

Suppose

Suppose it's a mystery we'll never understand.

Suppose reasons, explanations, blaming others for their inability to satisfy our needs, will ultimately not explain our actions.

Suppose trying to explain or understand is a waste of time.

Suppose it is best to simply accept who we are as incomprehensible, a mystery, a wilderness beyond the understanding of our human minds—and leave it at that.

Suppose we follow our hearts, see where they lead, and leave explanations and understandings to the higher forces.

The Beauty and Necessity of Self-Control

Yesterday, on our trip up to the farm, everything went wrong. We left two hours late, Bernice got sick, we stopped in a shopping mall for a half-hour bathroom stop, later another mall stop to buy special foods. At the express check-out counter, another half-hour delay caused by a computer problem. By the time we drove off, I was so furious that I exploded in anger. "I'm so damn frustrated!" I screamed. "Everything is going wrong today! I'm so tired from jet lag " One minor annoyance after another was killing me. As a final frustration, guests arrived unexpectedly at the farm, ruining the hope for peace on this rare vacation.

But something good came out of it. I realized I was out of control. My mind had been out of control not only today, but for the past six weeks. Suddenly, I saw the beauty of self-control. Then I saw the necessity of self-control. I needed it not only to keep my sanity and sense of self, but to keep my good loving as well.

How do I maintain self-control and loving at the same time? Is it possible? Do I even want to?

Can I keep my ardor, passion, within the confines of self-control? Or do I have to destroy myself every day in order to recreate myself anew? Is periodic self-destruction and self-creation a necessary element in the creative process? Are pain and suffering a necessary element? Can I experience a modicum peace along with my ecstasy and joy under the aegis of self-control?

It "only" took thirty years to discover that the center of my guitar playing is not in my fingers or wrist but in my stomach.

Solar plexus is my power center.

Everything else is a footnote.

PERFORMANCE

Guitar Power

It is not only my right index finger but my right arm and shoulder through which the power of masculinity flows. Perhaps it is also my whole right side. Witness the yad hazzak of Elohim Himself, the power of the right hand of God. Also, remember the "division" of my love in France where my left "feminine" side, divided off.

Perhaps it is time to recognize my right side, the side of power and masculinity. My power is expressed through the right index finger but does not originate there.

One with the Guitar

Notice how my right side connects with my stomach. The solar plexus, power, and masculinity connection.

Connecting My Body to My Mind While Playing Guitar

I pump strength and power—and love—from my solar plexus up my right side, through my right shoulder, arm, and wrist, through my fingers and index finger into my guitar. One flow, one thought, one movement.

The stomach pumps power.

Masculine Guitar Playing

Touch lightly, but do not lean or press the right below-the-elbow arm on the hip of the guitar.

Pressing cuts off the flow of power from the solar plexus. It divides me. I want a straight line, a direct current from the solar plexus, through the right side, right arm, elbow, wrist, and fingers directly into the guitar.

It is the masculine flow of power into the guitar.

BUSINESS

Yes, it's true, Roger is my teacher on this tour. Roger, and perhaps later Doris. Let's start with Roger.

Yesterday we visited Tabor, the home of Jan Hus and the Hussite movement, the town where the Reformation started, where Protestantism originated. I have always like the town with its impressive public square. I imagine Jan Hus burning alive at the stake in that public square, even though the real event happened in Switzerland.

We were touring through the catacombs under the public square. Right in the middle of the tunnel the lights went off, offering me a moment of stark terror, lost in darkness many feet under the earth with minotaurs charging out of corners and from behind tunnel turns, tearing my flesh, eating me up; lesser rivulets of fear also ran through me. Finally, to my relief, the lights went on. When we got out of the tunnel, I said, "Now that's an experience in stark terror! They should program it into every tour. " I said it an with enthusiasm touched with naivete. This quality of enthusiasm and ability to see the moment as something fresh and new is an endearing quality and one of the attitudes that makes not only my tours, but my life interesting. However, Roger didn't think so. He said about my enthusiasm, "We're taking you on this tour," implying that instead of leading my group, my group was leading me. The implication was that I was an incompetent as a leader; I didn't know much about the Czech Republic, even though I had been there many times before; I didn't work hard enough as a tour leader, that instead of being the shepherd, I was acting like one of the sheep—an enthusiastic and naive one.

It stabbed me to my heart. I walked away feeling awful. Old insecurities quickly rose from my unconscious and flew in my face.

I took a walk alone through the twisting back streets of Tabor; I sat down on a bench under a tree in a peaceful public square facing buildings that looked like a movie set. I had a talk with myself. Somehow I had to figure out a way to handle Roger. He had already made several subtle and not so subtle digs at my leadership in public. I didn't want him to embarrass me; I also I didn't want to make too much out of his comments. How should I handle this?

Slowly an idea came to mind. I would answer: "Yes, Roger, you are taking me on tour, you are bringing me to the Czech Republic and Slovakia; without you and the rest of the group I never would have come here. I need you. Without you there would be no tour. On the other hand, without me, there would be no tour either. You need me, too. It's a perfect combination: I need you, and you need me."

That was a beautiful answer! I'd acknowledged Roger's feelings, defended myself gracefully, and included all of us—the entire group—the final solution. A wave of inner peace swept over me. Then I forgot about the whole incident.

I may never have to say any of this to Roger or anyone else in public or private. But, most important, I think it. That's what gives me the power. Saying is only secondary.

Roger's "criticism" helped me discover and verbalize a deep truth. Once again I recognized the limits of my power. But I also recognized the limits of his power. Ultimately, we need each other. And that's a good thought.

Next comes Doris. She's sweet; I have soft spot in my heart for her. But she is always late. I told her about it last night, and she got very hurt, and upset. I hope she starts coming earlier. If she doesn't, I don't quite know what I'll do about it. We'll just have to wait and see what happens.

My writing is moving fast, easily, and naturally in these early mornings. I am writings the unexpurgated first words I think of. I just wrote two and a half pages in fifteen minutes. Pretty good. Is there is a qualitative shift taking place? Barry said I've been writing in this journal style so long, it is becoming natural and easy. Perhaps that is the shot of confidence I need to let things flow. We'll see. But as I say this, I realize it is true.

A fear I have been denying since December is the one engendered by the sty in my eye. What an ugly bump! When I look at it in the mirror, I not only get disgusted but worry about what others will think. How can I look them in the eye? They will see this ugly disgusting bump and think, What a freak this Jim Gold is. He may be a nice guy with a handsome head and svelte body, but, with that sty, he is too disgusting to look at. Once I thought he was perfect. Now I can see that nauseating imperfection rising at the very mirror and doorway to his soul. How can someone with such a disgusting imperfection lead a tour?

So far, not one client has said a thing. Bernice says my sty is not even noticeable and I should forget about it. It's possible no one notices or even cares about it. But I do! No doubt, the sty is a teaching in disguise; actually, a teaching in disgust. We'll see where this leads.

Many things to talk about this morning. Let's start at the end of last night. we heard a beautiful concert given by the Bohemia Musica, a famous group from Prague. It was given, along with a mime performance. The first third of the concert was classical music, then came mime, then folk music. Wonderful performance! And all given in a magical castle in the fantastic fairy-tale town of Cesky Krumlov in southern Bohemia. We must book our hotel there next year.

A few hours before the concert I was sitting in an outdoor restaurant sipping coffee, and gazing into the fast-flowing Vltava river. I was thinking about how this Cesky trip is opening up new directions, pointing to a return to classical music, and incorporating it into my tours and back into my life; I thought about how to reach the lovers of Dvorak, Smetana, and Janicek, how to become a lover of art once again and visit the Metropolitan Museum, joining the pictures on the wall as I did when I was a child, how Bohemia offers beautiful architecture, classical music, and perhaps intellect. Once again I realized how a tourist learns about a country but a traveler learns about himself.

As I sat writing and thinking, Joe and Sue Livak, from Reno, Nevada, entered the restaurant. First she asked if I'd like to be alone; I answered, Yes, that was very sensitive of them. But soon we began talking and I moved over to sit with them. I spoke about transcendence, classical music, and about playing the gorgeous classical pieces of Smetana and Dvorak on the bus as we drove through the bucolic landscape of south Bohemia. Then, to my great surprise, Sue said she had been a child prodigy on the violin and piano, had given concerts, played all the big concertos, but had given it up completely at age seventeen when, during a performance, she forgot a piece twice; she walked off stage never to return to performing or playing violin or piano again.

We spoke about stage fright, nervousness, and my fears of listening to classical music. Then, after the Bohemia Musica concert, she gave me the following note:

> *Jim,*
> *God has given us the window of artistic ecstasy through which to glimpse His force. To close that window or turn our backs on it is to deny the miraculous value of the gift.*

Now that is a paragraph, a thought, which says it all! I should remember and think about it not only for the rest of this tour, but for the rest of my life.

God has given me the gift of artistic ecstasy, the gift of a window to glimpse His force and all-mighty power. I absolutely love Sue's wording! Who put her on this trip, anyway? All the books I've read on self-improvement, self-help, searching, looking for answers and new directions cannot match the power, truth, and majesty of Susan's statement.

It is the perfect reason to listen to classical music again.

There is nothing else to write about this morning. When one has heard it all the only thing to do is walk around the block.

Hopelessness, Insecurity, Pain, and Harold in Piestany

We crossed the border into Slovakia last night. This morning I'm sitting in the beautiful Magnolia Hotel in Piestany overlooking the flowing Vah river. I could get used to this. The room is lovely; the service is lovely; last night's supper at the Koliba Restaurant with gypsy musicians playing was lovely; our dancing of To Ta Helpa was lovely; my sleep under the open window with the cool breezes blowing off the Vah was lovely: all in all, a lovely twelve hours.

Last night in the restaurant I sat opposite Harold. When we got up to dance To Ta Helpa I jokingly said, "This is the first and last dance we'll do on the tour." He answered in all seriousness, "I hope not." I realized that, up to now, we've had no folk dance workshops so far. Yes, we saw a Slovak group perform in Prague, and yes, we're going to the Vychoda Folk Festival for two days. Nevertheless, we've had no "hands-on" dancing. And we've got a real folk dancer on this tour. I realized Harold was right. We'd better have some dancing—or else! Then, to the happy speedy surprise, I moved away from my terror position—that my tourists will hate me, be dissatisfied with the lack of dancing, never register for another tour again, complain to their neighbors and friends, and basically bad-mouth my tour, to the position that I personally believe we should have some dancing, that it would be fruitful, fun, and profitable, and that I want to have this group-unifying experience. Therefore, I decided, come what may, to find a place to dance tonight. First, I thought about finding a room in our Magnolia Hotel. Then I realized that, by the time supper finished, it would be 10:00 p.m., that we have to get up early the next day to drive to Vychodna Festival, and that people would be tired after an afternoon of touring Bratislava. So I came upon the idea of dancing in the restaurant after we ate supper. Now that's a good idea! All we need is for there to be no gypsy musicians, few other customers, and some minimal dance space. Dancing right after supper is the "perfect" solution to the dance problem. True, you shouldn't dance right after eating. But this isn't dancing in its highest sense of transcendence of self through the art of movement. Rather, it is a social experiment, a form group cementing where we can experience some togetherness through the dance. We will do slow, easy dances that everyone either knows or can easily follow. That will be fine. Post-supper restaurant dancing may be a future way to go.

The quick leap I made from free-fall terror to the power of personal choice is a good development sign. All my tours should be based on personal desire. From there, tour services will radiate out. Giving up free-fall terror in exchange for power of personal choice is a very good thing.

I hope I can do it.

I read a great line this morning in Pema Chodron's book When Things Fall Apart about hope. This book is must reading for every human being; even animals would benefit from it. She says, in a chapter on Hopelessness And Death, that If we're willing to give up hope that security and pain can be exterminated, then we can have the courage to relax with the groundlessness of our situation. This is the first step on the path. Further, she says, ". . . . 'Totally fed up'. . . . This describes an experience of complete hopelessness, of completely giving up hope. This is the beginning of the beginning. Without giving up hope—that there is something better to be—we will never relax with where we are and who we are."

Now that is wonderful Buddhist life concept and philosophy of life which I thorough believe in and would love to follow forever. Hopelessness, giving up, fearlessly falling apart into the creative pit of groundlessness, is the way I want to lead my life, and the way I want to lead my tours. It is always good to verbalize and keep my goals shining in front of me so I remember them.

The free-fall terror I felt from Harold's comment acted as a pointed reminder: I will never be free from terrors; all I can do is deny and try to forget them. But that is impossible to do for long. Therefore, it is better to accept they will never be eradicated, dive into them, and deal with them as best I can, realizing at the same time that these terrors are only a few of many terrors on the upcoming chain of mini-terrors and errors that will follow me, like the Greek Furies, plaguing me for the rest of my life. So be it. My ground will continually be washed, whittled, and hacked from under me. No end to fear, terror, living on the edge, insecurity—and creativity. It is up to me to remember that hopelessness, insecurity, and pain are the only way to go. However, if somehow I can't remember, I have people like Harold to remind me.

Thus, as a corollary, when I look in the mirror and see how ugly I look, how my skin is wrinkling, my hair turning white, my eyeball filled with that disgusting cysty lump, my body wrinkling, aging and falling apart, it is a good sign. It is part of the lesson: to learn how to live in the pain of the moment. It is also part of the lesson on how to live in the pleasure of the moment. Falling apart or coming together—it's all part of experiencing hopelessness and insecurity, and, in the process, learning how to appreciate the beauty of living the groundless life.

Feeling Good

I'm feeling so good this morning I can hardly write. What is there to write about if you're feeling good? Nothing, really. After all, I write to feel good. If I'm feeling good already, then there is no urge or reason to ex-press myself, to press out those miserable and confusing thoughts and feelings that comprise the negative backward flow of events in my mind.

Why do I feel good?

Two reasons. First of all, the concatenation of events at yesterday's Vychodna Festival was fantastic. The way God worked things out to give us a perfect day was nothing short of miraculous. Look at the order of things: our original plan was to go the festival Friday night and Saturday only, the highlight was to be the afternoon parade of folk groups through the town. On Sunday we had planned to go rafting on the Dunajec River in the High Tatras near the Polish border. That had been our program for nearly a year. However, it was all changed when the downpour on Saturday washed out all Festival events. We decided to give up Sunday rafting in favor of returning to the Festival to see the international groups perform and the Festival Finale at 2:00 p.m.

What happened?

The weather cooperated beautifully. Even though there was a

threat of rain all day, not one drop fell until the Festival ended at 4:00 p.m. It gave us a perfect cool day. That was miracle number one. Miracle number two was the performances by both international and Slovak groups. Terrific! And imagine, we wouldn't have seen any of them if Saturday had not been rained out! Ah, the plans of heaven versus the plans of men! The performances were personal eye-openers for me. The Italian folklore group from Calabria in Southern Italy was the first Italian folk dance group I had ever seen. Although the choreographies and dance steps of their Tarentellas were simple, the singing, music, and spirit was elating. Suddenly, I "understood" why I had never had an attraction or interest or even any knowledge of Italian folk dancing. Most of the steps seemed to belong to in American square dance category with a few extra sashes to the right. The "essence" of Italian folk dancing was in the singing. And, of course, the spirit. But the singing, ah, the singing! No wonder Italians are known for their opera. Each country has something special and unique to offer. Just as Bohemia offers dull dances but beautiful Habsburg-Baroque architecture in every town from Prague to the smallest village, and Ireland offers the wonderful turns of phrase and use of the English language, Italy offers singing. You don't go to Italy for the dancing, but for singing!

After the Italian group, the Portuguese group performed. Even though I love the Portuguese, their dances aren't that interesting. Nothing dramatic here. But after the Portuguese came the dance group from Ossetia in the Caucasus. Their folk dances, like those of their Georgian neighbors, is the most dramatic and powerful dancing I know. While Italian songs open you up and make you cry, the Ossetian (and Georgian) dances squeeze you so much with their incredible control and fire that they make you cry, too. The knife dance by their leader put the audience into a frenzy of ecstasy as he first held knives in his mouth, on his eyes, and on his forehead, before throwing them onto the stage where each one stuck straight up on the wooden stage floor.

The came the Brigham Young group from Provo, Utah. Unfortunately, I left for their performance, but I hear they were terrific, too, concluding their program with a great clogging finale.

After the international groups came all the Slovak groups, one more sensational than the other. When the program ended at four, all of us felt mesmerized and stunned by the high quality of each performance. Why have I never heard of Slovakia before? Where have they been? Where have I been? I felt humbled by my ignorance of this country. It is a treasure chest of folklore, folk music and dance, and performed on the highest level. I'll have to learn more about Slovakia—and come back again.

That's one of the reason's I'm feeling good this morning.

Here's the other reason: After the performances, when I was feeling high and open, Harold said the quality of the dancing was much better than the Bulgarian dancing at the Festival in Koprivschtitsa in 1995. I agreed. Then he went on to say he comes on a folk dance tour to see dancing and to dance, not to go rafting on the Dunajec or anywhere else. He said he could raft anywhere. He went on "complaining" in this manner for awhile. I quickly interpreted it as a "complaint" about my tour; no doubt he was been unhappy because there wasn't enough dancing. I first defended my tour concept, explaining that Folk Tours have more than folk dancing—we visit sights, castles, churches, towns of historic interest, plus crafts people like wood carvers, glass blowers, potters, etc. because all this background helps you understand the people and their folk dances. Folk dancing is more than dance steps; it is a culture expressed through the dance steps. If you don't understand the culture, how can you really dance? All you can do is follow steps by rote and make hollow movements?

After I explained my tour philosophy, Harold agreed with me. But it was too late. My tour and tour concept had already been "attacked". I felt insulted, hurt, angry, and defensive.

So why am I feeling good? Because I was able to figure all this out within two hours. I quickly realized once again that it is impossible to please all people. Yet, in spite of this fundamental truth, I keep feeling bad whenever someone complains even in the slightest and most unthreatening way. Why is this? It is because I slipped into my old habit—an over abundance of ego: my miserable ego says I have to power to please them forever and completely. Therefore, when they are not pleased, it is my fault, my own personal failure. Overabundance of ego, indeed! To my satisfaction and credit, I realized my mental descent, caught myself quickly, and righted it. I returned to my serendipitous state, knowing once again that other people's satisfaction and happiness is their own business, their own affair, their own choice. I can do little to nothing about it. I can only do what I do in the best way I can do it. That is my offering; that is within my control. Beyond that, it is up to each individual and their relationship to the higher forces. When I realized this fundamental truth, my ego retreated. I felt great again.

All in all, a great day.

I wrote this after only a sip of coffee. Could I be onto something new here?

Joe Livak said most Basques in America live in and around Reno, Nevada. They have Basque folk festivals there. Something to explore. Also folk festivals in France. This could open up Folk Tours to France, Spain, and the Basque country "in between."

Historic Flooding in Moravia

We left Moravia after the historic rainfall and flooding had destroyed much of its Valasske southern region. I've never seen such flooding. I had to make many leadership decisions, including cutting our program and leaving our lovely Vlcina Hotel in Frenstadt immediately after breakfast and one day earlier. As Vladimir navigated our bus over flooded roads for a short time I thought we wouldn't make it out. I used humor, denial, and strong decision making to decrease the possibility of group and personal panic. I did a good thing. I made the right leadership decisions. Working together with Gabriela, Vladimir, and feed- back from our group, I decided to leave Moravia no matter what, even if we couldn't find a hotel rooms in Prague. Better to accept the small annoyance of sleeping overnight on the bus than be stuck in Moravia for days, even weeks—or worse, the threat of a serious flood accident with loss of life.

About nine hours of torturous driving later we arrived safely in our ILF Hotel in Prague. After our people had been comfortably settled in their room, I met Jasan Bonus in the lobby to discuss the tour. Suddenly, I got my first tour headache. Not because of Jasan but because of the Moravian flood decisions and the realization of the danger we had narrowly averted. In fact, we found out that, half an hour after we left Frenstadt, all roads we had traveled on had been closed. Prague weather was beautiful and sunny. But the radio told us that in Moravia it was still raining, the flood waters had risen higher, and the catastrophe had worsened. A narrow escape for us. No wonder I had a headache.

When I met Jasan almost the first words out of his mouth were, "You did things the hard way on this tour by traveling many extra miles. Perhaps next year you should begin the tour in Slovakia by first flying to Kosice."

Amazing. For the past few days I had been thinking about how to add Kosice to next years's tour; and this even though this year's itinerary was as close to perfection as I can imagine. I wanted to add to my knowledge of Slovakia by visiting Kosice. Some of the best dances come from the eastern Slovakia region, of which Kosice is the capital. What a startling coincidence that Jasan should mention Kosice almost immediately. But I have learned there really are no "coincidences." They just seem that way to our narrow minds, lost in their ego-stroking constructs. Most, if not all things, are pre-ordained, ordered, and run by the higher forces. We follow along and even make what we think are our own decisions, often mistakenly believing that the decision making power and the events that take place have something to do with us. On a lower lever, they do. But on the Upper Levels everything has been set in motion long ago. Half-blindly or completely blind, we follow the paths with an occasional visit by a burst of visionary light or enlightenment.

Perhaps that is why the angels descend from heaven creating turmoils guilt, abandon, inner chaos, and wonder. Why do these upsetting events keep happening? Isn't it a teaching in disguise? Is it disguised? Or is the disguise only on the lower levels of understanding?

Perhaps the angels descent on a personal level mirrors the chaos created by the Moravian flood.

Leading a Tour Is like Making Love with the Brakes On

"Here's to a wonderful tour with unforgettable new experiences!" That was the toast we made last night in the Santa Klaus restaurant. I couldn't agree more!

I am the tour leader; I have my followers.

But on a higher level there are no leaders and followers. On the higher level, leader and follower blend into one.

Same with giving and receiving. On a lower level there is a separation between giver and receiver; but on a higher plane, there is none. A giver cannot give without a receiver; a receiver cannot receive without a giver. There is only a partnership between the two. Same with tour leader and his followers. On the lower plane there is separation; but on the higher one, there is none. Leaders cannot lead without followers; followers cannot follow without a leader.

Tomorrow we leave Prague and fly back to New York City. Today is free. I took my usual end-of-the-tour walk. I wanted to talk with my many selves about this tour, future tours, and life in general. I often break down. I cry over the beauty we have created. But during the tour, I cannot think this way. Running a tour is like making love with the brakes on. Sometimes I'm 51 per cent into the love making part, but more often I'm 51 per cent into the brake part. I hold myself back, contemplate our next itinerary move, think about uniting our tour participants, creating a oneness out of the chaos of their many personalities. My mind is so occupied with these thoughts I can rarely step back and look at the beauty I have created and the beauty we are creating. But today, our last day, my mind is free to wander into fields of magnificence, mansions of unforgettable experiences, towns, valleys, mountains, people we have visited, experiences we had both through our individual minds and through the new group mind that we have created.

Our group mind is transient; it will only last for the two weeks of the tour. It will disintegrate forever when our tour ends.

Or will it? Perhaps it will leave a lasting impression on the scroll of history that winds round the world; perhaps it will live on in memory of our tour participants.

What beauty we have seen! From walks through the architectural masterpieces of Prague and Cesky Krumlov in South Bohemia, leisure days in Piestany spa in Slovakia, incredible folklore, concerts, and dancing at the Vychodna Folk Festival, narrow escape from the Moravian Flood. Angels have watched over our tour as so many events coalesce to create this beautiful experience.

Tour leading may be love making with the brakes on, but, at the end of the tour, when the brakes come off, a visionary orgasm of beauty unfolds. It is breathtaking; it rips off the straight-jacket of my old thinking patterns, annihilates my harried and ancient self, breaks me down, tears me into a searing cry, then molds me a new self with its tears of ecstasy.

Remember the Moravian Flood!

If I cannot keep promises to my travels, maybe it is stupid and unrealistic to make them.

Look at my tour itinerary. So many promises are made and broken. I promise events. But situations change so suddenly. Decisions that were so certain and wise a moment ago suddenly no longer seem so.

How then can I make promises?

On the other hand, if I don't, who will come on my tours?

Promises may be merely temporary itineraries. Fragile human tour leaders cannot play God even though many tour participants may expect it.

There is nothing noble and elevating about my promises. I make them so I won't be hurt. They are part of the "deal:" Don't hurt me and I won't hurt you.

The tour of life is in the "what might happen" category. You can plan all the detail but God and His plans often get in the way, mess you up, humble you, and teach you about the weakness and limitations of our power-striving ego.

Making promises to clients many of which you cannot keep will not protect me. The best I can do is make my promises in good faith and try my best to keep them.

Thus, "lying with a light touch" is a good way to navigate through life. Although the Moravian flood waters may sometimes overwhelm you, by sticking to "Lying with a light touch" in public" and telling yourself the truth in private, you can get along.

One has to let go of everything in order to find what is indestructible in oneself.

I'm leaving for Romania today.

What should I think about while I'm there? What mental project and direction should occupy the upper and lower stratas of my mind?

1. Think about masculinity and its attributes of solar plexus and right side.

2. Think about running tours from my solar plexus.

We arrived in Bucharest a few hours ago, checked into our Dorobanti Hotel, and took our rooms on the eighteenth floor. Not bad. It even has air conditioning.

I slept rather well on the plane. Now I'm in my room at six o'clock with coffee and computer.

I lay down in bed with a headache. Then I thought of sweet eye-massage with soft hands caressing my face. My headache lessened. Then I envisioned the middle way, and life in the abyss between two cliffs. I focused on my headache getting soft as it floated in the abyss. I didn't ask for my pain to go away; I didn't even want it to go away. I only wanted to notice it, watch it, witness it, see it as part of my cooling loneliness.

My headache softened. Notice, it didn't disappear, it only softened. But that's pretty good.

"God Forbid It Works!"

Yesterday we had a fantastic day in Bucharest. After meeting our guide, Radu, and visiting the Village (Satalui) and Peasant Museum in the morning, we went, in the early afternoon, to the twenty-first floor of the Intercontinental Hotel to meet our Romanian dance teacher, Remus Giurgiu. The dance room was beautifully decorated with folk dance costumes; to our right was a table laden with drinks, ice, and water; to the left was another table covered with folk items for sale. A band of four folk musicians and three dancers in full costume greeted us and offered us the traditional Romanian welcome of bread and salt. Mihai David introduced Remus as his former colleague in the Romanian State Dance Ensemble. Then Remus, a man with a large belly and white hair, stepped into the center of the circle to teach us a simple dance from Romanian Moldavia (Moldova) called Hora de la Putna. Suddenly, the hotel management burst through the door. They told Mihai the whole group would have to move to another room. He handled the whole situation calmly and with humor. While the musicians and dancers dissembled the setup and carried everything down to a stuffy first floor room, he said, "In Romania we have a saying, 'God forbid it works!'"

I love that saying.

I also learned how to shout: Ne mia pomenit! (Not more remembered): Fantastic!, at the end of the class.

The Road To Madness and Masculinity

An Important Truth About The Source Of My Energy Supply

Go for the madness!

Let insanity be my rallying cry!

Madness, off-the-wall, craziness, and insanity could be my energy source. Could it also be the base, center, and source of my masculinity?

I put this in the form of a question. Usually, when I ask such questions, part of me already knows the answers. My questions are often answers in disguise.

But I don't want to rush to judgement. The relationship between madness and masculinity is such a profound idea.

Is there such a relationship?

How does it affect me?

If, in the crucible of my personality, madness and masculinity are related, have a direct link and line to each other, then I would have to change my entire attitude and approach to life.

I am in that process anyway.

I would like to believe there is such a direct link. Doesn't wanting to believe it make it true? Isn't there some kind of truth in desire?

I want to believe I have hidden and repressed masculinity and madness for a long time. Perhaps all my life. Oh sure, I haven't always succeeded. Dribbles and hints have always leaked out, filling my life with conflict and glory. But I have never been at peace with such leakages. I often apologize to myself or others for being forceful, strong, and dynamic on the masculine side, and for being crazy, off-the-wall, and insane on the madness side.

It is time to end these apologies. I am at a new life stage.

As I write, this idea of a direct link is crystallizing. In fact, I'd better simply accept its truth and move on.

Done! Accepted! Now what?

How will such acceptance affect my life?

First of all, after pondering this thought unconsciously all day, I woke up this morning with a bloody eye. It could have happened the moment my coffee maker didn't work. I got so "mad." I started to cry in frustration and anger. Crying in blood-red angry colors. Anger, rage, frustration—and sadness, all expressed through a burst blood vessel in the eye affecting the way I "see" the world.

Do these two minor irritants, broken coffee pot and bloody eye, symbolize anything? Are they related to resistance of the relationship between madness to masculinity? Are they a test of its truth?

At the moment, I don't know.

This marriage of the two m's will alter my life. Broken coffee maker and burst eyeball vessel are temporary annoyances. (Besides, I shook the coffee maker and then it worked. Perhaps it was knocked around too much in transit. We'll see.)

Another minor victory occurred with Hal and Ginny. They said when we make a bathroom stop on the bus I should point out exactly where the bathrooms are. I was stunned. Do they really want me to lead people by the hand right into the toilet? They said yes. I didn't know exactly how to handle such an infantile request. How to say no with tact? I still don't know what to do about it. I don't want to infantalize my clients. They must remain adults even thought some of their deepest wishes may be for me to take care of their every need. I am first and foremost father to myself. After handling that one, I can move on to becoming a father to others. Maybe the best way to be their father is to leave them alone to make their own decisions and find their own bathrooms.

After all, just as you can lead a horse to water but can't make them drink, you can lead a human to the toilet but you can't make them shit.

Thus ends my first day on the road to madness and masculinity.

Later: I got home from our long touring day feeling tired and low. But why? The day wasn't so bad. Many in our group said it was a good one. They liked our morning walking tour of Sibiu, our visit to the Bruckenthal Museum, our drive to the village of Sibiel for a lunch at a peasant's house, and the finale, a visit to the gigantic Astra outdoor museum featuring Romanian craftsmen, potters, woodworkers, painters, and more. All in all it was a long hard but magnificent day.

So why did I feel low?

It happened when our guide, Radu, said: "This tour is very hard."

I knew we had a very ambitious plan combining both a full touring program with the full folk dance Mihai had set up. Immediately, I heard the voice of my mother saying if it's hard you shouldn't have to do it, you can't do it, it will make you sick, it will make you tired, you are too weak to do something hard, things must be easy and fun for you or you cannot survive. On and on this voice from hell, along with the witches of Sibiel, kept haunting me, speaking to me from the background. Slowly it depressed me.

It is hard to escape from old voices. Even though I know I'll survive this tour and even flourish, voices from the past keep trying to push me down.

It is not the voice of masculinity, power, competence, and take charge I want to hear. Nevertheless, I heard it.

Time to dispel this voice of weakness, powerlessness, helplessness, and passivity. Time to let the masculine Priapus rise.

Romanian Rushing

Rush, rush, rush, from dinner to supper to restaurant, to hotel, to and through villages north of the Danube, to pleasant pheasants flying above peasant towns. Flying, flying, flying; birds soaring, soaring, soaring. I too am soring, soring, soring, aching with the rushing pace of this tour. So angry was I about changes in schedule when I realized that four one-night stands had entered our repertoire. But after returning from the long drive to and from Belis and plopping into bed after one a.m. I realized that even this semi-torturous tour-paced existence, this life on the wing, is merely another disguise of the abyss between the cliffs. I am trying to avoid a floating life by hiding in behind a wall of frustration, anger, and rage at the fucking Romanian and Balkan tour companies that disregarded my minimum two-night stand wishes.

The tourist learns about the country; the traveler learns about himself. The winged bird learns to fly anew each day.

If I am living the life of maya why not enjoy it? After all, I am adjusting to a life lived in, on, and under the ruins.

This morning for the first time I have a slight interest in learning Romanian. Perhaps I am adjusting.

Coffee Maker

Love comes in all forms. This morning I love my coffee maker. It is so compact, well-developed, and cute; it feels so good under my hand. I love to caress it, hold it, run my fingers down its back and sides. Especially, I love what it does for me and to me, how it cares about me, fulfills not only the needs of my stomach but my extended solar plexus as well. From that third center of energy it moves upward to awaken and satisfy the deepest yearnings of my early morning soul. That's why I love her this morning.

We get along so well. She appreciates me. She listens carefully to every word I say, taking these verbal vibrations deep into her bosom, thinking about it, meditating, ruminating, and cogitating deeply before regurgitating them in a boiled down distillate of dripping dark brown heavenly elixir poured into her beautiful extension cup. Although those contents can be separated from her, she is always present. I take her deep into my mouth, taste, love, drink her up, digest, and remember her, if not forever, at least long enough to jump-start my morning with a full head of steamy hair. Dripping and wet with furious passion, I am ready to charge into the day.

I thank my lovely coffee maker for these blessings. Beyond that, the maker of my coffee maker, the company that produced her; beyond that, the genius engineer who conceived her; beyond that, the Maker of the maker of the maker of my coffee maker.

Yes, I am thankful this morning. My coffee maker has awakened in me a deep passion, not only for the sublime, but for the ridiculous as well. All visionary extremes of the emotional prism have been seen and released. In her small, compact, and transportable form, she is a blessing to me. Even when she is hidden deep in my valise, packed on the bus or plane, even when I leave her in America, I think of her. Even when she is far away, I kiss her plug, caress her seminal vessels, purr besides the image of her coffee spout, the swing of her well engineered hips, the sweet lips of her cup.

Although I am ostensibly alone on this tour, I am not alone. As long as my coffee maker is with me in body, mind, and spirit, I will never be along.

Male must be complimented by female. There is nothing like a coffee maker to keep you warm and cozy in the Maramures town of Baie Mare close to the northern Romanian border.

Compliments, Praises, and Hosannahs: Birth Of A New Attitude

We arrived in Cimpulung Moldovanesc in Moldavia about seven o'clock after a long, fast, hard drive through Maramures. En route we stopped in villages to see wooden churches. Beyond that, the day was spent whizzing through the Maramures countryside. During the drive, our guide, Radu, hardly said a word.

I'm getting tired of his silences and apparent sullenness. Although he has flashes of sweetness and will try to accomplish almost anything I ask, his attitude is nevertheless so withdrawn, quiet, perhaps even angry and hostile. But I don't know for sure. Part of his silence and sullenness may be due to competition with Mihai; or it may be due to the messed-up nature of our tour program, the sudden changes, the many one-night stands, Mihai's sudden additions—and subtractions—of dance workshops and performances both existent and nonexistent.

I can't figure Radu out. I'd like to work with him again next year. He will know what kind of program we want. But he may also be a downer. So far I see no sense of humor, fun, or life in him. But that may change. It is hard to say. Perhaps his is a characteristic of Romanian guides who grew up under communism. I just don't know. I'll wait to see how he acts after Mihai leaves our tour in Brasov. Nevertheless, tomorrow I'll push him to explain more to our tourists. We'll see where that gets me. You can ask a stone to talk and sometimes it will for a short time. But the nature of a stone is to remain silent. Is Radu a stone? Or is there a gold mine hidden underneath? I always wonder who will be the whiner and complainer on my tours. There is always someone. To my surprise, Ginny and Hal are turning out to be the ones. Perhaps it is because they know me and feel they can say whatever they want.

I do not disagree with their complaints. But that is usually true of anybody that complains. How can you disagree with a complainer? After all, it is their feeling, their personal truth. So there is no disagreement with Hal and Ginny's complaints that this tour is too fast, that Radu doesn't say enough, that we don't stop enough for pictures, bathrooms, or whatever, that we need some more free time to walk in towns, etc. I agree with all of it. In fact, to me it is so obvious, it's not even worth mentioning. It is largely due to the inherent mess our itinerary has become. First of all, the tour company changed my two-night stands into one nighters; second, Mihai's additional dance classes have added an extra load to the timing of our itinerary. I sensed all this might happened before the tour began. Every tour has its difficulties, especially a new one. Our first Romanian tour is bound to have some problems. Next year, based on my newly acquired knowledge of Romania, I will insist on more days in each town.

I cannot say Ginny and Hal's feelings, complaints, and even observations, are wrong. Yet they still hurt although not as much as usual. The dictatorial part of me wants absolute power along with compliments, praises, and hosannahs about how wonderful I am and how wonderful this tour is. In fact, the new personal element, this time is that, even though it has problems, I still believe I should be getting compliments, praises, and hosannahs for running it! A new addition is my desire and even belief that I shouldn't get any complaints! I realized a few days ago that I want such absolute power. I want compliments, praises, and hosannahs. After running tours for fifteen years, I don't want any more criticism. None! Zero! Only praise! Look at all I've done, put myself on the line, put my ego in daily jeopardy, taking a chance leading a strange group of people to a strange country; look at all the countless hours of preparation and study I've put in. No one on this tour has put in as much work and preparation as I have. Yet they have the nerve to complain! They should be thankful—and only thankful, not only for the tour I have created, but for their ability and capacity to even come on such a tour and appreciate what Romania has to offer. Yes, I am sick of complaints about me, my tours, or my other creations. It's time for the compliments-praises-hosannahs. If I can't get them from others, at least I'll start giving them to myself.

Of course I know there will always be criticisms and complaints. They only way I can avoid them is to hide in a closet. My only controls are over my attitude. In the future, my attitude toward criticism and complaints will be to reject ninety to ninety-nine percent of them. Perhaps I can even move up to one hundred percent. Let my clients, friends, and family focus on compliments, praises, and hosannahs. Let them sings songs of praise for everything I do. If they don't, fuck 'em. At least I can do it for myself.

Ah, it is so good for me! Val was right. Such a new attitude is miracle that God has sent.

Yes, tourists can learn about the country if they like. I'll focus on learning about myself.

Compassion Revolution

Last night I went to bed somewhat low. Why? At supper I sat next to Linda who once again complained about our tour in particular and Romania in general. "How can you come here again?" she asked. "Without dancing, what does this country have?" A subtle complaint, but a complaint nevertheless. Every tour usually has a complainer. To my surprise, even amazement, this one has Linda. Sam, too. I feel somewhat stabbed in the back when my friends complain. Nevertheless, they are customers, too. Such is the nature of entrepreneurship and leading a tour.

I have to congratulate myself for not taking this complaint as personally as I used to. Linda also complained on our first Hungarian tour in 1984. We took a long walk together and she broke down in tears complaining about something or other. Along with all her good qualities, she is also a complainer. To her credit, she speaks up. To my dismay, she speaks up to me.

My problem, as usual, is how to handle complaints. On this tour I've "advanced" from blaming myself for my customers complaints and pain to blaming them. But perhaps I could advance even further. How?

This morning's reading of Pema's book gave me an answer. In the chapter "Widening the Circle of Compassion," she says:

Compassionate action is a practice, one of the most advanced. There's nothing more advanced than relating to others. . . . To relate to others compassionately is a challenge. . . . It means not shutting down on that person, which means, first of all, not shutting down on ourselves. It means allowing ourselves to feel what we feel, even the parts we don't like. To do this requires openness, which in Buddhism is sometimes called emptiness—not fixating or holding on to anything. Only in an open, nonjudgemental space can we acknowledge what we are feeling."

This would be an excellent tour practice for me. Instead of blaming myself for Linda's complaints and pain, and instead of blaming her for them, I might practice feeling compassion for her. That would be a revolution for me. A compassion revolution. A Buddhist compassion revolution. This is a good way for me to go. Wrong. It is a great way for me to go!

Let's see if I can try it. Let's see if I can do it. Let's see where it leads.

I'm sitting in the Ara Palace Hotel in Brasov looking out my window at a lovely Carpathian mountain. It is six-thirty a.m.

This morning I am quite disgusted. Yesterday, after a long drive from Suceava, we passed through the Bicaz Gorge—so far the most dramatic scenery in Romania, visited the folk artist, Nicolai Popa, bought some lovely folk art works, watched the local children of his Tirpesti village dancing, and finally arrived late in Brasov at 6:30 p.m. in time to miss our folk dance workshop.

People were not unhappy about missing it. They were too tired from the long trip. In the evening, we went for dinner at the Carpathian Stag with music, wine tasting, and a folk dance performance. Good show but somewhat flashy. During the dinner, Mihai and his daughter, Aubrey, said goodbye to our group. They took the night train back to Bucharest. I felt sad losing him even though he hasn't worked too hard on this trip. And this for mucho money. We're also losing Flora, our driver, whom everybody loves. He has been a constant gentleman, jumping out at every stop to help people off the bus, smiling, friendly. A pleasure. Our guide, Radu, remains as grouchy as ever. I'm about to give up on him. I doubt he can redeem himself during the next few days. Only my belief in miracles might change that.

I might have even felt okay about yesterday, merely passing it off as a hard day or driving, except that when we returned to our hotel last night Ginny summarized the day: "Well, that's the second folk dance workshop we missed." She held up a medallion from the Carpathian Stag. "We'll use this design for our next T-shirt. It will say 'I survived the Romanian tour with Jim Gold.'" Not a positive statement.

In any case, I'm beginning to expect negative comments from Ginny and Hal. Strange, theirs are the only negative comments I've heard. Others have either said positive things or, mercifully, nothing. I appreciate that. Perhaps they are enjoying this tour in spite of its hardships, missed workshops, speedy drives, one-night stands, etc.

Stan is now so sick he wants to return to the USA tomorrow. Dorothy and Paul are sick, too, but they are hanging in there. I called Stan before the show last night. He said he was feeling better. Maybe he'll stay with us after all. We'll see. The lightning tour pace, the one-night stands caused by the fuck up at either J'Info or Balkan tours, has certainly made it extra hard on my tourists. Perhaps it is one of the reasons some are sick. But they might have gotten sick even if we had stuck to the original schedule. But the tour scheduling fuck-up is certainly the cause of my disgust and feeling of betrayal by the tour companies. It is the reason we have missed two of the folk dance workshops.

In any case, we're starting fresh today. I'm thinking about changing tour companies and guides next year. Perhaps I can work directly with ONT Carpati and Carmen Pricop in Bucharest. Or maybe Adam Molnar can set up a tour to Transylvania and Hungary (although I doubt this.) Perhaps I can clear up the mess with J'Info and still work with them again next year. We'll see. Everything is now in flux.

Hubris Rising

Is it really August 24th?

We're getting close to the end. Thank God. I can't wait for this tour to be over.

I reached my limit yesterday. I was hoping to have the afternoon off. Instead, our tour of Bran Castle, Poina Brasov, the Brasov synagogue, and the Black Church lasted until three p.m. Then I spent another two hours sitting in MacDonalds talking to Aurel Pavel, the owner of J'Info Tours. He is tall, wiry, and full of sleeping energy, with a sharp-turned entrepreneurial semi-communist mind, a former engineer and computer specialist, I was impressed with his sharpness, dynamism, and analytic mind. He seemed competent, opinionated, and knew the Romanian hotels and travel business very well. He's probably a good person to work with. We'll see. We sketched out next year's tour itinerary. He thought ending our tour with two nights in Brasov was sufficient. I sensed three would be better. Later Ginny confirmed this. It is good to remember I have intuitions and opinions of my own.

Last night at supper our group sang a song written by Paul Kerlee. It was called "The Jim Gold Diet Plan." Everyone gathered around my table and sang. It was a supposedly funny song about how people can lose weight touring with me, eating two meals a day, sitting hours on the bus, etc. I suffered through most of it while they sang. I never had a song written about me. Also I wasn't sure if the song was friendly or a critical. Actually, I felt it was critical. I smiled like crazy to counter my public embarrassment as my tourist sang out my name over and over again in the chorus.

I could be wrong about this. But I think I am right. Basically, I felt it was a Jim Gold roast.

How embarrassed and sensitive I am at hearing my name in public, especially when I hear it thrown around in what I conceive to be a critical manner.

Well, let me accept the idea that is was a critical song. I even agree with some of it. I myself have lost weight on this tour. But, of course, I don't eat much either.

In any case, as long as I try to create something and bring it to the public, public criticisms of me will never end. Such is the nature of public—and even private-life. Therefore, my question has to be: how can I stop myself from suffering such public embarrassments and humiliations when these criticism occur? An old question. Nevertheless, I could use some new answers.

Perhaps one would be accepting the truth that I live in the middle ground between right and wrong. That was the essence of the Pema writing I read this morning. I can never be completely right or completely wrong. I only grab at right and wrong when I'm want some security. During the Jim Gold Diet Plan song, I believed I was personally responsible for the food, itinerary, shortcomings, and personal pain of my tourists.

I am responsible for trying to do the best job I can. But responsibility for the pain of others is beyond my power. When members of my tour suffer under the Jim Gold Diet Plan, when they are criticizing me publically for running this tour in whatever half-assed, incompetent, disorganized, messy, and difficult manner they conceive of, I must somehow learn not to take their complaints personally. Yes, I can sympathize with them and feel compassion for their plight. But it is hubris to think I can takeresponsibility for it, hubris to believe I have such power.

Yet for some strange reason I do not understand, I believe I do.

Yes, folks, sad to say, I do take responsibility for the feelings of others on my tour. I'm slowly learning not to.

Perhaps it takes years of dealing with such hubris to eradicate it.

Perhaps it will never be eradicated but only softened.

A New Gear: Birth of Romanian Study

Yesterday we took our last long bus trip, an all day ride from Brasov in Transylvania to the Dobrugan town of Tulcea in the Danube Delta. On our way, we stopped to see Peles Castle in the spectacular Muntenian town of Sinaia. It is probably the most magnificent interior I've ever seen with incredible wood carving, painting, and designs. Outside the castle, a classical guitarist sat playing a beautiful version of Recuerdos de la Alhambra, followed by Leyenda. Luckily, our people needed a bathroom. While they experienced yet another Romanian toilet, I listened to this magnificent guitar player. Afterwards, I took his name and address. He told me that every summer, his teacher in Bucharest organizes a guitar festival at Sinaia. Something I might including in my touring program for the future.

Our stay at Sinaia took longer than expected. Radu was upset. He said we wouldn't arrive at Tulcea until eight or even nine o'clock at night. Another day of long and miserable bus ride with some of our travelers getting even sicker. I gritted my teeth. However, it was

Sunday, with hardly any traffic on the road and no truck traffic whatsoever. To my astonishment we arrived in Tulcea at 6:00 p.m. A Romanian miracle!

About a half an hour from Tulcea, when I realized we would be arriving early, a wonderful wave of freedom passed through me. Over! Finished! Free at last! The main travel hardships of our tour were over. And adding to my happy sensations was the atmosphere in Dobruga. This Danube Delta area felt soothing and relaxing. Perhaps I should plan to end next year's tour here, or at least offer a three or four-day Black Sea extension.

This morning, for the first time on tour, I had a desire to study Romanian. I have been resisting it all trip. In fact, I have been resisting all Latin languages. Why? Too easy? Not enough challenge after Hungarian, Greek, Hebrew, Arabic, or the Slavic languages of Bulgarian, Czech, Slovak, and Russian? Perhaps the alphabet itself bored me? All these seemed like good reasons. But more true, I was probably blinded by more important considerations. I had to first survive the Romanian tour. It was top priority. Now that I have "discovered" Romania, I see it is a good travel destination, a fascinating country to get to know and explore. Also, by studying its Latin language, I'll be preparing for our tour to Sicily and Italy next February, and, in the future, the general Latin world of France, Spain, and Portugal. Eventually, I may be able to fuse the languages I've studied and see connections between the Slavic, Hebrew, Greek, and Latin families.

It feels like a new day, a fresh start. I'm moving into a new gear with some peace and quiet at my back.

Why Solve Problems?

Why solve problems when new ones only come up to take their place? Isn't it better to learn to live with problems than to constantly place yourself under the pressure of solving them?

Fight the urge to solve my problems and those of others.

Only one day left! I can't wait to go home. It has been a difficult but successful tour. Yesterday's overnight in Tulcea and Danube Delta boat trip was peaceful, relaxing, and fascinating. But the resort area on the southern Black Sea Romanian coast so far is shit. Our three star Riviera Hotel is quite mediocre even by Romanian standards. I hardly slept last night. Too much noise outside. Luckily I have my fan to give me some background white noise humming.

I'm at the end of my writing in Romania. Perhaps I should take a break and read.

Problems are to be lived with, not solved.

By leaving "home" and stepping into the abyss, I am standing up for myself. Three stages of standing up:
1. Doing whatever others want.
2. Fighting for equality.
3. Making requests and strong demands for myself.

INVENTIONS

Witch Gazing

Tom gazed into the awful eye of the Wicked Witch of the West. Blue-black melon tits leaped out of each cornea; three vaginal penetrations leaned listlessly in the corner; beneath a tear duct an old man waddled willows while to the right, a horse sat fishing in a brook.

What a strange melon-eye she had. Why was it mottled? Melanoma? Or was she suffering from megalomania of the titus gland? One never knows with witches.

Her yarmulke was on backwards.

Tom Walked

Tom walked through the delicatessen window to examine a display of newsprint on an adjacent frankfurter.

Sure enough, Felix Frankfurter was appearing on a column beyond the Nile.

At last those beautiful Delta leanings could be pluned. That only a camouflaged wineplop could appear.

Tom's Job

Tom's job was to create the world. He began each Biblical Exegesis morning by bereshiting.

Yes, he created his world. First he rolled around in bed, creating earthquake rumblings in the mattress springs and a few primordial oceanic waves, trying to muster up a few seeds for the dawn of creation. But it was too early. Nothing worked yet. He sat up, abdominal muscles propelling his torso first to the left, then to the right. Suddenly, whambo! straight out of bed into upright simian pose. On your feet, boy! Up and standing and ready to bereshit.

He turned to his favorite morning madame, Mrs. Coffee and drank up her delicious a.m. elixir. Bubbles started bouncing in his stomach, discharged stray endorphines into his spiritual tunnel system, and set him ready to bereshit. Then, he meditated upon the caffeine filled archetypical liquid whose water had originated during the great biblical flood where Noah, his ancient ancestor, had first practiced the placement of couples in health-giving, loving, and long lasting relationships.

Tom began every morning this way. His job was to create the world.

Pointing the Way

Tommy went to the park. He tossed his balloon into the wind and watched it float upwards.

Suddenly, his right index finger left his hand and floated away!

Tommy was not used to body parts falling off and floating into space. He liked control of both his eight-year-old body and eight-year old mind. Index floating had to stop! But how? Can you control a rebel finger?

He watched helplessly as the finger travelled an independent route, separating from the balloon and floating even higher. It passed a cumulus cloud, crossed San Diego Bay, floated over the Rockies, settled one hundred feet above Nevada, then headed back to San Diego.

Suddenly, it pointed straight at him. He could see digits vibrating clearly, the skin glistening and wet from its passage through the cloud.

Then the index finger spoke:

"Oh mortal Tommy, travelling lost and alone through this confusing world. You may fool others, but you can't fool me. Your hiding days are over. I'll find you wherever you are. That's why it is best to travel Brutal-Honest Road, which runs past jagged cliffs, insurmountable boulders, thorns, poisonous snakes, savage lions, and caterpillars bursting with iron butterflies. Fear radiates fear, but Brutal-Honest Road eats up fear and turns it into a friend. That's why when you meet Mr. Fear along the way, say hello, talk to him, invite him into the kitchen of your mind for milk, cookies, and even ice cream. You'll soon get to know each other; you may even become best friends. You'll see that Brutal-Honest Road is nothing to hide from; it's not as brutal as you thought. More brutal is Hiding Road where darkness, fog, and confusion lead to the Land of the Lowly located just south of Camden, New Jersey."

Tommy's index finger floated down to earth, then whispered into his ear: "Don't worry, I'll point things out. You can have me back once you know the way."

Tommy contemplated the vacant space on his hand where his index had once stood. Where should he turn? He pulled down his balloon, deflated it, put it in his pocket, and took a thoughtful walk around the park, looking for the future in the palm of his hand.

When he returned an hour later the shadow of his index finger stood behind a tree pointing towards Middle Road.

Asking

"Do I fly or crawl this morning?" Tom asked. "Am I a lark or a worm? Do I take breath-defying leaps into the unknown where slithering dragons dwell in plenitude, well beyond the Waves of Pleasures and Pacific Pastures of Known Joys? Dare I leap past illusion into the black mystery of Chasm Ocean beyond? Can licking bring a platypus to Orgasm Peak? Can sucking turn a jelly fish into a sturgeon?" These are questions Tom could not answer before he carried out the garbage.

He shook his fist at the sky. "Where is the perfect carnivore diet?" he shouted. "What happens to vegetarians in hell?" He davened at a frantic pace before falling to his knees in a mixed grill of religion, frustration, genuflection, and meditation.

Dental Musician

Tom was a dentist who wanted to expand his cavity of knowledge. As oboe and bassoon soloist for the San Diego Orthodontial Symphony, an orchestra specializing in serial (cereal) music extractions, he needed to know the art of music from all ends. Teeth were his business by day but at night he dreamed of intestines.

When he entered the aviary section of the San Diego zoo, he asked the guard: "Please let me hear the sound of canary intestines."

The guard promptly handcuffed him to a rest room post, dialed the Aviary Intestinal Research Institute in La Jolla on his cellular phone, and asked for the director of the Fowl Intestine Department, Dr. Jonas Fawk, who immediately sent an ambulance filled with canaries. The guard handcuffed Tom to a back seat monorail—protecting the canaries from the threat of unauthorized dental work—and sent the hawk-faced ambulance driver back to the lab. As they stalled, bobbed, and wove their way through the Freeway rush hour traffic, Tom heard plenty of the sound he was looking for. When they finally arrived at the institute, he emerged from the van, smiled as he thanked Dr. Jonas, and ran down La Jolla mountain as fast as he could.

October–December 1997

WRITING

Terra Firma in Sight

During the past ten weeks I've had no desire to learn or pursue any avenues of my miracle schedule. Falling apart and lost have blanketed my world. Not bad as a beginning or as the Big Guy said, a Bereshit. However, I'd like to move beyond bereshit to the bara elohim, to creating a new world. This morning I stand at the border of a new land. I'm almost ready to cross over and move on.

What an important week I had! It all began September 22nd with our walk, talk, and decision to continue living in the abyss between two cliffs. At that point my mind stopped its swirling descent, its plummet into the bottomless reaches of the black abyss; it steadied itself but still trembling at the edge of foreign cliffs and precipices. Then followed our Sunday night group meeting and "Do you want to split?" debacle. With that question I reached the bottom of the bottom. It was a question asked from strength not wimphood. I wanted to know about my future direction, what would be right for me. A new core of self started forming, forged in the molten asking of the "split" question itself. A new strength was circling my former cesspool of self. I took infant walking steps, raising myself first a chlorinated pool of self with a misty future vision of a fresh mountain spring. Then came my first writing class with Barry. Once again I looked at my New Leaf journal and what direction to take with it. Next day came a therapy session with Dave where I took a fresh look at myself.

That evening I took a two-hour walk, a blast of leg moving through the streets of Teaneck, Bogota, Ridgefield Park, and back to Teaneck again. I walked around block after block, and thought thought after thought. Finally, I concluded with a new vow: forget so-called faithfulness to others. Rather concentrate and dedicate myself to fulfilling all my potentials, to being the best and fullest self I can be.

Next day I spoke to Barry about *New Leaf*. He came in with a whopper:

"Connect yourself to formal prose."

"What does that mean?" I asked.

"Write with the intention of someone else reading it," he said. "Think about influencing and enlightening others. This will also help you organize *New Leaf*. Cut it by first putting entries in piles of subjects, then eliminate repetition and keep the best one."

Major ideas are entering my mental vacuum! I'm taking my first steps on solid ground again. Slowly, painfully, I'm starting to walk with a new stride; a new purpose and direction is forming. It includes elements of All-Is-One, accepting love from others by exploring and accepting self-love, a new vow of self-expansion, and the expression of all these directions through a new outward purpose in writing—and playing guitar: that of influencing and enlightening others.

I don't quite know what many of these directions mean yet. But many of the butterflies in my stomach have stopped flying around; the jumps, twists, and turns in my intestines have slowed; In the mist up ahead I seem to see terra firma. A couple of months ago I had an intuition that I wouldn't know or understand my new directions and purposes until mid- November. We'll see if I'm right.

Lost in the Physical World

This morning I just want to write. I don't know why or where I'm going.

I hardly slept last night. Turnings, tossing, rising, falling, over and over criss-crossing the interstices of my mind, listening to intergalactic rumblings in my mental factory, interpsychic disturbances of a subtle and dark nature.

Why am I rumbling? What slender stalks are twisting, gyrating, turning, growing, pushing from my stomach? Is it a new layer of growth? Does the serendipitous nature of sticky non-entities attacking and swelling my abdomen harken to a former reality? Or does it sit before me dressed in wolf's clothing wearing the smile of my future sun?

This morning my body feels tattered, beaten, and lost. Why does every leg I own ache, every toe feel displaced, every thigh cooked in a furnace, every kneecap blown to bits, every nerve, vein, and muscle in my lower back rooted in tightness, and singed in bound blood knots?

There is a psychic disturbance going on and I am it.

Dave said I'm disappointed by the outside world. He's on to something. But what does it mean? I'm not ready to know.

But there is a rumbling voice beginning to crack through the molten rock hiding my physical core. Perhaps some day I'll grab the earth and hold onto it for dear life.

Grab the earth; grab the transient? Is that the way I want to go? The inner world of my spirit can light transcendental lights. It can fly to the moon and back in one second, visit endless stars and planets, create and reverse hundreds of universes, and all this in only a few moments. How can I compare such intrapsychic creations, such lunar and lunatic powers, to the shadow movements and crumbling transience of the outside world? Why must I accept or even deal with the pains, longings, sufferings, beatings, whippings, losses, and loneliness of the earthen physical world if my lofty inner spiritual one offers such lights?

I came into this world encased in a body. Like it or not, I have to deal with it. Like it or not, the physical world is my bridge.

I still don't know what this writing is about. Perhaps it will become clearer as I move through the day.

I want the crying thrill of early morning coffee to remind me of why I am alive and why I want to be alive. Sure, it's a drug high. But what else will give it to me? Especially when I am feeling down this a.m.

Why am I down?

Easy. On the surface, it's the annoyance of all my medical tests. But, deep down, it's because I'm not writing.

I've "momentarily" replaced writing with happy finger guitar therapy. I'll just have to ride the therapy horse until it runs out of hay.

But I am also building two new writing bases:

1. I'm caring for my temple. Looking for a healthy body through diet, acupuncture, medicine, reflexology, and etc. studies.

2. I've made peace with my New Leaf Category Organization.

The above are not inspirational bases, but care bases. They are necessities—like earning a living—but they do not have spark. For spark, I must write.

Of course, they might have a small spark. I'll have to look for it.

LANGUAGES

A Visit to the Latin Kingdom

I woke up this morning thinking about our Sicilian tour coming up in February. One month away and so far, I have absolutely no interest in going. Too bad. Can't I find something of interest, something to inspire me to want to go?

In the past, language inspired me to travel. But now I am studying medicine and health. How can I combine medicine and health with my Sicilian tour? Is there any possible connection?

This morning I found one: Latin. In medicine and health, I see the language base is mostly Latin and Greek. Here's my chance to study Latin— through Italian! This study immediately expands to include ancient Greek, Hebrew, and modern English. Why? Because not only is the medical and health vocabulary is based largely on Latin and Greek, but I know, from Isaac Mozeson"s Word, that many Greek and Latin words used as roots in the English language come from ancient Hebrew words. Thus, my Sicilian inspired, Italian language study is based on a wider study of the three basic Western classic languages and will ultimately include modern languages such as Italian and English. I find the poetry of medicine and health in the study of language.

LIFE

All-Is-One: The Vision

Yes, yes, yes! I will stand up for my No, no, no! In the beginning, a small voice filled with spark and light spoke from beyond a dark corner in my mind: "No, no, no! I refuse to return to the old ways. Never again! I'll find a new way of thinking, a new attitude, a new approach to living! Or I'll die first. I will never think my old thoughts again! That voice has been speaking for months and is still speaking.

At first it was covered up—but not silenced by the hardened crust of ancient habits and attitudes. You can't break through the thirty-foot thick walls of Ancient Habit Castle so quickly. You've also got to get over the moat before you even start the break down process. There's lots of work, time, and effort involved. The twins, determination and patience, must work together.

But I stood up for myself. I spoke to the guardian at the gate during my quiet walk around the block. I told him "It is not a failure, weakness, or blow to my masculinity. It is something I "decided" to do. And this because I wanted it to guide me somewhere, to lead me to a new approach and attitude towards life. My body spoke up for me, saying, I refuse to go backwards, to slide downhill into the old, worn-out, useless valleys where I once lived. Onwards and upwards to the Land of Goodness, the Land beyond guilt, shame, and embarrassment, beyond put downs and humiliations, the Stand-Up Land where Goodness and Love shine equally upon me. Yes, that's where I want to go; that's where I'm heading; and no goal-oriented process is going to stop me.

When I reach the Land of Intimate and Ultimate, the Land of Goodness and Love, I want to be in all directions! Like a ripe juicy pomegranate falling one-hundred and ten floors from the top of the Empire State Building and splattering on the sidewalk below, I want my seeds bursting everywhere, planting and fertilizing the world for not hundreds, thousands, or even millions of mile but beyond measurable distance into infinity. Limitless, infinite, ultimate orgasm! That the bursting I'm looking for. I want my seeds traveling not only in vaginas and fallopian tubes where they will visit friendly ovum, but I want them fertilizing my fingers as they play Recuerdos de la Alhambra, Leyenda, and Bach Suites, fertilizing the written words pouring across the pages, fertilizing my dances as I choreograph up a Romanian, Hungarian, Greek, or international storm, fertilizing my relationships with the worldly souls and bodies populate my life. Yes, I want a full seed-burst, a full flowering. I'll settle for nothing less. If I have to wait a few weeks, months, years, or lifetimes, so what? Sometimes you have to wait a long time before the best stocks rise. When my stock rises, when my pay-off comes, not only will it last for an eternity but it will also reveal the Infinite in an explosive, gastrointestinal, cacophonic, metaphysical, multiphysical, apocalyptic, All-Is-One vision.

Visiting Goodness by Putting the Critics to Rest

She's standing arms akimbo, eyes false, blood-shot, shaking her wild and accusing finger at me as she screams: "It's all your fault! I'm sick. It's all your fault! I'm dying. It's all your fault! You did it. My heart, bad back, bad leg, bad shoulder, bad brain, bad psyche, bad finance, and bad luck—it's all because of you and what you did! I'll never recover from all of this! You're guilty, evil, and bad, bad, bad!"

On and on goes the litany of blame. Who could this be screaming at me but Ma. Who else could have such power over the infant part of my brain? Who else can reach out to touch me like this even from the grave? Oh sure, she comes in many "modern" forms, shapes, and sizes taking the body of wife, tourist, client, weekender, dancer, audience, or whatever. But these are mere apparitions, phantoms, imaginary dancers pirouetting in my mind as they manufacture illusions before my eyes. Remember my Route 80 Vision. Critics are like raindrops falling on cellophane: they strike and roll off. They can't touch me. Critics can only penetrate if I want them to, if I let them. Do I agree with them? Maybe, maybe not. But their criticism is only as true as I see it.

So much turns on the concept of goodness! My mind spends thousands of hours wondering whether I am good or bad. It has been the great and everlasting moral quest and question of my life. For years I have been living under a cloud shaped like a whip. It flays and shreds and beats the shit out of me because of a fundamental belief that somehow, deep in my soul, I am bad, bad, bad, and wrong, wrong, wrong; that when I look at others and painful things happen to them, it is somehow my fault. If only I were better they would be better. What power I give them! They can, at any time, point an accusing finger at me and shout: "It's all your fault!" And imagine, part of me will believe them! Truly, this is insane. Yet I have thought this way for years. Thus I lived always on the defensive, ever ready to pick up my gloves and fight for my goodness turf, to scream and yell and kick and punch whoever would dare tell me I am wrong, bad, and their pain is my fault. Why would I fight them so much? Because I believed them. Well, a part of me believed them. But you only need a spoonful of poison in the goodness drink to sicken the drinker. A little belief in the blame poison, a few blows of the "It's all your fault!" hammer, a few swallows of the "You are responsible for my pain!" poison pill, a few chops of the "If it weren't for you I'd be better and happier!" axe, and you can well end up sick, hospitalized or even dead.

How could I have believed in such an illusion for so long? How could I have believed that raindrops falling on my cellophane raincoat could not only wet my skin but rot my body, mind, and soul? It is amazing how long an illusion can last. When it is planted early and deep in your soul, it not only grows and grows, but can survive for years, decades, a lifetime, even for centuries.

But terrestial lastings are different from eternal everlastings. Eventually they end. Finality finally strikes. The great illusion of "It's your fault!", the constant critic and judge of my life who ever waited in the wings to pounce on me, died in my Route 80 Vision. That Vision was a beautiful shock to my system; it will take months to digest. But I'm starting down Digestion Process Road right now. I'm hoping to reach the town of Reveling soon.

November 1st Day: Giving Up Directions

A few months ago I said that by November I'd know more about who I am, where I'm going, what my new "directions" are for the year. Well, today is November 1st and somehow I've put it together. I am steadier and more peaceful. My sense of "direction" has been established.

Why do I put "direction" in quotations marks? Because my new sense of "direction" is that I have no direction. I have "given up" directions. This in favor of process.

A good example is in my New Leaves. After taking a week off from writing, establishing a firmer, steadier, mental base, an old leaf has ended and a New leaf has begun. If I followed my old habits I would be starting a New Leaf. Instead, I'm simply continuing the old one. This symbolizes the continuity of process. Rather than finishing leaves, moving from level to level, from New Leaf product to New Leaf product, I am, instead, flowing one Leaf into another. Products, levels, and endings have ended. In their place is a continuous open-ended flow. I've exchanged progress for process.

New direction is a paradox because it eliminates the very concept of direction.

What does this mean? How do I express this new sense of peace and stability in my life?

I no longer have any place to go. I am aiming nowhere. Take guitar, for example. I see myself moving steady along with no stops on the way. The path seems upward but with no end in sight. After many years of frustrating practice, I have finally gotten the tremolo, can play Alhambra and Leyenda with pleasure and satisfaction, play my other pieces with tremolos and arpeggios; I can enjoy the new control and power I feel in my right index finger. But I no longer see this as a breakthrough or having reached a new playing level. In fact, I don't see it as a level at all but simply part of the upward flow.

My approach to the guitar, the way I practice and play it, symbolizes my new approach to life. Practicing guitar is a good-in-itself; playing is its own reward. I have dropped ulterior motives. I no longer practice "to improve;" I am no longer goal-oriented; I am no longer imbued with purposes like mastering the tremolo, conquering the virtuoso guitar world, or giving a concert. I have no desire to give a concert. I have no sense or vision of the future. My only "desire" is to be, to play in the present, to wallow and luxuriate in the sensuality and beauty of playing the guitar.

This attitude extends to everything else I am doing. My former sense of purpose, my drive towards a future goal, my desire to conquer and excel in other disciplines, be they yoga, running, language, philosophy, or whatever I would drain out of my miracle schedule, have vanished. I sit in peace and contemplation of the every day.

This new practice, this "discipline"—a discipline which by its very contradictory and paradoxical nature is not a discipline—feels like it is surrounded and bathed in love. What is love but total immersion in the present? I am in the present. It feels relaxed, peaceful, and beautiful.

I am not used to this state. I don't know what "to do" with it." Once again, a paradox. Obviously, you "do nothing" with it. It is a do-nothing state which forgets becoming and is born in being. How do I express such a state to others? Should I bother trying? Probably not. It is better to just luxuriate in it, let it radiate out. Then others can pick from it whatever they want.

That's where I am on this November 1st.

Progress and Process

Progress is an up staircase.
Process is a flowing river.
In the bible, Jacob dreamed he saw a ladder going up to heaven. Each rung brought him closer to God.
The rungs represent progress.
Where then is process?
In the beam of light.
Jacob's ladder—Sulaam Yacov, is the concrete material representation of the light beam (in ladder form). You ride the merkabah beam, you ride the ever- flowing light-drenched chariot of process into heaven.

In Buddhism, instead of riding, you flow downstream through changing forms towards a universal oneness represented by the Great Ocean.

Different religions use and adopt different symbols. But the final resting place, the "goal" of losing the ego, the self, in a pulsating sphere of oneness, never changes.

A Day of Reflection

Yesterday, in writing class, we talked about reading books "by the pound weight." There is evidently a readership for books of many pages. People like Barry's mother buy these heavy books and spend a year or more reading. The thicker the book the better. They read a few pages a day. These sagas and mini-epics become part of their daily lives.

Why did I like this so much? Because it opened up the idea of reading books again. It introduced the idea of "slow" into reading. This relates to my Route 80 experience of criticism as raindrop-on-cellophane experience.

This quasi-primal experience "freed" me from constantly defending myself against criticism. It allowed me to play guitar at my own pace—which often is slow. In so doing, I am discovering nuances, dynamics, and new levels of expression I never found before when I lived under the Tyranny of Speed. With audience criticism dropping away I can now explore at my own pace—in public as well as private. Actually, much of the distinction between private and public is also dropping, too.

How does this effect my reading?

I've always put myself under the same speed pressure in reading as I do in guitar playing. It is amazing how "speed" and "fast" have affected my life. Go, go, go, fast, fast, fast, speed, speed, speed! Everything must be done at a rapid pace. No time to linger, taste, rest, or savor the deliciousness of the moment, or the fragrance depths of knowledge in a work of art or anything else. Speed, speed, speed, move, move, move. No wonder I don't want to read a book. No wonder I focus on learning languages: they, at least, stop me from speeding by forcing me to look up and focus on word after word. Language study is my forced exercise in slowing down.

In any case, by allowing myself a year or more to read a book, by slowing down and just reading a few paragraphs or pages a day, I've brought a new pleasure to my reading. With the pressure to rush gone, I will want to read again.

It is amazing and wonderful how my Route 80 criticism experience has opened up my world.

Last night I started reading Metamorphoses by the Latin poet Ovid. In 8 A.D. he was exiled by Emperor Augustus to the backwater Black Sea town of Tomis. Today Tomis is Constantsa in Romania. I visited it on our Romanian tour this summer and saw Ovid's statue standing in the town square. A good reminder that he was once human, too.

My year is beginning to form a direction. I am standing on firmer ground. The route-80-criticism-experience along with my vow of fulfilling my potential and my growing acceptance of moving slowly are beginning to take.

But I am amazed at how these movements towards strength and power are interpreted. When I expressed them, my biggest fear was initially realized. Become strong and you lose the ones you love.

Rather than congratulating me for my new discoveries and the new base I've found on which I can build and fulfill my talents, I was told such strengths excluded others. I defended myself beautifully. Better, I didn't "defend." I felt no need to. Rather, I explained myself. My new strengths, rather than excluding others, would include others, and this even more than before. Why? Because I would no longer be defending myself against them, no longer live behind defensive castle walls ever expecting enemy attack. My defensive walls had fallen. I was open not only to seeing others as they are but would be able to listen to them and see them as separate people with their own wants, needs, and views. I would be able to accept all this even if they were attacking me.

This is an absolutely amazing discovery and personal advance toward an All-Is-One vision. As I see it, others can only benefit from what I've learned about myself. It can't be anything but a win-win situation.

Tantric Judaism

As I took a short run I thought about the pleasures of the flesh.

Flesh is of the earth. It is subject to gravity. Thus, to focus on it can pull you to earth and sometimes even lower, and therefore, bring you down—especially if you get lost in them.

But that does not mean we should dispense with flesh or its pleasures. Rather, to defend against downward movement we need to change our focus to upward. How can this be done especially with flesh?

Answer: instead of pleasures of the flesh, focus on pleasures through flesh. Flesh then becomes a means to an end. Like a guitar or flute through which you can play divine music, flesh becomes an instrument to reach the divine.

Thus you can jump in bed with flesh, fuck it, love it, luxuriate in its warmth and radiance, screw it, caress it, soak it up, wet it down, wallow in the sensual fragrance of its nostril-enhancing emissions, bathe in the soft lotions of its touch. But whatever you do with flesh, by flesh, on flesh, under flesh, over flesh, remember, ultimately your lasting pleasure and meetings with eternity come through flesh. By playing all your instruments, you too can hear the divine music of the celestial flesh-filled fuckulent orchestra.

This is the essence of the esoteric Eastern doctrine of Tantra. However, I am Jewish. What is a Jew doing studying Tantra? Shouldn't he study Torah? How about Tantra Torah? How about combining Torah and Tantra in the Judaic Torah Tantra?

What would Tanta think of Torah Tantra? What would Moses say about Tantra? Did he ever practice it? Did he receive anything else on Mount Sinai? What did he do in his spare time?

Is there such a thing as Tantric Judaism? If not, isn't it about time for it? I can see it now, "Oi vey, vat a fuk!"

Ten-Minute Rule

I followed the "Ten-minute rule" this morning. I played guitar for ten minutes which, not surprisingly, ran into forty minutes. Not a bad start.

The ten-minute rule is such a good idea. It helps fool the mind into low commitment and easy thinking. "After all," it say, "anybody can do ten minutes of almost anything." I can certainly do ten minutes of guitar playing, writing, calling, sales, yoga, running, Hebrew study, history, philosophy, or whatever. Ten minutes? What's the big deal? None, really.

So I get started. That's the most important thing. The ten-minute rule is my starting spark. Once I begin, then the hypnotic process of work itself slowly starts to take over. Ten minutes easily turns into fifteen, twenty, even thirty, forty, or beyond. Once you're hypnotized, mesmerized, you can go on and on. But first you must start. Starting is often the hardest thing to do. Once you conquer it, the rest is easy.

Yes, the ten-minute rule helps you start. Witness this writing. I expected to write only ten minutes. Instead I've already produced on page. And I'm just warming up.

What else is new?

Yesterday Barry made an important distinction between my daily New Leaf writing—the raw creative process in action—and the question of what to do with my piles of old New Leaf Journal. He said what to do with them is a professional question, a question of professional standard, of what and how to turn New Leaf into a publishable work.

I like that distinction. A professional question. It makes things more abstract, gives me more distance and perspective, puts the organization and publishing of New Leaf on another level. On a daily basis I can keep turning out new leaves knowing this has absolutely nothing to do with what to do with my pages and how to do it.

The professional standard, the professional level is something to think about. And on a new avenue, too.

Yesterday I began calling my clients, rustling up business, making sales calls, and re-entering the market economy. I even had minimal success. A couple of people were interested in my February tour of Sicily.

I'm trying to synthesize work mode with the process mode of the past few months.

The ten-minute rule got me back to work easily. I expected to do only ten minutes of calls. Instead, I lasted an hour. Once again, I fooled my mind, that big bad fucker shining in the internal sky of my brain. Sometimes it is my friend, sometimes my enemy. But whatever it is, I must deal with it. Fooling my mind may be a good way to go.

"The market makes fools of us all." Well, so does the mind.

Lover

I am an artist, scholar, and lover of study and learning. That is my passion. Everything else is a footnote.

I went to bed at 10:00 p.m. I woke up 4:00 a.m. this morning with a solid six hours sleep behind me. Ah, I was refreshed. Hey, hey, feeling good!

Why did I feel so good? The realizations of who I am are crystallizing. Priorities are falling into place. That's why I woke up at peace with a feeling bordering on wonderful.

I am an artist, scholar, lover of study and learning. That is the dominant aspect of my new wise, knowledgeable, and strong self. At heart, I always have been. My wise, knowledgeable and strong self has always been with me. But it has often lain dormant, or hidden under the rock, drifting in and out of consciousness. Certainly I have never verbalized it.

It has been partly covered up for the past thirty years; it has been submerged by my struggle to earn a living. My need and desire for financial security has forced me to put parts of this wonderful self on the back burner. Now I am at a different stage of life. The specters of financial ruin, inability to make a living, poverty, and homeless no longer haunt me. My children are paid for and out of the house. Bernice is working and making good money—much more than I, in fact. Financially, I have no one to care for anymore. Finally, I can focus on my own needs, on my own self. True, my finances are still low and I still lead an insecure financial life. But I have enough to get along on. My gut feeling is that somehow I'll survive. If I start to worry again I'll hearken back to my February vow of poverty to help me remember my values and priorities.

Yes, I am at a new stage. I can focus on the self I live with and what does it wants.

In my heart, I have always known who I am and what I want. But I wasn't strong enough or knowledgeable enough to stand up for it directly. Instead I would fulfill my needs in the corner hidden away from others. Publically, I twisted in the wind, trying desperately both to please those around me and, at the same time, please myself. I retreated into jokes, humor, outlandish thoughts and behavior, anything to get away from boring situations, remember who I was, and be true to myself. For some reason, self-survival behavior caused others pain. I simply accepted that my thoughts and behavior would bother them, did it anyway, as subtly as I could. I turned my mind inside out whenever they brought it up as I tried to rationalize what I was doing. I never directly stood up for myself because I was never sure I was right. How is a mature, wage-earning father-figure supposed to act, anyway? I wasn't sure. My models were the so-called stable social types like executives, public school teachers, social servants, bureaucrats, post office workers, administrators. Basically, it was just about anybody who held a steady job. But they were so boring. Even though I tried, I just couldn't act like them. Artists, writers, Hasids, and crazy people were my deepest inspiration; off-the-wall nuts, lunatics just out of the insane asylum, eccentrics, and over-the-edge types were my heros. How could these madmen with half a foot on the steady, stable, unshifting earth and the other foot and a half in the fires of hell and passion furnaces of heaven compare to the banal, hollowed out, half-corpse molecular brain structures of bureaucrats, public school teachers, administrators (ugh!), coffee-drinking executives, and stable job holders I pictured in my mind.

Inwardly, I tried imitating parts of their boring life style and attitude for thirty years. I partly succeeded. But, thank God, I partly failed, too. Luckily, I couldn't kill my soul no matter how hard I tried, no matter how hard I fought against myself every day.

Now I stand at the conclusion of that long process, the find-out-who-I-am and stand-up-for-myself stage. I am ready to jump straight into my passion fire, into the molten bloody resurrecting pits of artistry; I'm ready to ride into the center of the earth on the swirling whirlpool of scholarship; I'm ready to bathe myself forever and ever in the burning bath of learning and study. I simply love, love, love it! Why hide anymore? Never again!

I have not yet explained myself to others. And this because I could not explain myself to myself.

But those dark days are ending. Explain, explain, explain. People will know me. And if they don't, can't, or won't, at least I'll be able to explain myself to myself and know who I am.

It's Nice To Know I'm Right Even When I'm Wrong.

How can I plug into the ancient knowledge?

New beginnings. How I love new beginnings.

Of course, every beginning is a new beginning since it is fresh, bright, and born in freedom. An "old" beginning is really an ending in disguise (which, of course, is another "new" beginning.)

I'm sitting in the living room at David and Jeannie's house in Santa Fe. Zach and Zane are still asleep. It is 5:30 a.m.

In David's library I discovered a book that knocked my socks, shoes, pants, shirt, and even underwear off: *The Hebrew Vowels and Consonants: As Symbols of Ancient Astronomic Concepts* by a German scholar, Ernst Ettisch. It was published in 1987 by Branden Publishing Company, 17 Station Street, PO Box 843, Brookline Village, MA 02147. The reason I've written down so much publishing information is because I'd like to buy this book. I'll call or write to the publishers. Perhaps they have a catalogue of other works. Or perhaps they're already out of business and have nothing. This book is so way out, so unique in perspective that it is, no doubt, already out of print. Someone once said ninety percent of books are out of print, and the best ones are surely out of print.

In any case, Ettisch's book connects the knowledge of the ancients to the Hebrew vowels. He writes about the secret teachings of the ancient Egyptians, Babylonians, Pythagoreans, and yes, Hebrews, and says all this knowledge was kept secret, maintained only by a small select group of priests and scholars, and, most important, that most was transmitted orally. Writing was only used as a tool for memory, not as a tool for learning. Slowly, this oral tradition "seeped" down to the more general public, and then, after the fall of the Temple in Jerusalem in 70 A.D. the oral tradition was written down in order to preserve it during the diaspora.

Why is this all important to me?

It confirms that my imagination, thoughts, ideas, feelings, and the resultant knowledge I derive from them, is as important, true, and wise as what I read in books. It confirms my visions and give me more faith in myself, in the knowledge and wisdom my feelings, thoughts, intuitions, hopes, plans, and mystic insights bring me. It tells me the ideas born during the travels of my imagination are "as good as anybody elses." They are "as good, as valid as" the great scholars, religious leaders, kings, politicians, and philosophers of the past. "Good," I say, not better, not worse. Since every human being is an experiment of one, their thought processes are unique and incomparable. Sure, ideas can be refined and expanded through specific study; there is infinite room for growth and development. Nevertheless, at any stage of development, my insights and visions are "as good as anybody elses." Yes, they may be primitive and elementary when compared to experts in the field who have spent their lives studying these subjects, but that does not necessarily mean they are less valid. They may be "right;" they may be "wrong." But, if you look at the history of ideas and scholarship you will always find varying points of view, disagreements, and arguments between great scholars, philosophers, and leaders of the past. Often they take exact opposite points of view. If these experts, after a lifetime of study, can see the world so differently and disagree so vehemently while using their lifetime arsenal of learning to buttress their opposing points of view, then why shouldn't my opinion be any worse or better. It can only be "more primitive," "more elementary." However, even "primitive and elementary" can sometimes be an advantage. The freshness, naivety, and openness of children often enables them to go straight to the center of truth. They are not yet "clouded" with so-called facts, theories, and intellectual baggage.

It's nice to know I'm right even when I'm wrong. It give me confidence.

Writing, Hemorrhoids, and God

In *Conversations with God*, the book by Walsch, God says, " I speak to man through feelings, thoughts, experiences, and lastly, words. Words are the worst form of communication, since they are so easily misinterpreted."

I agree with God. Feelings, thoughts, even experiences, can only be communicated indirectly. And speaking of indirectly, I'll begin with a thought I had when I started writing this morning but didn't mention: my goddamn hemorrhoids are still killing me! Yesterday I spent all day in bed. Not an inch of progress. This morning I feel a tiny bit better. That may be either because I am used to the pain and expect it, or I have improved.

I had planned to visit the Urgent Care today. I imagined the doctor examining me. The thought of poking an examining instrument up my ass absolutely rocketed me through the pain-filled roof! I'll never be able to stand it! I'll probably faint during the exam. I slept fitfully in two-to-three-hour stints, woke up at 2:30 a.m., then took a shit which made me gasp with pain. But it felt slightly better. Then I fell asleep again and dreamed one nightmare after another. Finally, I awoke a 5:00 a.m., dressed, and drank coffee while I read about the Hebrew vowels and consonants as astrological concepts. I ended up taking another shit. Although again I almost fainted, I still succeeded. Soon I was back to reading.

So goes the story of my two-day travels through Fecal Valley and the Anal Land of Shits. Better is the Anal Land of Shitz. "Shitz " has more class than the common street word "shit." Why not put some class in my shits? I can do it by turning shits to shitz. The word has a Hebraic ring to it, a biblical tone. I can hear Abraham, Isaac, and Jacob using it; I can even hear God saying it. Hey, why not? It's part of His universe.

Moving on: I learned a lot in my nervous moments of silence with Dr. Mac. It taught me how uncomfortable I am when I am silent with others, how I feel pressure to perform when I am in their presence. Ultimately, it taught me to value, use, and accept my silence; it taught me I ought to experience, feel, and remain silent in "public." It is wonderful to know that my silence with others still communicates something to them. It may even communicate more than if I spoke or "performed" for them. I have always been afraid my silence with others, especially when it is one on one, cuts off communication; it alienates me from them; ultimately, it is impolite. Now I am thinking differently. Acceptance of my silence "in public" brings a wonderful new freedom. I can "be true to myself" in public. I can think my deepest thoughts and feel my deepest feelings in their presence. I no longer have to retreat to my room before I can "be myself." Only a few moments of nervous silence in Dr.Mac's office revealed this to me! I am thankful for this Thanksgiving Day gift.

But perhaps I will receive an even better gift: self-confidence. The gift that I know myself best; the gift that my intuitions about myself are valid, wise, and true. I could receive this from the "Hemorrhoidal Moment of Truth." This "moment" which has already lasted two days. The "pain-in-the-ass" truths I wrote about in Visiting the Kingdom of Hemorrhodia, if proven correct, will give me greater confidence in my intuitive ability to diagnose myself.

Did I really create my own hemorrhoids? Did I really "manufacture" this sick nd painful situation so I would be able to take a day off, sleep for a day like yesterday, and take a rest? Did I really manufacture the situation so I could have an excuse for a day of freedom, a day escape from this claustrophobic family situation? It's possible. Why else would I "want" to get sick? I doubt I'd get sick at home where I have wonderful work to do, responsibilities to live up to, loves in which to bury myself.

If my hemorrhoids or hemorrhoids will they abate over time? Will I prove myself right in my hemorrhoidal vision of the psychological causes of their creation?

Wait and see. The next adventure may reveal new truths.

Fissures: As Above so Below

Things are terrible this morning, absolutely terrible! I cannot wait for this "vacation" to be over.

Yesterday I went to Urgent Care. They sent me to the Emergency Room where Dr. George (Dr. Anyle Fisher, Anyle Fissure) examined me. Sure enough, hemorrhoids were not my problem. I was suffering from an anal fissure. Ah, how I wished it were hemorrhoids. There is no comparison in pain quotient. At least I was relieved to know the cause of my suffering. Dr. George said to take sitz baths, anal inserts, and that it would take me about a week to heal. Well, that was nice to know. I went home, took a sitz bath, put in my inserts, and went to bed. For the first time since Tuesday I felt somewhat better. For the rest of the afternoon I slept on and off, interrupted only by a delicious Thanksgiving dinner cooked by Jeannie.

I have a headache, too. Could be my miserably anal condition. I defecated this morning and almost fainted from the pain. Is this progress? Yesterday, before visiting the hospital and getting my curative ointments, I also almost fainted after defecating as well. Was this morning's quasi-faint "better" than yesterdays? I don't know. Dr. George said it takes a week. We'll see. Meanwhile I'll try to lead a "normal" life while I'm on the mend.

I am suffering from an anal fissure and a brain fissure. Life here is totally divided. The word "fissure" is its best symbol. My anal fissure reflects my brain fissure; it is a physical expression of my mental state. Perhaps my mental state caused my physical state. It certainly made me prone and open to creating it. Did I create my physical fissure—anal fissure—in order to avoid the greater pain of facing my mental fissure, and my subsequent imprisonment in the land of Santa Fe. Is this possible? Am I pushing psychological explanations too far? But I believe in power of mind; I believe we create our own destiny, our situations, and our defenses. Could my anal fissure, even with the fainting pain it causes, be less painful than the pain of my mental fissure?

What exactly is my mental fissure? Anything more painful than my anal fissure must be looked at. Besides, I'm hoping that if I find a psychological explanation, my physical pain will abate, then go away.

Here I am really combining bottom and top, anus and brain, lower world and upper world. Am I just playing with words and ideas? Or am I really onto something? I'd like to think I am.

Breathing into the Pain

Yesterday my Comedy of Pain and Errors continued. We took Zack and Zane to Toys Are Us. Bernice's idea—a good one.

After we finished and I drove out of the parking lot I cut my left ring finger on the car door—a deep gash. I yelled, "Oh, shit! There goes my guitar playing. Shit, shit, shit! First, I can't dance. Now I can't play guitar! Fuck! Shit!" I raged on in this manner until Bernice said, "Don't talk like that in front of the kids."

"Why not?" I screamed. "Shit, shit, shit! Everything on this fucking vacation is going wrong! What do you expect me to do?"

"Why don't you practice what you always tell me? What are you learning from all this?"

"Oh, fuck you! I give up. You tell me. What should I learn?"

"Patience. Don't take yourself so seriously. Have a sense of humor."

Good ideas. I liked them.

We drove off for pizza, then headed home to David and Jeannie's. At the last turn I veered right, took a side road, and, in spite of the kids yelling, "Wrong way, wrong way!" headed for the Dalmatian dog's house. "I scared off this huge Dalmatian this morning with my 'No!'" I told the kids. "Now we're coming back in full force with a van full of people. We'll show him. " I drove past the house. The Dalmatian was nowhere in sight. "We scared him off. He's afraid of us now, Nah nah, nah, nah, nah nah." I sang as I taunted. Then I realized I was feeling better! My first sign of life in two days.

The rest of the afternoon went smoothly. Happily, I sat in the sun besides the house reading my Hebrew Vowel and Consonant book. The kids played together quietly in the living room; Bernice took a peaceful walk down the road. What a nice afternoon; what a pleasure to feel alive again!

It lasted until nine that evening. Suddenly, I had to go to the bathroom. A terrible shit ensued. I nearly fainted with pain. Discouraged and in agony, I spent the next half-hour lying down. Finally, I took my sitz bath, suppositories, prepared tomorrow's coffee, and went to bed. Bernice said she understood and sympathized with my pain. She had had it off and on for the last nine months. The best thing to was to practice breathing, try concentrating on something else, use it as a focused meditation.

I liked what she said. A positive approach to my misery. As I lay in bed I vowed to fight by both "giving in" to the pain and using it to focus on breathing, concentrate on a spot inside my head, and send wonderful warm curative relaxing blood to my anus. Also, I decided to follow each shit with a short sitz bath.

I like this breath and concentration approach. Perhaps I can use the sadhus of India as my model. At the bookstore in Santa Fe last night, I read through a book called The Sadhus of India and about the practices and austerities of these holy men. The book had pictures, too. One showed a sadhus who had held up his left arm for twelve years; another was of a sadhus whose practice was holding both arms up for twelve years. Over time their arms withered into useless sticks. If they succeeded in bringing them down, they arms remained useless for the rest of their lives. Another practice was to stand for twelve years. These sadhus all slept standing up. There were other practices, too. One showed a sadhus carrying fifty to one hundred pound weights hanging from his penis.

Granted these practices are extreme. I doubt I could adopt any of their austerities to my life although learning to stand in place might teach me patience waiting at bus stops. Nevertheless, if sadhus can perform these herculean mental and physical feats, why can't I at least focus on my breath and concentrate when I take my pain-filled shits. If their human mind is so strong, why can't mine be? Actually, mine is. It's mostly a question of motivation. One arm, two arms, standing, weights hanging from a penis, or breathing through the pain of an anal fissure. They all hurt. Nevertheless, it is a question of attitude.

Riding the Black Cloud into Hell

How do you handle bouts of meaningless and existential angst?
By riding the black cloud into Hell.
Step on board

Ride straight into Hell!
Enter the Underworld.
Die!
Roast in the furthest reaches of Hell.
When you are cooked and ready
You will pop out
Fresh and reborn.

No, no! I don't want to ride!
Help! Save me!
You cannot be saved
Except through the ride.
You must travel through Hell's jaws
Before you reach Heaven's gate.

But to smooth your voyage
Keep your practices, rituals, and routines.
Even if done in misery, dejection, and hopelessness.
Their shadows remind you of the Good,
Thus, for travelers
Riding the black cloud into Hell
It never hurts to nestle for awhile
Within the safe restraints of discipline's iron band.

Conflicts are creative. Some should never be healed.

Jewish Meditation

Last Tuesday at the Paramus Jewish Center I told Miriam, the head of the Hebrew Day School, about my new book on the Hebrew Vowels and Consonants as Symbols of Astronomic Concepts.

"Study something serious," she said, "Read the Torah or commentaries on it. Don't waste your time with that other stuff." A man stood next to her wearing a black suit and yarmulke. She turned to him, introduced me, and said: "Jim's trying to study alone. It's very hard to study alone."

The man agreed. "It's very hard to study alone."

So much for Miriam's concept of vowels, consonants, and astronomic symbols; so much for her broader approach to Judaic studies. True, the concept in my new book is off the wall. That's why I like it. Who knows whether it has actual "truth;" if the Hebrew vowels and consonants are "really" astronomic symbols. But, no doubt, my new book has poetic truth Now when I look at vowels and consonants, I see parts of the universe in them. It gives the letters and vowels a beauty they never had before. Astronomy widens my scope and appreciation not only of the Hebrew language but of the universe itself. Thus, to me there is no doubt that, on the deepest of levels, astronomic concepts have poetic truth.

I'm using some of this poetic truth in Jewish meditation. I got the idea from a video tape by Rabbi Marcia Prager. I saw at Kripala Institute in Lenox, Massachusetts. She took the Hebrew name for God, Yahweh, turned it sideways, and made a human being out of it. The yod became a head, the heh became the arms, shoulders and the outer core of the upper body, the vav became the human spinal cord, and the final heh became the lower part of the torso and legs. Then she said to focus on neshemah, the breath. A good Jewish meditation exercise was to inhale, focus on the first two letters (the head (yod) and upper body (heh), then to exhale focusing on the spine (vav), and lower body (heh). Thus you inhale and exhale God. He is being spread throughout your body on the inhalation, and cleansing your body and connecting with the outside world on the exhalation.

A beautiful concept and meditation. After hearing it I thought about it for months. Now however, I have a reason to practice it.

The only answer to yesterday's fissure torture seems to be meditation. I called the doctor; he "helped me" by saying he could do nothing about my condition. "Take sitz baths and try to relax, " he said. "That's about all you can do."

Hearing that from the doctor marked the end of the medical approach line. I had been improving until yesterday's rage. My rage had worsened my condition; it brought me to the end of the road.

I've always avoided breathing and meditation in my yoga practice. Somehow they were always "too boring." But there was nothing boring about my pain yesterday! The screaming it caused stimulated my creative juices like no other torture chamber.

The best place to practice my daily meditations is in the toilet. What better way to connect the lower world to the higher world? And I can do it every day, often several times a day. Who would ever think that my best way of reaching the top is through the bottom.

We'll see where this Jewish Road of Bathroom Meditation leads.

Pain

Will this *New Leaf* ever end?

Why do I want it to end?

Because this has been my New Leaf of Torture or, as the nurse in the hospital called it, "discomfort."

Holy Name Hospital was amazing. I screamed out every holy name I could think of as the "kind" nurse tortured me. In fairness, she did "warn" me by saying, "This catheter I ram up your penis may feel uncomfortable." If "uncomfortable" is the term they use for patient torture, I wonder what it means when they say it will *hurt*. Maybe they only use it when you die.

In any case, I am writing this morning only in the hope that my writing will help cure me. This has been one of the worst, one of the most traumatic weeks of my life. Even the deaths of my parents were not as bad. Now that is a horrible thing to say. But at least when they died, their torture ended. So did mine. Sure I mourned; I cried on and off for four years. Nevertheless, this was "only" emotional pain. Emotional pain may hurt but it is nothing like physical pain. At least with emotional pain, I could focus on other things for short periods; I could step beyond the pain. But screaming howling God-forsaken physical pain absolutely incapacitates me. Not only does it make me feel helpless, but I am helpless. It reduces me to sitting in terror in my corner, squirming in agony in my chair, or lying absolutely stone dead comatose on my bed waiting, hoping, praying, the pain will pass.

What have I learned from this torturous adventure into the Land of Pain?

Nothing is worse than physical pain. It is the absolute bottom of the pain perspective.

Pain works. It succeeds in terrorizing you, traumatizing you. The memory of your own screams, the crying, pleading with God to stop the pain, the bargaining that you will do anything, give up anything, crawl, humiliate yourself, give up sin, give up money, give up everyone and everything you love, become a slave, even kill yourself if only you, dear God, will stop this pain.

There is no nobility in pain. It reduces you to your lowest amoral molecule. And that molecule, bawling, crying, howling, screaming as it roasts in your personal oven hell-fire, only want one thing: Stop the pain!

What does this say about mankind's noble goals? What does it say about my noble goals, desires, wishes, and hopes for accomplishment? What does it say about the human strength and importance of my beliefs? How strong can our commitments be when such cataclysmic overwhelming physical pain can reduce them to ashes and wash those ashes into the gutter?

After a certain point physical pain becomes too powerful. It is impossible to fight. There is nothing you can do but give in to it.

I gave in yesterday. I canceled all my folk dance classes for this week. We'll see where this leads.

Pain and Loss of Faith Leads to Getting My Shit Together

Overwhelming physical pain has caused a loss of faith. Or is it a loss of arrogance?

Has physical pain "softened" my "hard" self.

Is freedom from arrogance the spiritual lesson of this anal episode? Did I have to scrape bottom before I could find the top?

It feels right. It seems so.

The hard self is the arrogant self. It says, "I can do anything; I am in complete control of my life; I can take care of myself; I don't need anyone or anything; I don't need any help."

The soft self says, "I need others, I hurt; I can't do it all myself; I need higher and lower powers; I need others to make it through. I need the grace of God along with lots of earthly help."

But asking for help, whether it be from God or man, is most difficult for the hard self.

Asking for help is where the hard self cracks.

But the soft self can ask. It rolls with the punches; it easily accepts human weakness, gives in to it, and lets the healing process flow.

I saw all this in terms of shit. As I saw my hard self crack and my soft self emerge, I also saw my hard shit crack and soft shit emerge.

Hard shit fissured me, burst my hemorrhoids, and spasmed my urology. In soft shit, I saw a loosening. My soft shit was not a pushy shit.

It was free from arrogance.

Independent Mind

Why is my mind so disobedient? Why won't it obey me? It has an independent will, a mind of its own.

My mind has been on vacation. Since September it has wanted to do exactly nothing. It only wants to sit back and reflect. Well, that's just great! I've got bills to pay, a business to run, plus desires of my own. But my mind just doesn't pay any attention to what I want. It goes on its merry way practically oblivious to me. This year it wants to take off. To hell with bills, it says; to hell with diminishing bank and stock accounts, to hell with my limping tour business, mediocre weekends and folk dance classes. To hell with what I want. My mind has made up its mind. This is its "do-nothing" year.

What can I do about such a mind?

Basically, nothing. Without the input and energy of its operating system, my program won't run. But I can't call up Bill Gates for new hardware. Although Dr. Dave can help me understand and even accept my mind, he can't force it to act. No one can. My mind simply has its own agenda. This year it refuses to act. It just want to sit and observe, ruminate, meditate, cogitate, and philosophize.

Not a damn thing I can do.

Let's look at my present situation. Physically, I'm feeling better. That is wonderful! But why did I get sick in the first place? My mind played a large part. It enjoys entertaining itself often at my expense. When I went to New Mexico it didn't have much to do. It got bored. Then it decided to fool around with my body. In its own perverted way, it enjoyed ripping my anus to shreds, sending me for screaming visits to Santa Fe's and Holy Name Hospital's emergency rooms.

What can I do about it? Basically, nothing. I just have to wait around, and let it play until it gets bored. Then, when it's got nothing better to do, it will release me back into the handsof health.

I hate feeling so helpless. What can I do to control my errant mind?

Well, there is something I can do. I can have a lobotomy. But, of course, after a lobotomy I'd still be doing nothing which is exactly what I'm doing now. So why go through the expense? Besides, I doubt my HMO would cover it.

Feeling Better Today

It is my first day back to work. I'm teaching folk dancing at Temple Emeth in Teaneck. I'm not looking forward to it. I haven't taught for almost three weeks. I feel out of shape; my energy is down. I've used to being off. I liked it. But I don't like being sick. Still, the idea of staying home, reading, studying, writing, playing guitar—it's not so bad.

Maybe I can do today's job in vacation mode.

Meanwhile, new signs of life seems to be raising their startled heads. Death has passed; resurrection is at hand. After an almost four-month slide, I'm getting new ideas!

Here are some:

Food and food study. There's a radically new one. It touches Ma and botany.

Look into Leviticus, foods, kosher laws etc. I went to Margabandhu at the Integral Yoga Institute in Fair Lawn for an alternative medicine consultation. After poking me a few times—and miraculously "curing" my bladder pressure—was it a miracle or common occurrence?, he gave me a new diet, some enzymes, pills, and teas, said I shouldn't eat before bed, drink water at meals, and that I should chew my food slowly.

This morning I thought: What does this have to do with being Jewish? Well, I looked into Leviticus and the laws of kashrut for a Jewish/Chewish connection. Surely there is one somewhere.

Yesterday's Knowledge

That was yesterday's knowledge.

To keep knowledge as knowledge, knowledge must be refreshed every day. Otherwise it loses its luster, ossifies, and turns into ignorance.

Couch Sleep

I had the most beautiful "couch sleep" experience in Dave's office. I walked out feeling peaceful, rejuvenated, blissful, and holy. I had a few such moments when he untied the Santa Fe flight experience knot a few weeks ago. But this time, the peace was much deeper and longer lasting.

Psychoanalysis with its psychotherapeutic offspring was developed by Rabbi Sigmund Freud. They all offer couch experiences. Could the bliss and peace I felt during my couch experience be the doorway to Jewish meditation?

The Truth of Sleep

Am I more "authentically" myself when I am asleep? When I am among others I am often, usually, always affected by their reactions and desires. I read their faces or body language; I am torn between their wants and my wants. I choose some kind of middle road and act accordingly. But I do not have this problem when I am asleep. Is there some deep truth experienced in sleep? I sense there is. Is sleep truth the same truth as the truth found in meditation?

Suppose a higher truth is experienced in deep sleep. Suppose the deeper you sleep, the higher is the truth you reach. Perhaps the meditative state is one where you are conscious of the deep sleep experience.

MONEY AND ITS BRETHREN

Beyond the Land of If

What an exercise in frustration is the stock market. Had I not sold National Patent so soon I would now be up $4000; had I not sold Telecommunications I would now be up $2000; had I not sold Handy and Harmon I would now be up $1000. That's $7000 I "lost" by selling too soon. If I had done nothing, if I had waited, if I had simply "held," I would now be way ahead. Of course, such hopes, maybes, ramblings, self-beatings, and mental fluctuations are all part of the "market experience." They are based on the great word: "If." Playing the stock market is my daily lesson in learning to live beyond the Land of If.

But I rarely seem to learn. Especially when the pain is so immediate. If after I sell a stock it simply sits, or, if I'm lucky, start moving down, that at least gives me a short respite to emotionally detach myself from it. But when they start moving up right after I sell them, I just kick myself every time I read their stock quotation.

Kicking myself is an old habit. The stock market may not bring it on but it certainly does exacerbate it.

PERFORMANCE

Limitations Versus the Limitless

Considering the audience limits me.

In my desire to connect to them, by reaching them, I am reaching for a limitation.

Do I want to go in this direction?

Do I want my goal to be a limitation?

Do I want my aim to be for limitations?

Isn't it better to aim for the limitless?

On one level, that means "giving up my desire for an audience." It means aloneness.

But on another, it may open up the doorway to Oneness, Love, Eternity, Infinity, God, all vocabulary names to symbolize the "ineffable Something" that cannot be said in words.

Do I see aloneness, rejection, and alienation from others as a result of being true to my wild and crazy self? Probably.

In any case, the "payoff" for such aloneness, rejection, and alienation, for "acting crazy, like a madman" is putting myself in touch with my eternal soul. I would be literally "living in another world" of light, liveliness, and deepest self-truth. Is that so bad?

Does focusing on audience and "trying to influence and enlighten others" limit me? Or does it help lift me beyond my ego?

I see only one way around this dilemma: If I see my audience—the one I "influence and enlighten", as a fiction I create, then it will both lift me beyond my ego and influence and enlighten. That vision is all- inclusive; it brings audience and self together in a trinity of Them, me, and Me.

This would be my own personalized "formal prose connection."

It gives me "control" over the fiction creation of my audience, too. Thus it removes limits and can help me extend my vision beyond limitations into the Limitless.

More important than "influencing and enlightening others" is seeing (the audience is) criticism as raindrops on cellophane. If and when I do, "influencing and enlightening" will happen anyway—as a by product.

Thus "influencing and enlightening" is secondary.

Criticism as raindrops on cellophane is primary.

If I keep this in mind my own Bourree musical vision will come through.

The audience is a footnote. Its criticisms are illusions.

I don't have to "prepare" for a concert. The concert is now!

Where Standing-Up-For-Myself and Audience Reaction Meet: "As Above, So Below"

It is arrogance to believe I know what the audience thinks.

It is arrogance to believe they are not listening to me.

Truth is, I don't know what they think or what effect I have on them. No doubt, some listen, some don't. Some faces beam and radiate. I assume it is because of my guitar playing. But how do I know? Audience members could beam because they are dreaming about a beautiful beach in California; or they could radiate because they just laid a good fart. On the other hand, the stolid faces in front of me who apparently react to nothing may be very deeply effected. Their impassive faces may hide a delayed reaction which may not emerge for weeks, months, even years.

Thus I can only "know" how I believe the audience reacts to me. I can only know my own mind.

Until now I have viscerally believed my audience will not listen to me; I am butting up a wall whenever I try to penetrate its brain and heart.

Now I see my belief is arrogant. A misinterpretation. Wrong.

I can only know what I believe.

I can only know myself.

I am surrounded by angels. But it is often hard to recognize them.

Vow: I will never again play a note on the guitar without passion. Ecstasy is out of the closet. Private passion and ecstasy are going public.

To focus on passion you have to go slow.

Delight is the road to ecstasy.
Can rage be a type of ecstasy?

Writing is taking dictation from the divine.
So is guitar playing.
It's a different "Leyenda" than anything I've ever heard in my life.

I'm taking a risk by playing it slowly. What is the reward? It is *my* "Leyenda."

I'm marching, but without a tune. Directionless, the barbarians strain to wonder what comes next. Must watersnips peck turnip for a living? Or can wind fester while forces beneath time's pillow reckon their undoing?

Why can't a longer linger faster? Please, please, let this spleen come home. Its speeding waters, born in Elephant River, can no longer hide the piquant odor of phosphorescent banana peels bound in pea pods. Why do they tune their rods to turn-infested squadrons?

I'd love to make a sales call but I can't.

My mind is in a vice.

I need ad-vice. Oh, the frustration. I'll ask my brain: "Mr. Medulla, can a worm ever find it's way past heaven?"

I don't know where to turn. Thunder and lightening piss my computer. I'd like something to improve upon, a direction, a discipline. All I can think of is going back to work.

Doing what?

Performing?

Even though I'd given it up.

Is performing my new road?

No other roads are opening up. My retreat years have just ended. I can't return the old way. I need a new charge.

Performing?

Why? Where? What? And how?

Chesed is compassion.

Compassion in my right shoulder.

Sometimes I feel it when I play guitar. It opens me up, loosens me.

Now I'll take a little chesed for me.

Missed Guitar Note as Idol Worship

My missed guitar note was idol worship.

Why?

In missing the note, I focused on the critics and what they think about my guitar playing. I took my mind off my dialogue with God; I took it off worship of the One.

That's how I slipped into idol worship.

No need to rush notes when I'm playing for God. He has all the time in the world.

Light and Shadow

Thumb (and bass line) equals light
Tremolo and arpeggios (finger accompaniment) equals shadow.

Tremolo Soul

Maybe I will never "solve" my tremolo and arpeggio problem. Perhaps my tremolo soul cannot be cured, only cared for.

"A sage does not rush,
Not even for a bus."
—Allan Watts

I've opened a completely different orientation towards guitar playing. Instead of asking, "Am I playing well, am I playing musically, am I playing fast, slow, or whatever?", I now ask: are my fingers happy?

In this approach I am no longer concerned with speed, tempo, dynamics, rubato, or musicianship. Rather, I am focusing on physical pleasure. Are my hands having a good time? How about my feet? Are my organs enjoying themselves? Is there any life in my bladder or does it need a tuning? Is my colon happy? What about my liver and intestines? How's their relationship? Is my heart tired? Does my thigh need a rest?

I like talking to my body parts. Talking is how we maintain communication.

Soul is expressed through my guitar right hand.

Suppose

Suppose I was not meant to be a classical guitarist or classical musician. Suppose my classical training always had another purpose.

Suppose the soul of my individuality was meant to be expressed in other things... writing etc.

Suppose my desire to prove myself through classical guitar concerts has always been a misplaced direction.

Yes, no question, my classical training and playing is good for something. But what is it?

This is a crisis question, a crisis suppose.

The Quiet

The Quiet is definitely a more profound state: A most profound state. It connects one to everything and everyone.

This connection is made in silence, in the stillness of one's heart. Thus it must include "audience" to be proper and complete. Here audience means everyone and everything in the world beyond the senses and stream of imagination, everything lingering deep in the deep sleep-filled world.

Relationship Between Self and Audience

See the audience as a part of God. I reach the audience, Him, through sleep meditation.

The relationship between the audience and I is really the relationship between God and I. A Martin Buber "I-Thou" relationship.

When playing "Alhambra," do I dare fall into God's hands?

To practice "falling helplessly" into the hands of God, focus on HaShem.

BUSINESS

Old Habits and Fears Return and Are Reexamined

Last night I got back from our opening folk dance night in Darien feeling really low. Why? It was a good opening night, good crowd, good dancing. I even made some money. Why then was I low?

Expectations. I was hoping to get registrations for my upcoming Smorgasbord Weekend. I got none. So far Smorgasbord only has six people registered. A potential disaster and embarrassment in the making. If I don't get more I may have to cancel it. My only "hope" is remembering that we had the same problem last year. I called Rama two weeks before the Weekend, told him we had seven people registered and that we might have to cancel. However, during the next two weeks thirty-five people late registrants came in! We ended up with forty people! Due to this sudden rise we had to move our Weekend from the Fallsview to the Nevele Hotel. Hopefully, the same thing will happen this year. But, of course, you never know. Nevertheless, I'm experiencing old familiar fears of embarrassments and humiliations due to low registrations.

I have been through these so many times before. I also want to give up my fears. And I will! Today is a new day. I'm living above a new foundation, a new base, a new structure built on my vow of poverty.

Why bother worrying? First of all, I'm doing about as much selling work as I did last year which is, namely, almost none at all. Only last year while I did almost nothing I nevertheless spent hours worrying about the low registration. This year I am hardly thinking about it at all. I've done what I always do, the usual, sent out all my mailings, put out fliers, even called a few people. Beyond that there's not much else I can do or want to do.

I'll have to chalk up last night's low feelings to the return of old habits. The familiar atmosphere of the Darien folk dance group brought back familiar expectations along with their concomitant familiar fears. But I'm looking at them in a new light. Time to readjust my vision upwards. Leave out old worries and fears. Focus instead on my positives, my vow of poverty along with the new goals, purposes, directions, and ideas I am now in the process of forming.

Combine Kabbalah and Tourism.

Gathering the sparks is the same as gathering tour participants for a tour; it is the same as gathering them for weekends, folk dance classes, concerts, or any event. Gathering sparks or gathering customers— on a Kabbalistic level it is the same.

According to Kabbalistic tradition, restoration of the world is everyone's holy work. Thus, I'm in the "business" of gathering sparks. I gather customer-sparks.

Ever since I was a child and burned down the Johnson woods, I've always liked lighting fires. Why should I be much different as an adult? Why should I not continue this love but in a different form?

First I gather kindling wood for my fire. The kindling takes the fleshy form of the body containers in which my customers live. Then my customers and I together light the kindling. Sparks fly! The resultant fire of restoration, of tikkun, I call a tour, weekend, folk dance class, concert, or whatever.

Tikkun Tours, Tikkun Weekends, Tikkun Tourism

Thus each person is both kindling and spark. They can light my fire.

Seen in this Kabbalistic light my tours become the "holy business" of gathering sparks. This service happens to make money. So much the better. After all, what is money but a green spark.

Tour Inspirational Ideas

Study of classical languages: Hebrew, ancient Greek, and Latin. This could keep the Italian tours going for three or more years. Also Greece and Israel.

I've temporarily (there's a non-closure word) run out of modern language interest. Root languages, classical languages, may be the way to go.

INVENTIONS

Progesterone Revisited

The beastie committee never sided with Lincoln. Oh no, not while rifles in the barnyard blossomed. Only a rent-controller would have such courage, such dastardly malnutrition, such inward levity to level the stretch marks on either thigh.

That morning mourning day in 1866 meandered towards a strict

Malthusian diet. Indeed, no Diet of Worms could precurse the prerequisite sites for such a nether buster. Nor could Worms precrastinate the procrastinators of Neanderthal protoplasmic bobobusters stationed among the Nilotic watchers. Why? Why, Why? Why on that day did pharoahs stand in line at the bar waiting for a Tutti drink from the hands of Pharoah Tutti von Karman, the only German pharoah to sink the erotic throne of Cairotic pyromaniacal genius?

Nevertheless, the protoplasmic count kept moving up. Pharoah Lincoln whacking away at the big-box guitar, singing out Neptunian tunes, true plutocratic cantatas of the sea whose white-tiled bottom and frothy brown top beat a blue tread towards the receding skyline behind the Messinian village hilltops. Lincoln stopped his boats as he floated in the straits of Messina between Scylla and Charibdis. Could Sicily be far behind?

It was an axial water day. Ploughs downed trees leaving rows of watermelons in lateral, bilateral, and graphic positions across furrowed gardens, wetting bed-fellows of bed rock and leaving behind a trail of longing that only a psychoanalyst could trace.

"Speaking of the brain hens," said the Gettysburg magistrate, "Can pecking at the lower orders of my mind shrink in a barnyard? Can a hen run a juicer or drink a blended marshmallow? Can it circumvent the common psychiatric clusters, distill the hollow center, and eventually conbobulate a whirlpool of discombobulated dissatisfied syrups and turn them into happy Coke and Cola customers, pliant and satisfied beneath the Caribbean gateway south of Haiti?

Most Kinengrobules and Nincompoopees never consider the rammings ramifications, the creams, or creamings of such bladders gone wild. They rest content in their Lilliputian stews, lying spread-eagled beneath their laurels waiting for Daphne and Apollo. Reaching deep into the Greek mythology, Abe pulled out strands of old wool, goat hairs, and pieces of souvlaki soaked in hams ram of butt. For the bedroom he found a fission ointment of tourniquet.

What of etiquette in such situations? Can a hen roll under its egg while pheasants dance under parchisi tables? Is one limelight enough for a rope to hang itself? Nevertheless, an unending bashhood is in order. How else turn darkness into light? Thus do I pluck day from the black sea.

Pithi Tuitary Gland Gone Wild

A whacked-off turbo engine of dueling banjos strapped inside my large intestine. It is turning pounds of vestibule clothing, rice, bagels, and shishkabob into fartogogic turbulence. From the distance, a blatant banana slit of tuba sounds a Jewish tinge of shofar melancholy. My kishkas ache. Only Mrs. Petting Priquehood, great organizer of the Women's Strike for Venus, could quiet such a disorder.

But Petting has gone, driven to Mars by way of Bergen poets. This afternoon the whole universe is out to lunch.

What to do when stew is ripe for a pickle? What to do when the hardened crust of a cyclopean burp roll its rock of gold down the hill, lolling, plopping, and pidoodling past virgin teeth and rounded sallow gums before lodging, in grand finale stook, hine, and finker, in a vacant oral cavity?

Most philosophers avoid these questions. Instead, they dine in Planetariums munching luncheon underwear.

But I will not be influenced by these callow mermaids, these pompous estuaries of furrowed war fields whose mines, molten and minded by Minos gold, can neither fathom nor surface the underside of a true bottom. King Anuus never knew a better crack. Nor did the pituitary gland sanctioned by Ramses in hieroglyphic Egypt when his stack was mixed with Pithes stew to build the Pithes Tuitary Gland Baking Pyramid.

Is this not why doctors go to medical school? Is it not why cadavers sit upright, lecturing on the after life to living pears and au peres?

The afternoon came to a close when the Great Burp Globule, a Hollywood star for over twenty years, burst forth from his zoo garden. Directors cooed. Hens laid eggs while roosters bloomed.

Graduation from the Criticism School

Tom graduated.

As a first grader in the School of Elementary Criticism, the arrows of criticism pierced my body; many went through him; affecting the way he walked, talked, thought and felt.

Then, in the High School Of Secondary Criticism he developed a protective armor which could deflect the arrows of criticism.

Nevertheless, the sound of their ping and ring as their iron-tips glanced off his Mogen David protective shield still affected the way he talked, walked, thought, and felt.

This continued right through his graduation from the Bilious Department in the College of Higher Criticism, where he received a Ph.D. in Protoplasmic Pin-Cushion Maintenance.

However, once he walked out the door with his degree under his badly mangled arm, something strange happened. Even though under a hail of criticism, the arrows never pierced his body; nor did they bounce off his protective shield. In fact, two weeks later when he saw arrows of criticism whizzing by, he tossed away his shield. They no longer seemed to affect the way he walked, talked, thought or felt. When they flew by, Tom felt a breeze; otherwise, he hardly noticed them. Criticism archers may need their arrows to shoot at him. But the good news is that he no longer needed them. Their barbs had turned into puffy clouds. True, their nebulous and cumulus forms, filed to bursting with bloated bags of angry bile and flying at incredible wind-swept speeds, often storm past the castle of his self. Nevertheless, they no longer ruffle his hair much less blow him down.

Santa Fe Santa Claus

Yesterday I visited Santa Claus. He lives in Santa Fe. Santa Claus introduced me to Mrs. Claus, whose first name is Bernice Claus. The two Clauses closed in on me, covered my mouth with tape, tied me up with a rope of feathers, then served me coffee and cake in a big cup shaped like a Buick.

I said to myself "This is crazy! I wanted to visit Santa Fe, not Santa Claus. It's not even close to Christmas yet. What are they doing here in town, anyway?"

Musical Screams in ER

Slabbed on the back table, sliced and scattered, lies the worn-to-pieces, half-clothed body of Jason Grelt. The nurses have already administered last rites and are now dressing what is left of him, preparing him to meet his heavenly Maker and alter ego, God. And this, while his penis sits in a sling, jettisoned, through the hunkered hospices of Merciful Hospital of the Holy Name where crucified figures decorate emergency room walls.

Indeed, Jason Grelt's body is prepared for the sacrifice. Thousands of fingers, each in the shape of a five-star hand, reach out to pull, tear, rip, shred, roast, burn, pillage, trample, macerate all unique and different part of his tortured body. They say his spirit remains intact, but no one knows where; they say his mind remains intact, but no one knows where either. The only knowledge available is the whereabouts of Jason Grelt's hacked-up body. It sits, hunched and forlorn, a massive mountain of screams, tortuous twists, ravines carved by gullies of urine, pock-marked pit holes chiselled out by turd-swirling dervishes slicing through the egg-beater nets of his interstices.

Can this be good? Can the Lord of Suffering have an ultimate purpose in inflicting such cruel lacerations on such an innocent body? Must salt be put in old wounds? Why must acid pour from ceilings into gaping nerve-lined orifi? Must poles, pinions, stevedore ramps, and posts be jammed up his helpless penis? Can this really be good for his health? And will the HMO okay payment?

Finally, daggers begin to flow between his instruments. A scissor, the hospital instrument of entertainment, slides out from behind a proctal lamppost. A handsome prostate stands at attention while a mother hen pecks at passing spermatazoids. She cackles with neurotic, happy wisdom: "I see a urethra so close. Can a bladder be far behind?"

A rooster strolls by, proud and straight. "Call it Holy Name Barnyard or whatever you want," he snittles, "but a rooster could never live in ointments." Then he piddles away.

It is 4:00 a.m. Old hens dressed in white hats and aprons push stretchers across the floor. Dawn is around the corner. Egg laying time. Patients are rolled behind the iron lung near the caterpillar hangings. An HMO screams in the distance.

Jason Grelt's body remains warm and erect among the icebergs. His lacerated penis has been shipped to the Midget Highway Traffic Division in Bismarck, North Dakota for future use as a highway post.

Minotaurs in My Feet: A Poem to Soak out Foot Pain

The minotaur lives
At the center of my labyrinth.
This flesh-eating monster
Devours my feet,
Tears my toes,
Burns my metatarsals.
Will he transform himself
To reveal
An angel in my sole?

GOD

Be True to Yourself

Being true to yourself is the highest expression of the love of God.

Abraham Abulafia believed in the kabbalistic concept of combining the letters to meditate and reach God.

Writing is my way of "combining the letters."

Joy

Joy (Simha) is not the best way to "express" God. It is the only way.

I like "express." It is the best word for artists. "Serve" is better for government functionaries.

Fame–Wealth–Happiness Versus Joy

Long ago I thought fame would make me happy.
Then I thought money would make me happy.
As Rabbi Gelberman says, there is a "tendency to forgo the joy of the God within to concentrate instead on the idols of happiness with-

out."

Thank God for an imperfect world. Otherwise we'd all be out of work.

I wonder if my right index finger is my God finger. I wonder if it is always pointing to God.

Conversations

I bought some great books in town. One of them was called *Conversations with God*. I'd never heard of the author but I liked the title and "feel" of the book. It spoke to me. I leafed through it, then bought Books I and II. I started reading it over lunch in the Plaza Restaurant. In the introduction, the author says he did not write this book. Rather it "happened" to him; he merely took dictation. It was dictated to him by God. He sounded exactly like me in describing his writing experiences. I also know that God speaks to me and through me when I write. I realized it again when I read this introduction. But again, it scared the shit out of me. I started to tremble. Why does the "fact" that God speaks through me when I write—and sometimes through me when I play music or even once in a while on tours and etc., scare the shit out of me?

At first I thought it was the "What will others think?" fear phenomenon: They'll think I'm crazy, off-the-wall; they'll cart me off to the insane asylum; only nuts and schizophrenics say God speaks to them. They're crazy, and you're crazy, too! Better drop this idea real quick, or you're off to see the assembly of Olympian psychiatric and psychotherapeutic gods practicing their magic skills on the Magic Mountain just south of Englewood, New Jersey.

I've been through the "What will others think of me?" fear phenomenon countless times before. But this time I questioned it. Am I really afraid of what others will think? What will they really do to me? Probably nothing. I'm just using them as an excuse. They are not my real fear, my real threat.

The real threat to me is me. What will happen to me if I accept, without reservations, the deep realization that God speaks to me? What will it do to me? How will it affect my purpose in life? Will it put iron into my backbone, fire in my soul, push me over the cliff into the blazing passion burning in the fearsome creative abyss, drive me absolutely crazy dancing with joy, burn up my ego, flood me with compassion, overwhelm me with a love I have never experienced or known before, destroy, transform, and transmute my entire concept of myself, metamorphose the "me" I know today into a totally unrecognizable "other me?"

Truth is, this is happening to me already. I am slowly and through sudden dynamic spurts experiencing a "slow birth" process. Slowly, I am being squeezed and being squeezed out of another womb. A new self is plopping out, falling straight into the obstetrician's arms. Lots of wet nurses around, too.

Thus my biggest fear is that my ego, my old self will be washed out of existence by a great biblical Flood, a Mabool beyond description, greater than Noah's Flood. The animals traveling in my soul, representing all the roads and byways of my old self, will be washed away, too.

Who will I be after this transformation? What will my name be? Who will recognize me? Will I recognize myself?

Of course, there is no stopping birth, no stopping the opening of the new road I will be traveling. If God speaks to me, and I must go public with what He says, so be it.

I'm like Moses here. Moses was afraid too: he said, "No, no, don't chose me. Don't speak to me. Can't you find someone else to do Your work? But there was no turning back for Moses. God had chosen him. He had to lead. God said he would help. And He did. Moses only had to open his mouth, become an instrument. God would speak through him. He did and the Jewish people were born.

I'm in a similar situation. Is it hubris? Am I afraid to compare myself to as great a leader as Moses? Such a famous man, founder and father of the Jewish religion, one-on-one communicator with the Lord, doer of His deeds, bearer of the commandments from Mount Sinai? Can I even come close to him?

But, although I am not Moses, I have to admit, my experiences are similar to his. Where will this admission lead me? I don't know. But I have no choice but to find out.

Chasidic Yoga

Let God into each yoga posture. Use biblical passages for inspiration. Thus I'm not practicing alone but with God. I'm developing Chasidic yoga.

How to combine guitar and Torah? Become a gui-torah-ist.

Love for another, the yearning for another, is a "disguised" form of yearning for and love of God.

Love

Is the pain of love caused by the realization that all is transient, impermanent, and sooner or later everything will change, modulate, metamorphose, and die. Is the pain of love really the fear of death in disguise? We know the pleasure of love connects you to the moment, places you totally in the present, the oneness and Oneness. Just as the joy of love connects you the most powerful forces of the universe, to life, the Life, to Chai, to the Oneness, God, higher forces, wouldn't the pain of love remind you of the opposite of this, of death, destruction, transience, and impermanence.

January–March 1998

WRITING

Keep a notebook on my person. Always. Keep it strapped to my hand, shoulder, or side along with pens, calligraphy pens, and any other writing paraphernalia.

Write, write, write, in all languages, in all alphabets, in all scripts, in all ways, at all times.

Learn to draw. It improves not only eyesight and vision but gives a fresh, down to earth way of seeing.

On Redundancy and Repetition

Are parts of my New Leaf Journal redundant and repetitive?

Could redundance and repetitiveness be its strength? Is there unseen power in redundancy and repetition?

"Redundant" may be simply a negative term for the positive benefits of repetition?

Are redundancy and repetition bad? Or a good in disguise?

Polishing the Jewels

I'm getting a sense of self-satisfaction and peace from editing.

Could editing become a form of meditation?

The word "editing" is so mundane and dull. Perhaps I shouldn't call it something else.

How about Polishing The Jewels.

I don't want to think of Polishing The Jewels as a place of closure, frozen and fixed, but rather a temporary resting place on the ascending spiritual ladder of evolution.

Enjoy the view then continue climbing upwards to the next rung.

Benefits of "You're Wonderful!"

I've taken the works of Eknath Easwaran and turned them on their head in order to make them fit me. He's given me cloth, I'm sewing the suit to fit my body, mind, and life style.

Let's take his idea of putting others first. I hate putting others first. I don't understand why anyone would want to do it. But I understand putting myself first very well. I believe self-interest rules behavior.

So how do Easwaran and I get together?

I see it in the "You're wonderful!" philosophy. I totally embrace it.

I heard four writers read their works at Hilda Bary's Poetry Reading in Bergenfield yesterday. All the readers were good but the last reader, Woody Rudin, was truly outstanding. His reading inspired me to improve myself.

During the afternoon reading I was feeling somewhat out of it, distant, blase, bordering on the edge of closure. Michael Friedman sat next to me with his Indonesian girl friend. At the end of the reading he asked, "Are you going to read again?"

"I doubt it," I answered. "First I want to figure out what direction I'm heading in writing."

Michael turned to his girl friend. "This guy really has way out stuff," he said. "You'd like it. It's off-the-wall wonderful."

His words sent an electric shock through me. Suddenly, I felt awake and alert. Wonderful! Me? Hearing such a compliment knocked down my closure walls immediately and filled me an energy bordering on enthusiasm. Imagine, me wonderful! What a thought. What a wonderful thought!

I reflected further. If I was feeling out of it, down, lackluster, energyless, beyond the loop, simply because I wasn't reading and putting myself on the line, and, if Michael's "You're wonderful!" had woken up and energized me, what did such a word mean?

As Michael was saying these fine things about me, he was smiling. When he said I was wonderful it made him feel good, perhaps even wonderful. My being wonderful, my wonderfulness, was making it wonderful for him. Something I had done, namely, giving a service, reading my work, expressing the creations of my inner life, not only made me feel complete, whole, good, and wonderful, but made him feel wonderful as well.

It feels so good when someone says, "You're wonderful!" because you are giving something to others. Putting others before you. Just what Easwaran says—only backwards. Your existence makes them feel good. That is why they say, "You're wonderful!" Often it has little to do with you and a lot to do with them. They have created, invented, imagined a situation, using your existence as ballast, which elevates them, makes them feel important, creative, and alive. They project it onto you. Nevertheless, despite this projection, you are still partly responsible for their feeling of wonderfulness.

"You're wonderful!" in the deeper symbolic language of kabbalistic mysticism, mean: "I'm wonderful!" It is Martin Buber's "I And Thou" all over again.

Looking for that means you are unconsciously searching for a way to help others. On the surface, it can appear egotistic and narcissistic. But that is only a materialistic vision. The deeper explanation for this phenomenon is: When you shine in your existence the light you create shines on others.

Thus, Eknath Easwaran and I are both heading in the same direction—towards the truth of Self. He starts by thinking directly of—or through—others whereas I start by thinking directly of—or through—my self. I call his the "intellectual" approach, mine the "artistic" one. Yet we are simply using different means of driving, different roads to the same castle.

Writing as Meditation

I love the idea of writing as meditation. It feels so much like the right path for me. Finally, after years of believing I have missed the essentials of yoga by leaving breathing and meditation out of my practice, I have taken a step through the looking glass. Writing as meditation is writing without the outer goals of publication, audience, or even improvement. No outer goals, period.

My only purpose in writing now is to understand myself, to dive into the inner sanctum and discover the well-springs, yearnings, and bottom lines of my being. What could that be but meditation? Indeed, I looked up meditation in the dictionary. To my non-surprise it is related to the Latin word for medicine and beyond that to the Hebrew root mida meaning "to measure." Thus, I have been measuring myself for years, trying to fit myself into this world, figuring out where, how, and why I belong. I'm tailoring a suit of clothes to fit me, sweaters, jackets, pants, and shirts to fit my mind, good sturdy underwear to fit my body, fine hats, socks, and shoes to fit the spiritual longings of my soul. I have been doing this all my life. But memory of my "measuring days" began when I started studying violin. What better way to measure? What better way to fit, squeeze, pull, and push ones way through the meditation musical measures of life? Is my life in three quarter time? Am I a waltz clothed in flesh? Is my life a two fourths march? Am I a parade displaying myself proudly before others, shoulders back, chest out, head high, marching up Riverdale Avenue showing my physical, mental, and spiritual wares before my unsuspecting neighbors? Or, perhaps I am a six-eighths jig type with an Irish lilt to my style? As an adult, I've discovered East European rhythms; Greek, Bulgarian, and Byzantine measures with seven, nine, eleven, and even thirteen beats to a measure. Am I those types? Do I meditate in these off-beat rhythms as well? Indeed, yes.

Thus I have been meditating all my life. Mine has been a yoga of music, sound, and beauty. I just never called it yoga.

What about breathing? I have been doing that all my life, too even though I never called it pranayama. Upon further reflection we'll see if I can also discover a unique approach to breathing that I have been doing all my life.

True Editing

True editing is rethinking my thoughts as I rewrite them.

LANGUAGES

Bursting in "Hiriq" Freedom

In ancient geocentric times, the center of the earth was thought to be the center of the universe. It's astronomic symbol was a dot, a Hebrew vowel hiriq.

When man is stuck in hiriq, stuck in the center of the earth, he lies in the "coffin of responsibility."

There are two qualities of a vowel: stuck and frozen in place, or roaring through the universe, bursting in freedom. As in the dual meaning and personality of hiriq, you can either lie at the center of the earth surrounded by darkness in the limbo coffin of responsibility or stand, surrounded by everlasting light, at the center of the universe bursting in freedom.

On the Hebrew Vowels as Astronomic Symbols

I see the sun flying around the Hebrew vowels, flying from holam to seggol.

Writing the vowels, my pen moves from right to left... just like the sun.

Hebrew Is Clicking!
Through the window of illumination
I saw a glimpse of light,
A moment of peace and joy.
Hebrew is clicking!
Hours of daily study suddenly paid off.
It pays to practice!
To put in the hours of unrequited time.
Daily, daily, daily,
Patiently, patiently, patiently
Without hope of reward.
Follow this path.
One day
The window of illumination will open.
For a delicious moment
I will understand!
And see the purple fluttering wings of glory
Shining in the Light.

It's Not Easy Being a Word

Latin is a highly inflected language. Thus it is riddled with declension.

Nouns, pronouns, adjectives, and verbs are inflected, bent out of shape, twisted, perverted, and diminished.

So diminished are they that the process of inflection is called declension—a deteriorating, descending, sloping, falling away, declining process.

Declension shows case, number, and gender.

Case, from the Latin cadere—to fall, is another "case" of diminishment. Here words are twisted beyond their true selves, partially stripped of their essential nature; they are pushed, forced, and enslaved, squeezed into strange forms to become subjects, objects, possessors, etc.

They can also lose their individuality and identity by being reduced to mere numbers—another form of debasement. Or they can be twisted and turned on the gender rack.

Changes in a verb are called conjugation. Thus verbs are better off than nouns, pronouns, and adjectives. They might even see marriage in their future along with conjugal visits. However, verbs can be tense and suffer from mood changes, schizophrenic shifts of person, voice difficulties, and even the same number problems as their noun, pronoun, and adjective cousins.

It's not easy being a word.

If you want to be tough, strong, and stable, be a noun.

If you want to be tough, strong, and mobile, be a first person verb.

Another look at Latin grammar:

"Infinitive" is the soaring word. Thus "to soar" opens limitless flight into the heavens of everywhere and forever.

Finite forms are in conjugations: I soar, you soar, he, she, or it soars. These are limited. First personal singular or "through the masks of sameness," (First—from Latin "per" through. Masks from Latin "persona" mask. Singular from Latin, "singularis" and Hebrew "semel," same, similar.)

The same limitations apply to plurals.

LIFE

New Year!

What better way to begin the new year than with the "parsha" approach to life. Making the ordinary holy, "normal" mysticism, eating and taking meals in meditation, uniting Leviticus with health and nutritional studies. Making "parsha" and daily Torah study a part—even the central pillar—of my life.

That is a worthy new year's resolution!

"It's all there in Judaism," Gene said. "Eastern philosophy, mysticism, love of God, and making the day and ordinary life holy."

Read the "parshas' in both English and Hebrew. I would (will) read them again next year—and every year. A life time and many life time process. Certainly this is non-closure at its best!

Also witness New Leaf Journal as a non-closure practice. It will never be finished, never end. Just like Torah study will never finish, never end. The life of the day versus the life of the forever.

> Sometimes I am running wild to a quiet spot.
> Sometimes I am running wild in a quiet spot.
> But I always want to run wild!
> Yoga is running wild in a quiet spot
> Progress is running wild to a quiet spot

> Perfect balance is right next to the perfect fall.
> Run With Lions
> The lion has broken out of its cage.
> The lion has broken free.
> Now he is running wild on the African plain.
> If I'm going to run wild
> I have to run with lions.

Can a running wild approach be born in magyar ashes? Can it be reborn on Hungarian soil? Or should I also add an African Safari, Arctic Circle Cruise, trip to India, or something else?

Yoga Additions

1. Hands through lotus legs.
2. Focus—gently
3. Squats—one leg standing posture.
4. Using the power of mind spread toes and "mentally" straighten my hammer toe. (Can I straighten my toes through mental power

and focus? What a good long-term project that would be. Develop powers of concentration.

5. Overall concept: Yoga is an exercise in focus!

Fears

We create our own fears to challenge ourselves and to grow.

I was having a great time. Then I thought, is she having a great time, too?

I was having a great time lying on the couch visualizing the word "strong" written across my stomach along with yod and a shadow of the Yahwah God- letters of the tetragrammaton. Then I thought, is he having fun, too?

Both times I interrupted my wonderful self thoughts; both times I stopped both self-giving and giving to others. By inhibiting joy and wild running I, on one level, inhibited their joy and wild running.

Years of "No!" almost took away joy and wild running. Time to get it back; time for repair.

"Crossing the Bridge of *With*

It will take months to absorb the message: Give to yourself with another."

"With" is the bridge word; "another" is the land beyond the bridge.

I looked "with" up in the dictionary. It means against, in opposition. "He argued with his wife."

"With" also means "by means of." "He stirred it with a spoon."

Thus you need resistance, opposition to cross the bridge of With. The opposition calls up your energy enabling you to cross the bridge and build the new bridge of "By Means Of."

Silence

Silence is part of expansion, assertion, and self-love.

BREATH OF THE WAVES

The breath of the waves
In and out
Inhaling... exhaling

The breathing
Of the ocean.

Adventure

Part of life's adventure is letting oneself completely fall apart, then seeing where it leads.

BALLAD OF THE VEGETATING MOANER
Why can't I have what I want?
Why must everything be so measured and calculated?
Why can't I just linger?
Where is my mother?

The Hebrew folk dancer's Pentateuch is the Toe-rah.

Adventures in Sad-Versus-Mad

Madness contain rage within it. But it also contains wild creative forces like running wild on the plains, the mad scientist, and the mad artist. I love them!
Madness is the way to go.
I want to keep my madness but I don't want to give up my sadness. It is too delicious.
I need both.
They feed each other.

The audience is pushing me to play fast.
But I don't want to play fast.
I don't want to be pushed around!
I am not responsible for their emotions and actions.
I'll play it my way.

Art

If I am an artist in my heart, mind, soul, body, and spirit, isn't it best for me to approach the Bible as an artist. As a calligrapher.
Isn't it best to approach everything I do this way?
Approach even money and business as an artist. And only as an

artist. My tours must be works of art.

Should my bank account also be a work or art? Is this possible?

Art is my life. I have no choice. My so-called "choices" like business, have only worked halfway, the artistic half way.

Go back to art. Go forward to art. Let everything else go by the wayside. Let debts pile up if they have to. I may die in the poor house but at least I'll die there as an artist.

Art is my God connection.
It is my love connection.
There is nothing else.

Read the Torah as an artist. Can I afford to be an artist? Must I go bankrupt in the process? But what else can I do? Do I even have a choice? God put me on earth to be an artist. It is my calling.

It means running tours as an artist.
Artistic tours.
It means doing yoga as an artist
Artistic yoga.
It means imbuing everything I do with art.
I has always been thus.
It means doing yoga as an artist

How can I make my tours more artistic? Perhaps I can start by writing great copy and adding good art work.

To Be an Artist

All these art realizations are nothing new. What is new? I am ready to deepen my commitment to the artistic way, the artistic life. I'm ready to become an "extremist;" ready to throw out everything and become an artist. Or rather, I'm ready to be an artist.

What Is the Payoff?

What is the payoff for one who keeps climbing?
One who accepts impermanence?
What is the payoff for not grasping,

Gathering no monuments to yourself,
And letting the life force flow through you?
What is the payoff for gathering no monuments to yourself?
What is the payoff for the spiritual ascent?
It is the pearl of joy
A glimpse of intangible truth.

Crossing the Tourist Desert

I read that Moses wanted to bring everything he owned—"not one hoof will remain"—out of Egypt. He didn't know what he'd need to serve God in the desert. Like a tour leader, he was situational: he'd know what method or tool to use when he got there. And, like a tour leader, he wanted to bring as much equipment from home to use "just in case."

I do the same thing when I leave home to lead a tour. I bring as many props "out of Egypt" as I can: computer, writing books, language and history books, all to help me survive in the tourist desert.

Perfection is a path not a place.

Reading Slowly To Reach All-Is-One

I felt down after reading about Moses in the original Hebrew. I read so slowly. I spent an hour on two sentences. At this rate, it will take sixty lifetimes if not more to finish the Torah.

What about accomplishments? What about crossing the desert and reaching the Promised Land, reaching that place of rest and closure where I can say "Look at me folks, I've finally made it!" I'll never reach that place. The more I read, the slower I get. Slower, slower, slower. True, by reading slowly I go deeper into each sentence, word, and vowel sign; I wring out meanings from each letter. Yet, I am still pursued by a fleeting panic. It's the "I'll never finish this thing no matter how hard I try," panic.

Can I accept the fact that I'm studying and practicing something I'll never finish? Can I accept my daily slide into the abyss of eternity? Can I deal with its terrifying vision of the infinite?

Can I accept even though there is no choice but to accept?

I am hung on the cross. The horizontal pantibulum is pain, the vertical stipiti is pleasure. As I hang daily, tied to the crossbars, dogs devour my feet and birds peck out my eyes. In three days of less I will die of suffocation.

Call that a life?

What else can I do? Is there really a choice?

I'll never finish Torah study in this lifetime or many more lifetimes. Yet, in my gut, I still want to finish.

What does "finish" mean?

It means reaching an ecstatic moment of awareness where, once again, I realize All is One.

Follow the Sun

Can my mind be controlled through meditation practice?

Do I want it controlled?

If I steer it towards positive thoughts, will riches be avoded by not plumbing its depths?

Is control the artist's way?

Is it better to follow storms than the sun?

The battle rages between clouds of impermanence and a beatific sun with secure rays of eternity.

Dedicate myself to the practice:

Follow the sun.

The Next Mountain To Climb

As I sat on the side of the road in Taormina, Sicily, I thought: I need a new mountain to climb.

Which one will I climb next? What upcoming projects shall I embrace?

1. Spain for May of 1999
    a. A guitar, dance, and southern Spain tour.
2. Study Latin languages along with history.
    a. Climb the Tour-Language-History mountain.

I can look for new mountains in yoga, guitar, history dates, and even writing. Writing? Perhaps gathering my writings and editing them into a publishable whole is my next mountain to climb. I'd like that to happen. But when I see it I'll believe it. Such a writing project may have to wait for a special calling. It has not yet come. But I could be wrong. Perhaps Climbing-The-Next-Mountain approach will encompass writing as well.

When the Climbing-The-Next-Mountain attitude flashed through me, I felt electrified. It filled me with energy and enthusiasm, with a power and desire to pursue endless possibilities. Climbing is a powerful attitude, wonderful for me.

I would be happy is such explosive, volcanic Mount Etna approach guided my entire existence. I can think of nothing better.

The-Next-Mountain-To-Climb attitude is a fitting climax to my tour of Sicily and Rome.

Feeling sorry for yourself has a bad rap.

Dacian Rumblings

I have returned. The doors are burning down and the cat is crazy running out of the house. My bowels are in an uproar and the furnace is lit with kerosene from distant Byzantine lamps. Only catcalls and caterwauls are flying backwards tonight even though it is morning.

I am working directly with my God connection. Finally, it has all made sense. Years of reading, studying, learning, dying, rebirthing, living in the stylistic light of backward and past years are slowly and steadily beginning to pay off. Yes, folks, I do meditate after all! I have been doing it for years; nay, most of my life. But I didn't know it was meditation. I called it art.

It any case, by simply turning a few words around, I find I am easily following all the dictates of post-menopausal meditation of the fornicating ant variety practiced by members of the pre-historic Module civilization living on the banks of the Danube. These ancient warmongers, comfortably nested in Danubian sands, forebears of the noble Dacian leader, Decebelus, practiced archery well before the Roman conquest. In later days, from his capital in Sarmogethusae, Decebelus diplomatic strung up fosters well with the Roman emperor, Domitian. Sarmogethusae, you say. And how do you spell that fucker, anyway? Is it Sarmogethusae, Sarmozegethuse, or what? I raced to look it up. Sarmizegethusa! That's it. It marches well with the first Dacian War, too. Decebelus won that diplomatic battle only later to lose to emperor Trajan. Victory column of Trajan, indeed. And to think I almost saw it in Romania last year. I should visit Sarmizegethusa once in my life. Imagine standing on the ground of the ancient Dacian capital; imagine Decebelus sitting on his throne, drinking Dacian wines, robbing the clitoral wine-pressings of virgins along with their social security numbers, and raising his third finger to Roman domination before succumbing to the ultimate Latinization of his language. What is Dacian and who are the Dacians, anyway? A Thracian tribe related to the Getae, of course.

After this brief foray into the back wards of history I am returning to my present God connected writing. Indeed, it is a pleasure to let the words fly across the pages again.

Torn between the motivating forces of self-loathing and asphyxiation. Self-loathing gets me out of the house; asphyxiation puts me back in.

Thank God for these forces. Without them I'd either be dead or crazy. With them, I am "simply" torn.

Mount Vesuvius belching smoke. Pumice ash raining down on helpless twats, vaginas gone wild with sea scum pumped from the volcanic eruptions on the island of Stromboli. Lying on Stromboli's beach, far from the Roman crowd, I wonder at the sight of distant Eolian islands lite by smoke, fire, and floating ashen chips their only hope beyond Roman baths is the Church of Saint Peter whose Vicoli chains never make it beyond the horns of Michelangelo's Moses.

Unexpressed rage is an energy clot. To unclot it, express it. But not necessarily to the person you are mad at. Feel and express it for yourself first. Then, when the proper time comes—if it ever does—you can handle it calmly and easily with the one you were mad at.

Visiting the House of Historical Loves

Yesterday I went to Barnes and Noble. I bought the Rough Guide to Italy and an Historical Atlas Of Ancient Rome. The Rough Guide series are the best guide books I've found. I'll glance through it with cursory interest. But the Historical Atlas is a book I'm enthusiastic about reading. It is a musical, mystical, historical, dream adventure as are most history books. Indeed, to me, that's what history is: a musical, mystical, dream adventure with "real" historical characters leading the drama. If history isn't a dream, it's not worth reading. I love dreams. I love life as a dream. I can never get Calderon's La Vida Es Sueno out of my head. Although I've never read it, the ephemeral mystery of its title always haunts me. Like the cloud of the Lord hovering over the Israelites as they crossed the desert, the dream is my cloud always above me, pointing me in the right direction, protecting me from the destructive concrete vision of seeing life as a permanent material reality. Yes, as Calderon said, La vida es sueno—Life is a dream, and I love it that way. My philosophy is: keep dreaming! Dreams are much closer to reality than the material existence of so-called "real" life events.

I almost never talk about my love of books. Could it be that, bottom line, I don't believe I'm smart enough, my thoughts not important enough, to talk about in public? Is it a lack of self-esteem thing, a holdover from my school days where I was a lousy student, spending most of my time in class daydreaming? My marks stunk. Sometimes I managed to get them out of the stink hole. But even with all my effort I could only raise them to average. I was never a good student in school. However, if you measured my dream capacity, my ability to fantasize in class, I would have gotten straight A's.

I still have a poor self-image of myself as a student. How can such a poor student dare to speak of lofty ideas, of wondrous, miracle filled tombs of history, philosophy, language, and whatever? I love to read these masterful books; I love the bathe in their visions and ideas. I approach study as bather. I love swimming in the ocean of learning. But bathers often get poor marks in school. How dare I, a bather, speak of historic events and lofty ideas! What is my pedigree?

Turning Anger into Compassion

Turning anger into compassion means turning shit into fertilizer.

Even better is to turn the shit others give you into garden fertilizer. Some day, many years from now, you can thank them for helping your flowers grow.

Yoga Morning
The loins are very primal.
Animal energy emanating from them
Connects me with the animal world.
Can such power be brought into the heart?

Visiting the Dark Emptiness
Deep and heavy
Clouds settling in
Gray, gray, gray.
Blank and barren firmament
A vast emptiness haunts my being.
Clinging to flesh softens the void,
Chases away the wolf howl and whorl.
But the vast, black, empty, universe returns
When flesh is gone.
I want to enter the paragon on Flesh Mountain

Lose myself in its folds

Hug and cover up, divest myself of my being, lose body, mind, and soul in the ever-increasing folds of warm, wet, wonderful, lose, bland, black and hair-filled liquid; I want to swim in the cockpit, wrestle with snakes, singe and sizzle in awareness of a deep blackened nothingness, yes, and cling to lovely fat and juicy folds where wet lips claim destiny and dominion over virulent magic.

Where did I go? Why do I want to lose myself? Why do I revel and rebel against my loses? What is the wonder, the attraction, the miracle of going down, down, down, exploring the bottom of the pit, tearing into the blackness with lightning rods and white-hot steel pins, thrashing and whipping up froth, and cooking the daylights out of nighttime habits?

Will I ever know? Is there no cure to emptiness, no antidote for psychic explosions or black waves of downtrodden flume? Probably not.

And yet this stream of snake words helps. It releases the venom of emptiness and brings the relief of sweet peace.

Ah, up ahead I see a ray of light.

What did I do?

I opened the flood gates. Snakes slithered away, carrying poison in buckets; horses with hoofs on fire flew through the night, whipping the darkness. I see it, I see it! A sparkle of sun!

What did I do to deserve this?

Who knows?

But it helps.

Mother's Arms

Why am I sick? Why is my throat sore? Why does my lower back hurt?

I am approaching major areas of conflict and major threats.

I am approaching the good mother, nice mother, loving mother; I am approaching the mother I love.

Most fearful is the mother I love. Mother loving upsets and overturns all I know, knew, feel and felt about mother, mothers, and women in general. To move from anger, fear, even hatred to love, well, that is something.

This warm, wet, and wonderful but simultaneously miserable, depressing, black, early afternoon post-lunch, downward "falling—in-love-take-and-destroy-me" feeling is really the sinking energy form of my beautiful mother in disguise. She lies in the bed of goodness pulling me into her heavy warm fat-lined arms to tarry, rest, sleep, even die; then to be reborn with new strength and power. That is a true loving mother. I have simply never recognized her.

And this because her love has visited me in "negative" forms, appearing as destroyer, restorer, annihilator, sopping up my energy, calling me to tumble into her loving arms, to lie in comfort and in the dark relaxation of luxury on her breast, giving up my struggles to conquer the world.

My masculinity dies on her breast; my powers drain, my moribund energies dissipate and vanish. Suddenly, I am transformed into a helpless, happy sleeping infant; gladly I return to her womb and even pre-womb. In happy flying fashion I glide into her channel, rowing deep into the dark recesses of my pre-universe, into that sleepy blackness where all is comfort, ease, rest, and non-motion. Ah, how I love it. How I hate admitting I love it! What a beautiful luxury! To give up the struggles of this world; to simply fall back, relax, rest, sleep, and die in the morphine embrace of mother's fructifying arms, to enter that sweet world of beyond and past where once I lived in mere potential with my expectations at zero level. That is true peace.

And with peace come beauty and truth.

There is beauty and truth in my sweet mother's arms. There is truth and beauty in rest, sleep, death, annihilation, depression, destruction, a sweet truth in giving up my struggles, dumping my desires to make a living, to function and survive in the outdoor streets of the mean, competitive worry-filled material world. Beauty and truth, don't I know it. Who wouldn't give it all up for a few moments of bliss and peace nestled in warm, wet, blissful comfort, cradled in mother's arms, your head resting on a warm, pulsating breast, your ear listening to a heartbeat that was once your own as your infant hair is stroked by the hand that once fed you. Only a few moments of such comfort and feeding is enough to send you back into the outside world refreshed and invigorated, ready to struggle anew.

I am taking another look at mother's arms, taking another look at my down times, depressions, longings, another look at my falling, loneliness, missing, hopelessness, and emptiness when power and meaning are drained from my being. Not a bad place to be, after all. Imagine, this formerly miserable location might, in the warm dark light of mother's existence, be a wonderful location, a prime piece of peaceful real estate, a miniature paradise.

I just never saw it that way.

I am torn between practical and passionate.
I need both.
Practical for my base,
Passionate for my soaring.

Stretched over life's abyss
Between the practical and the passionate
It is my destiny to be split.

Joy and the experience of God are the same.

Learn to be grateful for opposition.

The "Her" in My Old Self

"I don't want to lose her!" I cried.
But I have already lost her. She is disappeared along with my old self.
Who is "her" but my old self.
I mourn the painful lose of my old attitudes. Some were mean; but at least I knew them: My familiar old miserable friends.
I hate to lose a piece of my old self.
But replacement parts are coming in.
And what wonderful parts they are!

Shame is a doorway to expansion.

First you expand, then you exhilarate.

Do not push others.
Simply say what you want. Then do it.
The "I Want" philosophy works like a charm. And this, even though it may not be charming to others.
The "I Want" philosophy is a wonderful non-violent, non-hostile act of rebellion. Standing up for "I Want" pushes nobody, forces nobody, puts pressure on nobody. You have compete control over it.

True self-love quickly turns into universal love.
True self-love is love for others.

Learn to stop at the right moment: the beauty moment.

A Mountain Takes Longer
It took almost forty years to play guitar.
I wasn't brushing a pebble off my shoulder. . . or a rock.
I was removing a mountain.
A pebble takes a day. . .a rock takes weeks, or months.
A mountain takes years. . . even centuries.
Mine took forty years.
Yes, a mountain takes longer.

PERFORMANCE

Opening the Door of Concert Freedom

I gave a concert last night. I began with Villa-Lobos "Prelude Number 1." I played it beautifully. I usually do. It is an excellent opening piece and easy for me to play. Then I moved on to Gaspar Sanz' "Pavane," I forgot, and "Canarios." I started to fall apart on that one. To recover, I began Malats' "Serenade" but continued falling apart while my right hand froze. As I played the Sanz, I fought my lack of concentration. But then something new and different happened. As my right hand froze and my body refused to relax, my mind gave way, saying: "Fuck it. I'm so tired of these bouts of anxiety in public; I'm sick of fighting them. I'll just go with it." Then, right in the middle of the Malats Serenade, I stopped playing, looked up from the guitar, and said, "But then Malats thought his 'Serenade' wasn't romantic enough, so he decided to sing." Then I switched gears and sang the calypso "Love, Love, Love."

Although I was somewhat embarrassed from having once again failed in public—I'd never done such a switch before—I hid it well. No doubt, most in the audience thought I had "planned" this sudden change even. Inwardly, I still "knew" I had failed. Yet, somehow it didn't bother me as much as usual. Part of me vaguely realized that rather than fail, I had suddenly and subtly opened up a new door. Imagine, changing horses in midstream and all in the name of staying relaxed and at ease in public. Actually, I liked it. I was no longer chained to the concert form and order I had created. I was free to give the "concert order of the moment," free to follow not only the spontaneous dictates of my inner voice, but also the higher orders of HaShem Himself. No doubt, He is the one who made me fall apart in public. He had a higher calling for me—to be myself no matter how embarrassing or difficult it got. He even wanted me to get beyond my nervousness and anxiety and worship Him fully by living totally in His present moment. Well, changing my concert form and order on the spot in public was one of my first steps.

So I improvised in the moment. I swam, twisted, turned, made up a few off-beat outlandish stories to "explain" my situation, and moved on. People ended up loving it. Why not? I'm a professional and can handle these public ups and downs easy on the surface even thought inwardly they kill me.

But, as I say, this time they didn't kill me that much and I even was smart enough to realize a new door was opening—the door of freedom.

> What exhilaration, fun, and joy!
> Do something wrong for a change! Get used to it.

NOTES ARE PEOPLE IN DISGUISE
Notes are people in disguise.
Each note has an inherent integrity and speed.
I imagine, create, play, and express them.
Phrases, groups of notes, are like family.
In larger numbers, they become a concert audience.
Each notes has its own dignity.
Its own integrity and speed.

Notes are bridges between private and public, performer and audience.

WRIST POWER
Feel the power
Flowing deep within
My slow right wrist.

A juggernaut rolling,
Elephants marauding through my veins.
Have I been fearing
And avoiding it
All these years?

Guitar Flexing
I flex my guitar muscles
Luxuriate in fleshy digital sensuality
Feeling my power.
Love dozes warm on a rock beneath
Sunning itself like a seal.

Play Softer
Play softer
On a whisper level
The gentle level
Quietly, softly,
Whisper into the deep open,
To levels beyond comprehension.
I cry, break down, unleashing a flood.
"I-Me" is washed away.
I take my first steps into the realm
Of Heart-Worship
Then my heart chakra
Opens through my shoulder.

Displaying Myself to Others

I am a flawed and beautiful example of a work in progress.

The courage to appear, play, and display myself, perfections, imperfections, and all to others, will, I hope, inspire them.

Displaying myself thusly is a public service, a form of giving to others.

Questions are answers in disguise.

MASTER DANCER TEACHER
A good dance teacher dances in his shoes;
A master dance teacher dances in other people's shoes
Visible or not
His feet are in the Universal Shoe.

BUSINESS

Flying into Rome, I had the gift of three free seats next to me on the plane. Best transatlantic sleep I've ever had.

Then we flew into Palermo, met our Sicilian guide, Marco—I like him a lot. Drove into the city and settled into our Excelsior Hotel.

Let my tour business be an expression of soaring!

Business is never dead. It just goes to sleep for awhile.

I could use some good non-closure philosophy right now. I took a short walk through the main street in Palermo, past lots of boring clothing stores. Unimpressed, I returned to my room, took an hour sleep, and woke with the familiar tour feeling of "What the hell am I doing here, anyway? Why can't I be at home, reading the Torah, playing guitar, writing, studying, reading, running, loving, doing yoga, and all the wonderful things I can do there? Why am I here in the first place?

I often feel this way at the beginning of a tour. Perhaps I'm just tired. In any case, I am pushing for some non-closure fears, excitements, and bottom-falling-outs to put me back on the God-driven track. I want my world of flying between the cliffs and diving into the abyss. What happened to that world, anyway? I lost it on the plane ride over.

A great day! Our local guide, Pina, short for Joseph or Guiseppi, lead us on a tour of Palermo. he gave it lots of feeling. I sure felt bad for the Sicilians. What a history! But with only ten minutes to write, let's just say, the Jews, Arabs, and Sicilian nobility really got it in the neck. Especially when the Jesuit Inquisition came to town under the Spanish. Such damage and destruction can last centuries; it did with the Sicilians. A great culture in the middle ages! Palermo was one of the most important cities in Europe, the greatest in the twelfth and thirteenth centuries under the Normans, Roger of Hauteville, King Roger II, William the Bad and William the Good, the Hohenstaufens with Henry the sixth, and finally Frederick II. His reign was called Stupor Mundi! How I love that title! It means not Stupid of the World or Stupor of the World but rather Wonder of the World.

After trying to convert the Pope to Judaism, the 12th century Spanish kabbalistic Rabbi Abulafia came to Palermo. He spent five years here after leaving Spain. I went to a Palermo bookstore this afternoon and, after purchasing books on the Normans, History of Sicily, and the Sicilian Jews—all in Italian, of course, I saw a book on Frederick II written by, guess who? David Abulafia. Turns out he teaches history in Cambridge University in England. The book was written in English then translated into Italian. I dislike translations; that's why I didn't get it. I'll order the English version from Barnes and Noble in New Jersey. Perhaps David Abulafia is a descendant of the Abulafia family from which Rabbi Abulafia came.

Order: The "Only" Way

I overslept this morning. To my disappointment, I woke up at 5:30 instead of 4:00 a.m. I turned off my alarm, figuring I could wake up mentally. Wrong. I am still on jet lag time. In any case, after waking up late I decided that I would eliminate writing from my morning routine. I washed, had coffee, studied Torah in Hebrew, then began yoga. But I couldn't concentrate during my first Salute to the Sun. Writing gnawed at my brain. Finally, I took out my computer and wrote these pages.

What does this show? I must follow my routines in their proper order. If I have little time just spend less time with each one.

The Birth of a La Marco Tour Notes

First we visited Trapani and the Pepoli museum in northwestern Sicily, then drove 800 meters up a mountain to the medieval town of Erice. Shrouded in fog, it gave me a truly medieval experience of cold, wet, fog, dampness, low visibility; the thrill of Hamlet lost in Denmark on a cold night. We ate local couscous, returned to the bus, drove down the mountain and back to Palermo again.

Erice was really a thrill a minute. When I got back to my room and reviewed Marco's excellent history notes an idea:

Make my own a la Marco notes for future tours!

I could put years of history study and knowledge into practice, learning to verbalize it as well; I could make a la Marco notes for each country I tour, put the notes into my computer, print them out and give them to my tour participants. It would focus my tours on educating myself and, parenthetically, it might educate them as well.

That's my "new" tour philosophy. No longer to make money—although that would be nice. But for inspiration, purpose, meaning, and motivation, I'd best run my tours to educate myself. What better purpose than to fill my life with joy and the glow of personal expansion. Start by writing, and "publishing," my history a la Marco.

Foggy Sicilian Morning

A doubt crossed my mind. Was yesterday's history revelation really a revelation? It felt powerful and true; everything seemed to justify it. But this morning, doubt clouds my mind. I'll have to mull the idea over, then try to forget. If it returns to haunt me I'll know it is good, true, and rightly timed.

Turning out words now, trying to warm up, get in the mood. The historical significance of asteroids hurtling through space, turning machines into non-entities and waking up interstellar parlor games, flits through my mind. Must they be accounted for? How about the stellar limitations of our trip to Erice, haunting in their munificence, thrilled and perforated by a fog of narrow straits and isthmuses gone wild with herrings and baited mattanza tuna hunting breaths. Only the salvation of a Sicilian magnificence can haunt such a lair. Mental bombardments and warm-ups cannot necessarily hamper a historian whose calling smacks of chicken shit and odors wrapped in rooster cellophane before the barnyard fog of Trapani or Palermo.

Racing through inner tubes, turning intestines in brain fodder, wrestling with the giant questions of: Am I a poet or historian? Can I be both? Is it too late to change or have I discovered all there is of myself? Where do history and facts fit in? Can I take dry facts, turn them into wet noodles swimming in delicious sauce, and turn these succulent nutrients of a spaghetti fed environment into a last and first supper to feed both myself and my family? Is history writing just another passing dream, a momentary fantasy built over a Sicilian well of emptiness? Am I simply filling my barn with new hay for a day? Or am I onto something? Is history writing a new direction? Or is it simply a new cloud on the horizon that will pass as soon as this tour ends?

What about children's stories? What about my journal? What about my delicious verbal feeding frenzies, my flights of imagination, and my God connection? Hasn't that always been why I write?

Is there a God connection writing about history? Can I make one? Do I even want to? Will I ever? But if I can't, why bother writing about history?

All good unanswerable questions. Time will tell. But why I wait for time? Better act now. I'll answer my own questions. Sure, they'll only be today's answer's but who can do better than that?

If I am going to write about history I've got to discover my God connection in history. Perhaps I can find it through writing about history.

What do I like about history? What have I ever liked about history?

First, and perhaps foremost, I like the explosions of lingual velocity in my mouth as I pronounce the names of ancient personages and places. Mine is a musical approach to history, a velar and stellar approach. Then I like to dream through space. Flying backwards over time, letting my imagination soar, sailing across the Euphrates, visiting Babylonia, seeing stars shine under Phoenician nights as I make a quick visit to Carthage, jump two thousand years forward to Tunisia or backtrack two and a half millenia to visit Pythagoras at his home in ancient Crotona. My Greek is rusty, especially my ancient

Greek. Will Pythagoras understand me? Or do we need a translator?

How will I write about history? Will it come straight out of my imagination? Will I do research? Or both?

All good questions, unanswerable on this foggy Sicilian morning.

Idiots of the World

What can I do if Marge is a total asshole?

I came to dinner last night and sat next to Doris. The first thing she said was, "I'm so mad. Why weren't our festival tickets and performances arranged before hand? We should have gone to a performance tonight. Why did I come on this trip, anyway? You should have known about this festival program and made arrangements in advance." She said a few more things, but I got so mad that I didn't hear the rest of her vitriolic barb. This little fuck ass was criticizing my tour! What's more, she was criticizing me! Who does she think she is? What does she know about running a tour, anyway? Nothing, of course. But she didn't even bother asking. She simply assumed everything was all screwed up, that I wasn't doing my job, that the tour was disorganized, and that nothing good was going to happen at this festival, that she would be cheated and unhappy. So, in her atrocious manner, she blamed me for her bilious frustration.

I felt an immediate volcanic rumbling in my belly; the white-hot lava from my intestinal Mount Etna was about to erupt. But I restrained myself from strangling her,

I was about to defend myself by explaining how this tour works, but I didn't. Actually, I didn't know what to say because the beauty of my tours is that I don't quite know how they work. For example, I don't know yet what's going on at the festival. It's my first time here. But even if I were here for the second, third, or tenth time, I still wouldn't know what's going on. In fact, I even pride myself on not knowing what's going on. Then I seize the moment, grab the day, and find my way. Each situation calls for a different response. You really can't know exactly what to do until you're in it. Knowing what to do, working my way through the situation, handling the spur-of-the-moment decision, is not only what I like to do, but the best way to handle things. Too much early planning is often as bad as too little. But why explain all this to dumphead Doris? She's just too stupid and mad to understand anything beyond her childish tantrums and imaginary creations.

I wanted to get more information before I spoke to our group. I got up from my dinner, went to a phone and called Michelle Gallo, our local tour guide. He gave me more details, which I passed on. It helped. Marge, who had picked up on Doris's discontents, chiming in with her own worries, later apologized to me for acting so childish.

I don't mind Marge, Doris, or anyone else asking for favors or even trying to effect change in our program. But I absolutely hate their demanding, pouting, asinine, assumptive manner of blame and accusation. I don't take that kind of stuff anymore. That is one of the great pluses in my tour leadership development.

I knew how I felt. Now the question was how to act.

I called Michelle Gallo again and got more information. We set up a meeting with a local Sicilian folk dance group! Michelle said he would also try getting tickets to performances on Friday and Saturday night.

Another tour situation saved.

Later I asked Doris, "Do you feel better?"

She answered, "Absolutely not. This should have been arranged in advance. It's your responsibility."

A hearty fuck-you to you, too, I thought. Then I left our hotel to take a short walk around the block and meditate upon idiots of the world.

Mr. Down Faultline Meets the Supreme Sparker

Thank God for Aaron. And I don't mean biblical Aaron, but rather Aaron Kirchenbaum of Mykonos, who told me the shock I get from touching my computer comes because I'm barefoot. Current passes through me into the ground. Now when I use my computer, I wear shoes.

Yesterday, in Agrigento, we met our first Sicilian folk dance group. They performed a Tarantella, then taught us basic Tarantella steps with lots of enthusiasm. I made good dance contacts for next year. Working with our local guide, Michelle Gallo, we set up a 1999 tour program. We'll return to the Almond Festival in Agrigento next February, meet folk dance groups, visit a Sicilian village, meet the local people, and dance some more.

Finally, I had put my Sicilian tour together! I felt satisfied.

Then, as often happens after a success, I was visited by Mr. Down Faultline. He is the depressive gnome inhabiting the southern intellectual sector of my brain. He tried to kill my jubilation. "You can hardly call this a victory," he said. "You've done it so often. Putting tours together has become easy for you." Leaning on his stick, he tried making a hole in my brain. He went on: "It is also important to remember that you'll soon be dead. If not tomorrow, next week, or next year, certainly in thirty, forty, or fifty years. When doesn't matter. So why bother feeling good or bad about accomplishments? All will be forgotten. It all ends up down the drain."

At first I agreed. Then I realized Faultline is right only on one level. On a higher level, he is wrong. My victories are sparks of spirit in action, bathing me in holy waters. Down Faultline, as a representative of the fragmented intellectual sector of my brain, speaks to the other fragmented sectors, exhorting them to "be reasonable."

But I visit levels beyond. I travel in Lands Beyond Intellect, where sparks fly. The fire of my success carries me upward. In a whirling column of rising sparks, I ascend to meet the Supreme Sparker.

How To Prevent Sleep Walking

Later in the afternoon we arrived at Siracusa. We visited the archaeological park with an excellent local guide named Salvatore. However, I couldn't concentrate on what he was saying. I kept falling asleep. When I didn't, I wished I were somewhere else. How boring these wonderful archeological lectures are. How amazing that such knowledgeable guides imparting such important historic and cultural information put me to sleep almost every time. What a shame I can't concentrate on what they're saying. Yet even thought I like history, I can't help it.

It has always been thus.

But maybe, by expanding up a few helpful words from Paul Kerlee, I can find a way out. Paul fell asleep at the concert last night. He said, "I always fall asleep at concerts. I also fall asleep at lectures, during classes, and sometimes even when someone talks to me. That's why I started videoing: It keeps me awake."

I liked that. I understood it. The process of videoing keeps him awake. Paul is participating in and in charge of his own creative process. He has found a personal approach to staying awake through life, a way to handles times of stress and boredom. I could do something similar.

I thought: if creativity is my God connection, then I should keep this connection at all times. Creativity wakes me up and keeps me alert. Why not use it, in the form of writing, calligraphy, drawing or whatever, while tour guides are lecturing.

How can I access my creative self while touring? How do I stay awake? Here are some answers:

1. Keep a writing pad in hand while touring; keep on in hand while the tour guide lectures.

2. Use free form spontaneous writing while they are speaking. Use their lectures to "verbally take off."

Here's what came out of this approach first used in Siracusa:

Dionysus ear: Orrechio di Dionysus. Siracuse. Cir-a-kus-a. Cir-excuse. Slaves slaving, carving out today's paradise. Romans, Greeks. Read Thucydides. Thoo-sid-a-dees. Write Thucydides using Greek letters.

Write by hand. A free writing hand. Thus can I jump, writing many alphabets.

Learn to calligraphy and to write in Hebrew, Cyrillic, Greek, and Arabic alphabets.

Carry different pens on my person at all times.

Tombs of the acropolis, lava of Mount Etna, marine bodies stuck on the back of ancient graves. J'ai rencontre un homme de Bordeaux.

Eonus led the first slave rebellion on Sicily against Rome around 129 A.D. Spartacus was about 73 A.D.

"How I Wish This Tour Was Over"

I awoke with a terrible longing to get back home. It was a "how I wish this tour were over" morning.

I wish I was not going on the 4-day Rome extension. I could do it all next year with a Southern Italy extension covering the Naples area; I could include Sorrento, Almafi drive, Capri, and Pompeii. I don't have to do it this year. Of course, this is all hindsight—the best sight.

In any case, I have to figure out how to survive the next two days in Sicily and four days in Rome.

Focus on Quality

This morning I did a slow yoga, very slow. I decided to focus on doing postures only once concentrating deeply on each one.

Could I "avoid" warming up doing it this way?

Can intense concentration warm-up the body?

Can it replace warm-ups?

My intuition says, why not? Try it. If it works, and there is no reason to think it can't, I can apply this principle of intense concentration all day long.

By thinking about quantity, the number of times I do each posture, I do not focus as well as when I think about quality. Quantity is about self-improvement. If I do thirty push-ups I'll be better than if I do twenty; if I do three head stands then I'll be better than if I do two. Qualitative thinking pushes my thoughts into the world of future rewards. It does not necessarily put my attention on the present. But focus on quality does. Focusing on doing one good slow push-up, one good slow head stand, one good slow posture of any kind, anchors my thoughts in the here-and-now. The quality approach is better than the quantitative one. I'd like to follow it. Now I just have to see if my ego can stand it.

What else is new? We're leaving Siracusa this morning. We'll visit Catania, then head for Taormina.

They Can Hurt You

There is no reason to deny that some of my tourists frighten me. For example, at a gut level, there is something about Marge that frightens me. After she exploded in Agrigento when the festival scheduling didn't go exactly her way, I realized why my instincts were right. Although quiet and restrained on the outside, inside she is a volcano about to erupt. She erupts when things don't go her way.

I am right to be afraid of her. She can give me a very hard time. She could potentially ruin my tour. When I talk to her, try to be friendly, I realize I am trying to keep her volcano from exploding.

Who needs the trouble she can create? Certainly not I. Therefore, it is wise that I use my wiles to calm and keep her in her place. Potential loose cannons must have their powder checked. If charm, friendliness, and wit will do it, so much the better. It is only important that I know my feelings about her and thus know and stay in charge of myself and my emotions.

Thus it is wise to fear some folks. They can hurt you.

Nightmare Masking Possible Confidence

Last day in Sicily. We're leaving for the Catania airport and will soon arrive in Rome.

If feel a tinge of sadness. But tomorrow also starts the Rome extension. Best to prepare my mind for Roman challenge.

I awoke this morning after a nightmare. After attending a concert our group and all the other concert goers went outside the theater where we were attacked by a group of Sicilian gansters. Somehow I was the leader against them. My only weapon was a stick and some kind of hidden crazy courage. I waved it wildly, threatening them as I do the dogs that bark at me along my running route. It seemed to work. They didn't hit or kill any of us. They continued to shouting and threatening us. Then I awoke.

What could this dream mean? Does it signal a new confidence, an ability to gesticulate wildly against the dogs of fear, to fake fearlessness and thus protect both myself and my group? What threat do these Sicilian gansters represent? The threat of our upcoming Roman extension?

Good questions on my last morning in Sicily.

Improving

We arrived in Rome yesterday. I have a lovely room at the Universeo Hotel.

I'm sorry now I booked Pompeii. Should I go? Or take advantage of this beautiful room, walk around the city, take a rest, and visit Pompeii next year? Visiting it next year would give me something to look forward to. In my heart, I'd like to do that. But I have a group to consider. How disappointed will it be to them if I don't go? On the other hand, how disappointed will it be to me if I do go? Ever the conflict. At the moment, I'm leaning towards going. We'll see. . .

INVENTIONS

The Larry Henry Story, by Giant Rushmore the Third

Isn't this the time for the appearance of Larry Henry, famous biblical schizophrenic? They are also known as Larry and Henry, the only schizophrenic (s) to climb Mount Sinai with Moses. Larry—or was it Henry—tried to stamp out the burning bush. Biblical writers eradicated him. Not a mention of this split mind schemer anywhere, no Greek iota of print, not even a comma in the Septuagint, Pentateuch, Hamesh Hamisha, or anything else. They burnt his blood in calves' milk, then drowned him with his golden calf in the waters of the Nile. Hard to get portage on that one. Finally, Aaron carried off the Henry part—or was it Larry?

Schizophrenics are hard to carry for burial in the Nile.

How to Furyize

There Is So Much Energy In Fury! It Is Good for Me.

Enter the dicey inner sanctums of the juicy life.

I sit straight-backed at my meditation table, talons pruned, brainstem clawed, tail in perpetual hanging. Over my chair, a cathedral slumps. Its spires beckon towards Saint Peter, chained and spread-eagled, hanging from the hot seat. Indeed, sperm starts to run. Helter skelter through a maze of Jerusalem back alleys these little buggers fly; they stop at hand-carved twat doors featuring the practice of menopausal metaphysics. Can the cravings of such madmen be justified?

Why not? Madmen in metaphysical motion are a staple in the back alleys of Jerusalem where artichokes thrive and damsels, caught in the craft of craving, swing their hips and, with raven purity, juggernaut pendulous breasts.

Such sensuality must be rewarded! And indeed it is with cravings beyond the practical. Spires of longing reach down the Cathedral of Saint Longing; free breasts swing and beat against its two-thousand year old hand-hewn doors. No doubt a former basilica. But who cares? Breasts beat then too.

As ravens crow to the Latin corbus lingo, crows tingle, and crafty ships weave their way across steep-waved seas traveling to Cretan Land where the fresh flower flow.

I am tickling my brain this morning, trying to jump-start my mind into a furulent, purulent, prurient, verbal frenzy. All because the last thing I feel like doing is doing what I'm doing. I have committed myself to writing/meditation practice, doing it every day. Indeed, it is good for me. It keeps the oils moving, the brain in order with laminations and lamentations flowing from the back seat. Lots of gas here. And the Iraq crises affecting it not a wink. Only the power of the Euphrates flowing through the back door of my brain hints at a hedonistic politic hidden behind a branch of Noah's raven.

Imagine, hedonism is related to Edenism! Well, why not? Pleasure seekers all. As the uncooked intellectual parts of morning mind reach out trying to touch a star, I labor against fatigue and truculent creplachs sliced by a star wars mind. Can I change my mood? Probably impossible.

When I returned from my fucking bird flying class, I felt utter drained. My body ached, my feet were on fire, my brain slogged through muddy waist-water fatigue. But this morning I realize I wasn't so much tired as furious! My raging energy road, instead of directing itself at my fucking dancers who never showed up, instead turned and directed itself at me! I got tired, real tired.

Why was I so fucking mad? Easy. I gave a party and hardly anyone showed up. At seven o'clock starting time two people trickled in. The trickle trickled on. By eight o'clock, five people. I wasn't mad yet, only slightly depressed. I consoled myself by thinking that if others didn't come I could end the class early and have a semi-night off.

But then, as I was about to pack up my tape player, Bob and Ruth walk in. Don't bother paying, I told them, I may end the class in ten minutes. But two minutes later, Joyce came, then Ginny, then Bill, then Ruth. Soon we had a minyan sizable class. But by then it was too late. The mental raven had flown out of my thatch-roofed brain. I had given up the class. Now I had to recrank, call up new energy, and restart. I gave it my all for the next hour. It wasn't bad. But, truth was, the damage had been done. Sadness, lowness, depression had set in. And, of course, behind that, their counterparts anger, rage, and fury.

I didn't know this until I got home aching. When I ache with fatigue it is often because, deep beneath, I am angry—nay, furious! It is good to recognize this. Recognition of my fury energize me; it chases away fatigue, aches, and pains. Yes, I ride high on it. We're friends. Better furious, angry, enraged, on fire with passionate hatred, ready to break walls, kick down doors, slam fences, throttle birds, squeeze the living juices out of every animal, mineral, and vegetable, human or crawling, crush lawn grass, stamp out ant colonies, and pour my cauldron of hate-filled energy out than to turn this volcanic energy on myself. Such reversals make me sad, soggy, downtrodden, depressed, miserable, aching, weepy, and filled with logy tortellini salad. I dance tarentella tortellini in my Medulla Dance hall filled with cheese and fettucini Alfredo, a truly high cholesterol diet of artery stuffing internal hatred that stops ups the arterial energies.

Better to furyize than to turn fury on myself and become a stuffed cabbage.

Pegasus Soars

Ancient days return. I am flying through mortuary madness with clattering speed. Black, disgusting, puss-filled, heavy, eagle-clawed storm clouds are drifting in from the African horizon; south winds are blowing in swarms of locusts; each one carries a tickling change in their air-worn spindly feet.

Many changes in the air and at sea. The provinces are in revolt. Everywhere meditation madness is on the rise. The army has been sent in, but they can't quell the disturbance. Grain riots? Perhaps. Nevertheless, grain rebellions are not easily squashed. These started out small, real small. Jack the Ripper Africanus, famous Latin purple onion-headed squadron leader from Cyrenaica, lit small fires in back dungeons. Nobody noticed. Until sixty years later. Suddenly, one day, these fire pimples burst in heat-swelling. Parsley Simmons, Il Duce, the famous sequestered Italian historian from Naples-upon-

Nipple, whose classic study on papal apocalyptic apapolepsy, Vaticanus Interruptus, writes: "Fires lit in closets burst across the Roman Empire. Flames rose, conflagrations conflagrated, granaries went up in smoke. Never trust a match."

Small rebellions soon grew into a massive Latin Africanus uprising. Followers of Jack the Ripper Tomicus fanned out across the North African grain belt, extended hands to slaves and whipping posts across the Mediterranean. Soon rebels were dipping their toes into the frigid hydrocarbons of Firth-Upon-Forth. No stopping their expansive brain-popping leg work, no restraining their chain-bursting chest busting, no holding back their upward flight.

Rebels soared upwards, scattering hoof and skinny dipper alike. They flew through the barn door with Pegasus. Old chains, bits of harness, stray pieces of hoof manure, fell from the winged horse as he flew, nay soared through the clouds and higher into the brilliance sunlight, freedom clanging behind him.

"Free, free!" bellowed Pegasus, dropping a pile of chains upon the Tripolitan slave town of Boodie-upon-Tit. "I am free—and soaring!"

He winged his way across graveyards of ancient inhibitions. Above him the sun shone. But his fire was hot beyond sunlight; the sun dropped dead as he winged passed it on his way to outer galaxies, spreading his new wings of freedom, bringing his bellowing Roar-of-Soaring to compatriots, equestrians, and kumquats alike.

Witness Sitting for Larry

Larry sits amazed at how, on this bright and elastic morning, all the purpose has been sucked out of him. Perhaps that is because it is afternoon. Nevertheless, a slow descent into hell is once again on the horizon. Dogs bark as skiffs float past, skimming the breeze from behind wrapped curtains of island cellophane. In the distance, the caterwaul bird sings its ancient song of lost bell bottoms mooring under the hot tropulent trucucal Caribbean sun.

Can a weather vane stand idly? Can a cornucopia, braked by the suns rays, bracketed by earthen vases, stand the sweltering Capricornucopian sky? Sweltering behemoth crocodiles crawl by carrying bibles in their breasts. Their dilating pupils express: All seems lost in the realm.

And yet Larry spies a crust walking on the beach. Ringed by bell bottoms, it dips purple breeches in off-shore waters. Ballantine beer drafts drift in as foggy malt-driven tuna fish drift out. Soon only a mermaid remains.

Larry waits. Still no purpose has surfaced.

Suddenly, he spies a vacant purpose form, the Ultimate Witness of He-She, sweltering under the afternoon sun. This starry-eyed Creature with thirty-two arms from the island of Brain Surgeon, sits luxuriously between a wall of legs, witnessing the phenomenal passing of physical, mental, and spiritual events.

White herrings hang from ear lobes of pristine steel as the Witness of He-She sits on its perch of alabaster viewing androgenous peaks, ups and down, in and outs, along with lives of vibrant purpose or vacant drifting existences.

All is One in Witness Life.

The Witness sits in graphic splendor.

Shouldn't Larry?

Is he not a Witness, too?

Practice Witness Sitting.

Alabaster chairs never hurt.

July–September 1998

WRITING

Conversation: Why I Love It!

I like eating out. It leads to conversation.

I hate TV and movies. They detract, distract, and destroy conversation. . . and rumination.

Letter writing is also good. That's what my journal is: a long letter to my self and a few others who listen, read, and want to know the true me.

Is E-mail a letter?

I doubt it. E-mail is often written too fast. Slow forming of words, when written by hand, fosters reflection.

Writing letters is such a lost art!

They are better when hand-written. Painting the letters of each word by hand expresses yet another aspect and nuance of soul.

Why not make all my life fiction?

Let it have many characters.

It could one central character, Sylvan Woods, who meets many characters along with path of his adventures.

Yogi Schwartz is the yogi, Jimenez, the guitarist. These characters develop over time and appear in my journal as Sylvan's "new" friends. They could include the prophet of religion and mysticism, Catskill Moses.

Dr. Lume, or a new character, Trojam, the sex fiend, would represent his mad love affairs.

As I'm writing about these characters I'm bursting into laughter! I must be onto something big!

As I laugh, my laughter is turning into tears, then back again into laughter. What is happening with these characters, how they are all coming together with my writing and my New Leaf Journal, is all so beautiful! What else can I do but laugh and cry?

I might even introduce Dr. Zoltan Fok Dansz as Sylvan's new dance teacher, or perhaps even his travel and tour consultant. Or the tour consultant might be Petko. Or both.

LIFE

Doing My Miracle Schedule: Awe and Wonder "In Public"

The forked mind springs from my tongue as the seated lad waits for his porridge.

Ah, he is a beauty this grandson of mine. And I love him.

I am amazed I can write in front of him. I can remain quiet and somewhat meditative. And this because I decided my most important job was to love him, and I could only do it if I followed my miracle schedule in their presence. I cannot give up my love for my God-finding routine or for him. But I can add him—and them—to my love and search process.

I include them in my miracle schedule by following the schedule in their presence.

Blessings in the Divine Tickle

Fear hesitates.

It balks

But does not buckle.

If the divine tickling can be sustained, what greater powers can be unfolded?

Within fear lies the ladder.

Fear hides the ladder, and the potential ascent into heavenly forms.

Although impatience, suffering, and frustration are pains in the ass, they lead directly and indirectly to knowledge, even wisdom.

Who wants suffering and frustration? Who isn't impatient with the miseries, stops and starts, and the slow muddy path to wisdom carved into the mountain of suffering? Who does not want quick answers and easy solutions?

But it doesn't work that way.

The path to self-knowledge and wisdom is slow and torturous with bends, turns, and twists in the road. There are crashes along the way, the frustrations of storms hurling tree trunks, branches, and the stones and mud slides of avalanches across your rutted road. There are no easy paths down the infinite highway of self-knowledge. You have to fight, struggle, and scream for each kernel of wisdom.

If you do not push on in spite of all difficulties, you will be buried under mud slides, smothered by the fallen tree trunks, rocks, and the debris of the annual avalanche.

Self-Abandonment Strikes Artistic Creation

I stood on the square in Cesky Krumlov and thought about the beauty, inventiveness, imagination, and wonder of Mad Shoes. I was overcome by a melancholy and nostalgia.

I will die without ever having fully appreciated Mad Shoes.

I will die without every having appreciated myself.

How sad.

What a waste.

I write excellent books, deep and powerful journal entries, play beautiful guitar pieces, create exciting folk dance classes, tours, and more. But as soon as I create them, I try as hard as I can to forget them.

This desire to forget everything good I do is most evident in my writing—king of my soul. But it also effects other creative activities as well.

Someday I hope I can surmount this obstacle.

The Wheel of Life: Spokes Are Roads to the Hub of Oneness

How can you live in the present with ideas of future and past whirling and swirling about?

Must you live on two or more levels?

I doubt it. Unity does not mix with duality or multiplicity. Unless, of course, you see them as part of a greater unity.

Ideas of past and future are like spokes of a wheel. They emanate from the God center of the wheel, the hub of oneness.

It is experienced by living in the present where ideas become spokes on the wheel, roads leading to the center of life.

Going Public as a Footnote

It's okay to go public.
But it's more important to go private.
Going public is really a footnote to going private.
Most important is to keep in touch with my in-room private prayer world where outlandish, adventurous, and soaring imagination creates mountains of vitality havoc in my mind.

Disciplines, Directions, and Purpose

If purpose, discipline, and direction are now my "goals," what forms will they take?

1. Get my body back in shape.

Return to yoga and running with a vengeance. I have about two months of training time (July 27-about September 20th)

    A. One hour of a.m. yoga with morning and afternoon warm-downs.

    B. One to one-and-a-half hours of running.

    C. Use a.m. and late p.m. training times.

    D. Go back to the 50's and 150's. Push-ups, sit-ups, squats. Aim for September 20th to accomplish this.

2. Tour business and schedule Organize it. In the process, learn about E-mail, Web, and Corel 8.

3. Guitar: Aim for a concert by September 20—or to give it on October 10th. The program: Leyenda, Alhambra, Recuerdos de Seville, Alard, Villa-Lobos Prelude No.4, Bach Bourree, Sor Sonata, Soleares, Bulerias, Misionera.

Give a "private" concert, too.

4. Writing: Keep it up.

5. Study: Thomas Moore, Joshua Abraham Heschel, novels.

6. Language: (Hebrew and the bible?)

"Beautiful" Connects My Work to the Divine

I want to put together a beautiful tours schedule!
The key here is: beautiful!
Give a beautiful concert, a beautiful weekend, a beautiful folk dance class: It is always the beautiful that connects my work to the divine.

Feeling Good

I sent a perfect fax; I did a perfect E-mail.

Mastering the computer skill that made me feel so good.

Also, my 1999 tour program is coming together. I've added tours without my personal leadership, three tours a year to Czech Republic and Slovakia, Greece, and Romania. This expansion came effortlessly after years of thinking about it.

Somehow the creation, caring, expansion, and pruning of my tour program is also making me feel good.

Soon I want to prepare my fall mailing. I also want to learn how to do mailing labels on the computer. I'll call Bill Romano to give me some lessons and see what he thinks. Another computer expansion.

The walls are falling left and right.

I whizzed through the "her face" problem in a few hours instead of a few months. So fast, so easy. That made me feel good, too.

I'm feeling so good its upset my equilibrium. How does one feel so good and survive? But I'm learning how to take it. I've also gone beyond the It's too good to be true wonder feeling and the I can't take all this goodness feeling.

That also makes me feel good.

I am calmer and more accepting of the feel-good mode.

I am even starting to talk about it in public! I am expressing it verbally. Now that is an incredible step! I've entered a new realm, a new level, a new magic circle. I stand somewhat unsteady in it–the light here is so dazzling and new. But I'll get used to it. Where else is there to go? What better place is there to be? Where else would I want to be?

The walls are crashing left and right.

And this with a little help and loving acceptance from my friends.

The wet blanket is off. They are helping me give it the final shove out the window.

The Feeling-Good Paradox: Waves of the Soul

Trying to hold on to feeling good may be an unbalanced approach. That's why so often feeling good is followed by tears and mourning.

Tears and mourning are, paradoxically, part of feeling good. They are the other half, the shadow side of the sun.

Feeling-good, tears of both joy and sorrow, are the waves of the soul.

Thus, feeling-good is only one of the high points in the vast and varied expanse of the soul.

Forgetting Through Videos

Well, we're on the farm. I'm in a never again mode.

Woke up this morning minus my God connection. I lost it last night watching videos of Saturday Night Live. And this, even though Robin Williams was great. It's something about the nature of videos, movies, TV etc. I leave them feeling like I have lost something. Robbed and cheated. Upon reflection it is easy to see what I have lost. It is my imagination. And with it my God connection. Those electronic mediums are too overwhelming. They provide sight, sound, and a hypnotic buzz. After a few minutes of watching them I am in their clutches with no time for reflection. When their event is over I have forgotten who I am.

Do these mediums affect anyone else that way? Except for the book Four Arguments Against Television I've never heard of it before.

In any case, I've got to move back to my Imagination. By writing this morning I am starting. Imagination—the God connection mantra needs constant reminding and remembering.

Awe Challenge

What fun to fly on the computer and see my progress! I'm slowly mastering strokes and keys. I'm beginning to feel comfortable with it; I'm even beginning to feel I can figure things out myself! Computer panic is fading.

The only negative is the pain in eyes and shoulders. Those are the nail points on the cross of computer progress. Guitar is rolling, too. Nevertheless, I need new challenges. Every day an awe challenge.

This morning my direction seems to be reclaiming my body. This temple of shit is falling apart. I ache in every joint. As my mind expands, the aching painful process of its growth is reflected in my expanding body growth pains. My shoulders, eyes, and knee pains are pains of growth, too.

Pain is the dark side of growth coming up strong. It is the Marquis de Sade in growth clothing.

It Is a Wonder: No Wonder I Can't Believe It

What I've just discovered about myself through writing, about tours, awe, must, fighting, and old versus new neighborhood, is so extraordinary I can hardly believe it. Did I write that? Who told me that? Who is directing this right writing hand, anyway? Who is directing my brain? Who is the conductor of this orchestra?

The fact that I have made these discoveries is, in itself, awesome. A miracle and miraculous experience! Do I dare believe it, remember it, act upon it?

This is an experience of my mind being directed by a higher hand. If I dare to look at it, it is indeed frightening. Actually, it scares the shit out of me. But isn't that what awe is all about?

This kind of visionary experience makes me tremble to the depths of my soul. I am sitting on top of a volcano. It just rumbled. An earthquake followed. Who am I compared to an earthquake? Small. No comparison. Not much. Who is this insignificant ego-I trying to stand up to the mighty volcanic powers , the Vulcan Hephaestus forces of the awe-stricken, wonder-filled, bashing, crushing, destroying, remolding, recreating, recreational forces of the universe.

Well, that's what an awesome experience is. It shakes and shatters you to your foundations. No wonder I resist it even as I desire it. No wonder, when it takes place, I can't believe it. But there it is again in the sentence: the wonder and disbelief of the phrase itself: No wonder I can't believe it.

The Small Jim Gold Self

Naturally, my small Jim Gold self does not believe all the brilliant ideas and realizations I've been writing down.

Why should it? How can it? It is, by its nature, too small.

These awe-filled experiences are directed by higher forces. The small Jim Gold self is merely the instrument through which the work is accomplished. It does the work because it is a good boy and does what it is told. But it doesn't understand, accept, or believe it.

Well, so be it. That is the nature of small life on this earth.

The entire war, the must and fight, the struggles, ups, and downs, go on in your imagination.

You even believe, imagine, that the world itself is outside you.

The to do things are not the foundation. They are secondary. But they must connect to the foundation.

What is the foundation?

It is the vision of awe and wonder.

Visionary View from the Deck

I sit in Provincetown after seeing my uncle Jim Lechay's exhibition in the Berta Walker gallery.

A deep sense of sadness and melancholy invades my being. I remember Ma, Private Ryan. . .

More so it is Jim as an artistic legacy. . .and more so, it is a deep love and longing and melancholy and appreciation and love for the glory of. . . myself!

Yes, who do I miss most? Myself!

True, I have some loses, but not too bad. I've lost Jim as my mentor; I've lost Ma as a mentor; I've lost my belief in, need for, and love of guides. Ma, Jim, guides, all gone.

The only one left is my glorious guitar-flowing, write-flowing, yoga sprouting self.

I am sprouting and I love it! I can't think of anything better to do than travel down the front roads and back alleys of my art.

What is my art?

Kaleidoscopic.

Color patterns in my miracle schedule. But more than a schedule it's now a life style. A life style built on miracles.

The miracle of my guitar flow. . . and yoga flow. . .

Basically, I just love living in my head! What scenery and accommodations! Nothing beats it. And the visionary view from the deck is glorious!

What was my sadness, loss, and melancholy about? Strangely, because I had to face the fact that I was gloriously happy! Ecstasy is a mild word to express it. That's because it is beyond that. Basically, the sun is bursting inside me!

It's a metamorphosis, the cockroach is changing into a glorious, bursting sun!

Dawn and dawning. Learning how to live in the land of glory.
Sure Private Ryan, we'll all die someday.
But fuck it! It's just a temporary state, anyway.

I'm Rich!

The sugar plum pepperpusses are jumping tonight. Plastic petals paint dizzying crossbeams on light steel.

My coffee mate is singing.

The grand entry has been made. Crossing the bridge. Ayeiii, I'm in a New Land. New Found Land. I'm a flow meister now! Yes! And thank God for that! He's the one who's peppered my pinions.

How else can I fly on eagle wings? The black eagle balancing precariously on the cliffs of Meteora is the same yoga as the black guitarist carried, flying on eagle wings to the land of Him. Flowing with milk and honey on his wings. Flying with miracle based cellulose forming the protoplasm of enchantment.

Luck, luck, lucky me! My fortune and five tune has been made! I'm rich! Oh yes, at last, I'm rich! No money, of course. But rich in flow. I've received (what does kabbalah mean in Hebrew but to receive) a wealth of flow beyond my wildest dreams!

Never in my life could I have imagined, dreamed, or conceived of such riches. But, yes. Now they are mine! Where else is there to go? I am home—and everywhere at the same time.

Everywhere is home and home is everywhere. My head is in all things and vice versa. Glory be! The peepod has burst!

Lesbians

We were sitting in a restaurant in Provincetown when three good-looking, macho young men walked in and sat down at the table opposite us. I said, "I wonder if those guys are lesbians in drag."

Mike said, "Jim, you're reaching. Don't try so hard. Not everything can be a joke."

I answered, "I'm not trying at all. It bubbles up naturally."

But inside I sizzled. What a humorless bore this guy is, I thought. This is exactly what I mean when I say I need some new friends. I didn't say anything more to him because I didn't know what more to say.

But it bothered me for the rest of the night. I told Jutka about it. She agreed with Mike. She's a humorless bore, too. Finally, about eleven p.m. I took a walk and figured it out.

The best thing to say would have been: Not everyone can enjoy my imagination and sense of humor as much as I can.

I'll say it next time.

The whole thing is part of my endless attempt at bringing my imagination, sense of humor, wit, and enthusiasm public. I'm not defensive or defending it; rather, I'm taking a stand, taking my place.

Sure Mike made me mad. But giving in to this kind of shit is over. I'm brimming with defiant rage. But I'm returning from Cape Cod with both guns blazing.

Defiant?

Hell, I'm beyond defiant!

The Good and Beautiful Parts of Ma

I wonder is Russian, St. Petersburg, and Ma is a new direction. To study Russian as a language of Ma: mother Russia, love of Ma, dependency and neediness, a Ma Revolution.

Return to Russian? Hmm. For next year? Hmm. Russian is my heritage, my hermitage, my St. Petersburg return trip to the homeland of assimilated communistic Russian Jews—the good and beautiful dream of the Marxist communist, Jewish, messianic, secular apotheosis of the heaven on earth communist Jewish beautiful state dream. The good and beautiful part of the Ma dream with its love and passion for music, the arts, intellect, and culture.

Is this the initiation, the beginning of the "Love Ma And All The Good Things She Stands For" era?

Could be. At least the door is opening.

I won't forget the bad, but it may recede.

Whatever sadness I feel here has been controlled, promoted, and pushed by Mr. Should, his partner, Mr. Must, and their henchman, Mr. Either/Or.

Why not make myself master of my own destiny? Instead of doing what they want, why not do what I want.

Why not embrace my true heros, the family I love so well, Mr. And Mrs. Paradox (née Ambiguity) and their children, Larry Conflict, Priscilla Opposite, and Morty the Mess.

PERFORMANCE

The Beginning of My New Life

Yesterday, in the late afternoon, I went to a classical guitar concert. To my surprise, the guitarist was a woman, Milada Karezova. She gave an excellent performance.

The day before, in the late afternoon, I went to a concert by a string ensemble. Their program included a performance of the Seasons by Vivaldi. The musicians were excellent, the solo violinist, superb.

But the most surprising thing about both these concerts was my reaction to them. Basically, I had no reaction. I heard the superb violinist, watched my mind drift off into space, went into a deep state of relaxation, slept beautifully during parts of the Seasons. At the end of the performance I walked out relaxed.

But I was puzzled, too.

Why did I have no affect? Why did this concert not effect me? Usually I cry during such performances or soar into the heavens of wonder about my life. This time nothing happened. I left in a "normal" state.

The same was true of the classical guitar concert. Added to this was my amazing lack of jealousy. The guitarist played beautifully. She had an excellent technique, especially a relaxed and beautiful right hand technique. She played Leyenda flawlessly with a wonderful arpeggio flow. In the past, I would walk out of such a concert sick with jealousy, wishing I could have such superlative technical abilities, wishing I was adequate enough to give such a fine concert and be so comfortable in my playing ability. I would also wish for other things but I forget what they were. Attending a classical guitar concert usually made me sick with jealousy as I was forced to face, once again, all my guitar playing inadequacies.

But this time I felt no jealousy, inadequacy, no wishing to be someone else, no flights of fantasy or imagination. I even fell asleep when she played the Villa-Lobos Prelude Number One.

What do these new feelings mean? Or rather, what do these lack of old feelings mean?

Also, during the evening of the first concert I reached the 98% solution. Last evening after the second concert, I reached the 99% solution. That's after starting at zero one year ago. Doesn't this rising percentage rate point to a rising personal development? And this especially in the field of rewards.

Yes, it is easy to give to others. It is even harder to receive what others are giving to you.

It has been difficult to receive my rewards. I've always felt I have to improve myself first, that I must push to get better and better so that, at some future date, I'll be worthy of accepting that "better person" award.

Reward myself? You must be kidding. Accept a reward from others? Ridiculous. As a good actor, I might smile and graciously accept such awards in public, but inwardly, a small voice would always whisper, "You are not yet worthy."

That voice is fading. I would love putting it in the past perfect tense by saying it has faded. That has not happened. . . yet.

During this tour I've reached the 98-99 percent level.

Perhaps my reactions—or lack of reactions, to the concerts, reflect this new state. Instead of punishing myself by thinking what an inadequate guitarist I am, how much I still need to improve, and how I am still not worthy, I am now beginning to say, yes!

Yes, I'll accept my award now!

Yes, I'll accept my reward now!

Yes, I've done a good job. I deserve my reward. Even better than "deserve" is "Yes!"

It's a big jump from the "No!" and "Never!" of last year.

I don't know where will this lead. But on this tour, new pathways have been carved. This morning, in spite of my tours delicious aspects, I'm ready to return to America.

I'm looking forward to beginning my new life.

Guitar

A naily right index finger sound points to a masculine heart.

A soft, sweet, mellow right index finger sound points to a feminine heart.

That's why I resisted Segovia's sound. Too soft, too sweet and feminine. I wanted something rougher, tougher, more masculine and naily. That's why I like Julian Bream's sound.

Daring

Daring encompasses missing the notes—even forgetting them. It is part of masculine, naily, pine-needle Bourree playing.

Daring also encompasses looking backwards, sifting through the graveyard in awe and wonder, reading the tombstones headlines, and luxuriating in former deeds and energy bursts.

I love this naily, strong, powerful right index finger. It is so masculine, forceful, and macho!

I am getting more comfortable with its power.

More comfortable with the naily power of my right index finger.

More comfortable with the power of my masculinity.

Could my nay right index finger secretly be my God connection finger?

Underneath the hard, nay sound resides great beauty.

This also means that masculine, hard, tough, as well as feminine, soft, yielding, smooth, are paths to God, connecting links to the Imagination. That is why it has taken so long to find it. It is not merely a guitar playing and relaxation technique; it is a pathway to God.

And this, since the nay right index finger points to the heart.

Thus it is the meditation finger.

The Awe-dience

It is time to start using the audience. What does using mean?

It means using their reactions or lack of reaction as a means of inspiration. Somehow, as I play or read for them, I have to be both inner and outer directed.

Performing before an audience creates a sense of awe. It's like falling into the abyss. What will their reaction be? Always different, always a question.

When I perform for them it creates a sense of dread. As this dread twists between excitement and panic, I can faintly feel a creeping sense of awe and wonder. How did I get into this mess? What am I doing here? Where will this lead? How will I get out of this alive? What a frightening and magnificent creation is our universe! Why am I a part of it? Good questions for a performer.

It is good for me to perform, to put myself in such a vulnerable position, even though it usually scares the shit out of me. But isn't that part of awe? How awesome to see how fast all my ship runs out, to stand at the edge of the cliff and peer into the abyss of infinity.

That is the nature of performing, of my audience relationship, of all relationships, even the one to the world at large.

Nevertheless, I can't go around all day in a state of awe. Too exhausting. I need rest periods, long ones. States of awe are high points. They are the stars, nay, the sun, awesome, terrifying, and frying the brain as it points the way to the fiery land of Imagination, the awesome God connection.

What does this mean in terms of personal direction?

It means more public performances, more meetings with the audience, placements before the awe-dience. It means more concerts and public readings. It means a new look at New Leaf, rereading it with the audience in mind. This is the birth of a new public direction.

But I no longer need an audience to prove or improve myself. I need it to scare myself, scare the shit out of me, empty my bowels and bladder and fill the vacuum with wonder.

I want to create the conditions in which that can flourish, to bring

One-der into my life.

In this sense, an awe-dience can be One-derful.

Showing my deformities in public is a mitzvah. It makes others feel better and more accepting of their deformities.

I'm controlling and affecting my right index finger relaxation through my stomach muscles. Could this be an aspect of stomach, solar plexus, chakra power in use? It is power through the stomach, the solar plexus chakra. Been avoiding this one for years, too.

The power of holding lots of women in my stomach, lots of contrary ideas, lots of conflicting values and beliefs. Can I stomach it? Can I hold such variety in my stomach? Do I have the power? Is there even a choice? Anyway, I'm at that border.

Yesterday my old, torn, shattered guitar sleeve finally fell apart. I replaced it by cutting off a new sleeve from my silk shirt. Kabbalistically speaking, what does this mean? It came with the birth of "my interpretation only, please! Is it a silk new guitar sleeve for the new silk-like playing of Mr. Somebody Else?

I just flew through Leyenda and Alard. God, what fun to fly on the guitar! Twenty, thirty, forty years of practice—it was all worth it!

This is running wild on the lawn of guitar!

The beginning of Leyenda, and perhaps the rest of it, is kabbalah on the guitar. An artist is truly a mystic with skill.

BUSINESS

For-The-Joy-of-It Tour Experience Approach: Combining Travel and Love

I love is the soul flying through space, drifting into the belly, soft and round; it is fertile fields shifting with melancholy, driving rain sleeting the streets, washing windows, and pricking the drifting remnants of a star smashed on ice.

Our first day in Slovakia speaks of innumerable liaisons through Slovak suns, lifting dull norms, undressing before a multitude of Slovak serpents slithering through Slovak streets pushing their carts over newly painted municipal poem-buildings of Kosice.

Yes, such poetry bespeaks of our first trip to this capital of Eastern Slovakia. Although, at first glance upon arrival, Kosice appeared like a shithole lost in nuclear waste. And this, coupled with my afternoon wandering down an desolate Kosice street. It brought my usual first-day tour question to mind: "Why am I here?".

But on second viewing, great inner beauty appeared.

Our meeting at the airport with Jan Pumpr of Dvorana, the Czech agency of Jitka Bonusova with whom I work, and Jan's chance meeting with a dance friend in our Centrum Hotel lobby followed by a subsequent invitation to visit a rehearsal of his friend's Jahodna Slovak folk dance troupe, made our first evening in Slovakia a smash hit.

What a night! Another miracle manufactured out of nothing. Our exhausted dancers returned to their hotel rooms with smiles on their sleepy, hollow-eyed, jet-lagged faces.

It raised the question: how can I not return to the Czech Republic and Slovakia next year? I have such excellent contacts, itinerary, and events. The tour is a true winner. The only problem is, as usual, how to get customers to fill the bus traveling through this beautiful program.

Shouldn't all my dancers come on this incredible tour? Indeed, they should. It should be required for every folk dancers. How the fuck can they dance if they have not had this life-changing tour experience? Without it their vision remains shallow and superficial, even approaching the "Why bother? stage.

How to I communicate my enthusiasm? How can I transmit my belief in the mystical quality of these tours?

I don't know... yet. Yes, I'll add an optimistic "yet."

If I'm zeroing in on a for-the-joy-of-it life, perhaps I can incorporate a for-the-joy-of-it tour approach.

I like it: Touring for-the-joy-of-it. What better reason to tour?

What better reason for coming on one of my tours? A folk tour where serendipities of magnificent proportions occur and the mystical glow of folk dance fires burn Mosaic bushes before Sinitic eyes.

As I sat in the amphitheater in Helpa watching the incredible folk dancers and singers from central Slovakia including the fabulous group from East Slovakia, Zeleziar, many polyphonic, multifaceted thoughts and directions came to mind:

1. Back to languages! If I want to find a reason to run tours, an inspiration that will last all year long and for many years to come, I must return to the study of languages. They are my central core of study and inspiration. I realized it again when I bought my Slovakia T-shirts from a Hungarian in Helpa. First, he spoke to me in Slovak. Then, when he saw how I could not understand him he asked if I spoke German or Hungarian. I answered "Igen" (Yes in Hungarian.) As I dug out old quasi-forgotten words from the antiquated computer memory of my former Hungarian brain, I formed them on my lips and remembered the pleasure I always felt speaking the marvelous magyar tongue so full of paprikash and fire.

Learning and practicing languages on the local population has always been one of my central touring pleasures. Hungarian, Czech, Slovak, Bulgarian, Russian, Greek, Turkish, Arabic, Hebrew, Italian, French, Spanish, Portuguese, even Georgian and Armenia—I've tried them all. True, I can't speaking any of them. But who cares? I love them. They inspire me. That's enough.

2. My tours must go where the folklore is alive! They are, after all, folk tours. Folklore, especially folk dance, is what I love. Eastern Europe has the most developed and sophisticated folklore. Plus it is alive, hidden in "unknown" countries like Bulgaria, Slovakia, the back woods of Bohemia and Moravia, Romania, or along the less travelled paths of "known" countries like Greece, Turkey, Israel, Italy etc.

These were some of my basic thoughts. Now some new ones:

I've spent thousands of dollars and many years of travel in order to find the correct spelling and meaning of a folk dance from the central Slovak village of Helpa that we, in America call, Horehronsky Cardas. Slovaks call it To Ta Helpa. Hore means up or upper; Hron is the name of a river; sky is an adjectival ending for a masculine noun. Thus Horehronsky Cardas (write an inverted carrot or hacek over the c and s in cardas) means csardas from the upper Hron. Lower Hron would be called dolny Hron.

Also the sign on my T-shirt: *Horehronske Oslavy* means: *Horehronske*—djectival form for a plural ending; *oslavy*—east (a "singular" noun that uses a plural form).

Rewards, Here We Come!

We're leaving for the Prague airport in a few hours. I feel sad. Anxious, too. What will my "new life" in America bring?

Yesterday I was hit by the old travel anxiety block-buster. It's the "I hate to leave the safe haven of home" feeling. Over the past two weeks Slovakia and the Czech Republic have become my home. After the initial arrival in Kosice I've settled in. Slowly jet lag ended; the tour came together; I became comfortable with our problems and lack of problems. Gabriela guided us; Vladimir drove us; Jitka designed a fine program. I oversaw it all. I was in charge, watching to see that my tour plans were carried out. I carried the weight of this responsibility on both a conscious and unconscious level. The weight lessened slightly as the tour came together, but, in reality, it never ended, even during the last two days when my tourists had free time. Even though on the surface it may have looked like I was doing nothing, I was doing mucho. Only my work was invisible. The ignorant outsider might see an easy going tour leader enjoying himself on his tour. The insider, my "sidekick" and me, see a never-ending thought process going on inside my brain. Motion, growth' decay, future plans, the birth and casting aside of new ideas. This inner movement, reflecting in outer movement is. . . work! Never-ending work.

I am constantly working. No wonder I want rewards.

Rewards, here we come! I'm off to America.

Folk Dance Therapy Ad

Do you feel a stiffness in your thoughts?
(Do you find your thoughts turning stiff?)
Do you suffer from arthritis of the brain?
Then you suffer from the new (psychological) disease most recently listed in the DSM4 manual: *choreophobia*.

Choreophobia (fear of dancing) usually strikes at an early age but is often not recognized by either parents, teachers, principles, life guards, or school boards. It is an insidious disease, subtly and slowly eating away at the dance) joints until the sufferer or sufferant can barely dance a Greek folk dance (syrtos) or an Israeli or Romanian Hora. In 1998, choreophobia was voted (dance) disease of the year by the United Dance Association of Northern Jersey.

Do you suffer from choreophobia? Do you suffer from claustrophobia, depression, or schizophrenia? Do you suffer from choreoschizophrenia? (Do you find yourself dancing with a partner when there is none?) Do you suffer from leg abuse or foot abuse? Are you a podia-abuser? An ankle misuser?

Join our folk dance therapy group. We will never threaten you by asking you to dance or even teaching you. We simply stand in a circle and talk about how we feel about dances and dancing. The group is led by Dr. Jim Gold (have picture of me teaching folk dancing on a dark night..a la Dr. Fok.

INVENTIONS

Tchai-kovsky Loved Tea!

I am at the bottom where pit and pauper meet. I descend deep into the pit of darkness, alone, lonely, dark, dreary, fag and fig bottoms scraping the distance in an inner sanctuary of lust and longing and deep caterpillars digging in earthen earth works.

Oh, what kind of release is the deep cannon? Sputtering, it configures a confuming conflagration of earthly turnips and slantwise broccoli and bacon strips, born naked across the horizon with star scattered in the distance. Can an earthworm hug a tree? And can a butterfly, lost in the Flood among Noah's ark and arch-descendants every hope for an elevation beyond Mount Ararat?

Questions of somnambulance. My, my, how the hair trigger of an eyelash burns deep! Who could say that a bath of water words would ever cleanse the bath line of a tub? Well, fear not. I am moving off the mark.

My abandonment lies deep down and across and into the abyss. I hover above the infinity clouds, looking for a lining bent in silver. But I have given up hope. Life in the abyss is better that way. No one can save me today. Oh, I can call the Valerie girls or the Pectopod wings or the Dripping Sisters, or even the cumquats of steel twats. All would, no doubt, answer my call, whisper sweet dumplings into my telephone ear, take a dumpling out to lunch, find a Chinese sandwich in the Ridge Wooded areas of Brooklyn or the Bronx, sing a song between peanut butter sandwiches or walk a hot dog on Camb Ridge. But none would satisfy the deeply sliced rye bread wounds bounced through my gut by the Great Abandonment Issue and the iron bound monster hurtling down the tracks of Reject Train.

No, it's no fun being rejected, ejected, projected, or any other jects. Jections of any sort belong to the nomadic Madagascar Madness baking tribe of Henry the Eighth, grand king of the English Cutlery Renaissance. Here was a wench of a man, born to the steel, bound and proud of his earthworm lineage, a man bent by the will of steal and the won't of iron. Not a farthing ever specked his bottom. His mother, so proud of him! She reached deep into his tit and pulled out a sugar plum fairy to star in each Tchaikovsky dance of the Walnut Queens.

Tchai-kovsky, there was a man who loved tea!

GOD

God And Creativity

God is the Creator. Creativity is His tool, His method. All creativity leads to God.

God is creativity.

He is not only in my imagination and fantasy but is my imagination and fantasy.

What is the difference between in and is?

On a lower level, in describes a means to an end, a way, a bridge.

Is means you have arrived, you are there.

But on the deepest level, in and is are the same.

On the deepest level, God in creativity and God is creativity are the same.

But hey, I'm talking about God here. I know He is real. Why? Because I know the experience of creativity; know its fire and lightening; I know the calm, beauty, beatitude, and stillness that comes after its explosion; I know the oneness of vision that comes during the creative process; I know the peace and deep happiness that comes when you reflect on this stillness.

The stillness is God resting on the seventh day.

It is my personal shabbat.

In the stillness, I feel like God witnessing the world in its splendor, the world I created.

Yes, I said, I am the Creator. I am God.

Is this hubris? Is it idol worship?

I was created in God's image. The image contains the spark of creation, the spark of God. In that spark lives the Holy Fire igniting, lighting, and uniting the universe. It is that spark I am speaking to, acknowledging, when I say I am the Creator. I am God.

I radiate my God connection.

I have the ability to radiate my God connection.

I have charisma.

Charisma is the ability to radiate your God connection.

That's why I'm a good entertainer, folk dance teacher etc. In those public areas I am able to radiate the charismata of the Higher Forces.

The periodic weakness and trembling in my arms and legs is my defensive wall against the rising power of the Power. It is my dam against the oceanic transcendental tidal wave that is about to sweep over me and wash away the remnants of my old neighborhood.

I Fall into the Loving Arms of Imagination

If Imagination is my God connection then I fall, not into the abyss of insecurity, but rather into a net of support.

Forgetting

After I organized my day I suddenly felt sad.

Where did this sadness come from?

Perhaps, by focusing only on organization I forgot my God connection.

Judaism is about remembering the God connection.

Sadness is caused by forgetting my God connection. This is a definite bug in my divine web site.

Mine is a distraction and forgetting problem.

Do yoga, teach folk dancing, write my brochure, all while focusing on the God connection.

Through Shoulder and Knee

My shoulders ache from too much computer, my knees ache from folk dancing and yoga standing posture overuse. My body feels like its falling apart.

Yes, my mind and body are being rearranged.

How is this taking place?

On the highest level—or most profound—I'm preparing to see Imagination in everything and everywhere.

On the lower earthly plane, I am preparing next year's tours and schedule, learning new computer techniques and generally, through therapy and love, rearranging my attitude toward the world.

I have had wonderful insights, and this has lead to amazing insights and this has led to amazing developments. My body is aching because of them.

Can the pains in my body be similar to the pain of anxiety? Absolutely. It has to be.

Yesterday I discovered that anxiety is awe in disguise.

Thus the physical pains in my knees, shoulders, and cut foot must also be awe in disguise.

Is this possible? Can a block be awe in disguise? Can a cloud be the sun in disguise?

On the deepest kabbalistic level, yet. All things are one; all things are One. But on the terrestrial level, the analytical mental level of division, things fall into separate categories, pains and pleasures, good and bad, etc. On this level, my pains separate me from my higher self and hide my God connection. But through the energy my pain gives me, the thought rays that go into combating and handling it, I can find my God connection. Thus, somehow I must use the energy of pain, the energy my pain creates, to heighten my imagination and connect me to my Imagination connection.

How is this done? Ah, that is the question.

But first comes the realization. Answers will come later.

Judaism: The Study of Awe

What does this have to do with my aching shoulders and knees?
Pain creates fright and awe.
Fright is the lower level, awe the higher level.
Both exist in pain.
Look deeply into it to find the link;
The awe of pain is the God connection.

October–December 1998

WRITING

The Huge Play Pen

I should just write and write and write; it makes me feel so good! Writing chases away the pain.

I read from Inspired Talks by Vivekananda. What a splendid philosopher and yogi! He wrote: ". . .all our struggles are but play in God's eyes. This world is all for play and only amuses God; nothing in it can make God angry."

I sure need those words this morning! They certainly beat God's expulsion of Adam and Eve from the Garden of Eden just because they ate the wrong fruit. Now's there's an angry God. Of course, I could say man created an angry God and wrote Him into the bible. And that's probably true. Perhaps this angry God is simply a lower level version of the true unnameable God who is incomprehensible, a total mystery. And why is He laughing? Why is He amused by the world He created? That is a total mystery, too. But I like it. I want to be part of that laughing, amusing mystery. Just like God, I want the perspective to step away and view the creations of my mind, look at the torturous relationships, painful expectations, unfulfilled hopes, and see them all as mere amusements, mental playthings in the illusory world of Maya. Like a huge child, I create them, destroy them, then move on to something else. Ah, how I love that idea of the world as a huge playpen!

My journal as a huge playpen

My relationships as a huge play pen

My fears, worries, hopes, prayers, and expectations, all as passing players in my huge playpen. What an amusing way to look at the world! What a wonderful attitude! And this, especially because it is true!

Judgements

It's so hard to judge whether my writing is good or not.

If I'm in the right mood, it's good. If I'm in the wrong mood, it's bad.

Perhaps may be simply impossible for me to judge my work.

And I can't put my complete faith in others since their judgements are subject to the same fickleness as my own.

I have to plough ahead, editing, collecting, and organizing my writing without judgements.

How is this done?

LANGUAGES

Language Is the Path into My Soul: Follow It!

I have turned my tours into mass productions instead of opportunities to study. That was their original purpose.

(The other was to make money. Ha!)

What happened?

First, my desire to make money overshadowed my original purpose.

Second, I have "solved" or "resolved" the money problem by dealing with and giving up my fears of having no money.)

Third, I have been overwhelmed by too many tours, too many languages, too many cultures etc. I'm too scattered. I can't see a way out of the scatter.

Nevertheless, the prime purpose of my tours is: to give me an opportunity, motivation, and inspiration to study.

To study what?

Language and culture. . . But mostly language.

What happened? Why have I lost my way?

Maybe I haven't; maybe I've just put my tour path on hold; maybe I'm getting ready to return to its original purpose.

What is more important, language or culture? Of course, language is part of culture and vice versa. Nevertheless, language is closest to my soul. It has the sound of history, the tone of the culture.

Therefore, the study of language is my most basic inspirational. This study is above money making. Money will come "by itself" if I

follow the right path. But first, I must believe in my path.
Language is the path into my soul.
Follow it!

LIFE

It Is as Simple as That!

Total Reversal of the Abandonment and Rejection Concept

Abandonment, rejection, failure, stage fright, the black hole: all are reflections, other terms, really, for abandonment.

Now here's the killer: rather than my mother abandoning and rejecting me whenever I stood up, suppose it was me who abandoned and rejected her! Suppose abandoning and rejecting her was my way of standing up. Suppose I projected my abandonment and rejection of her onto her, so that, in my mind, it looked as if she was abandoning me!

And this life style of projected abandonment and rejection was projected onto others in the outside world. That means that I decided to abandon and reject them in order to do my thing; in order to protect it. I said to myself, imagined that they were rejecting and abandoning me. Thus, by saying this, I "gave myself more space." In this space that I granted myself I was now free to create even more things, to do my thing even more.

Thus, by abandoning and rejecting others, I protected the center of my creativity, that marvelous little room in my imagination.

If it is true that one imagines one's life into existence, then I have created a topsy turvy view: To reiterate: it was that others abandon and reject me when I stand up for myself.

The "new" view, born today, is that I abandon and reject others in order to stand up for myself and protect my creativity.

Aside from being the exact opposite of everything I have ever learned or thought, what is the difference between these two views?

The former puts all power in the hands of others.

The latter puts all power in my hands.

And I mean all!

Quite a difference!

Imagine, even two-year-old me had the power to abandon my mother, to reject her because she was not paying attention to my needs. Rather than give in and say I'm worthless (in Ma's eyes since she wouldn't recognize and appreciate my unique ways of doing things, my gifts, talents, personality etc.) I, in two-year-old fashion, screamed "Fuck you! You can't treat me this way! I'm taking control of the situation. I'm exerting the only power I have: the power to reject and abandon your view of me! I'm creating my own space, my own room where I can live independent and free, where I can be my own creative person unhindered by your narrow view of me, an inner chamber protected from your crushing heel. Even though I am only two-years-old you cannot mold and change me against my will! I will stand up to you even at two-years old! I will be me in spite of everything, and this, even if the outside world around me crashes down!"

This is a powerful two-year-old talking! This is a discovery, or rather a rediscovery, of the two-year-old me.

And why not? Why shouldn't a two-year-old have such incredible power! The two-year-old, in spite of his dependency, still lives in the powerful room of his imagination. That room is born with him. Nothing can destroy it except a voluntary act of self-destruction.

Thus did I stand up for myself by abandoning and rejecting the domination of others.

What a startling reversal of the power concept! This view gives me all the power! And I mean all! And this, because life is created and exists solely in the imagination! Yes, I said solely! That "solely" is again a statement of utter strength.

I am happily taking complete responsibility for my rejection and abandonment of others. It was certainly the way to go. (I say "was" because I am stronger now. I may no longer need this view.) But is was certainly the way to go. I secretly loved it. But I could never admit it or even see it.

The fact that I can see it now points to a powerful shift, a powerful example of emerging strength.

I run the world—my world. It is as simple as that! I create my mourning, sadness, anger, and madness; I create my alienation, dependency, and rage; I create my frustrations, wild visions, and beauty. I am in charge, not only of my room, but also of my vision of the outside world.

It is as simple as that!

This puts all the power in my hands. And I mean all!

I Am My Imagination

My life has been blasted out of the sky this month.

So what else is new?

Since all sadness, happiness, madness, abandonment, rejection, and stage fright is created in my imagination, and by me, this means I am the driver, the captain of my ship. There is absolutely no one else. Is this solipsism? You betcha!

It means I am in control, total control of my imagination. Of course, spontaneous combustion takes place. Thus the type of control I have is an out-of-control control. But it is control, nevertheless.

Control is power—and military success.

Where does all this leave me this morning?

Sad, distant, and somewhat dazed. On the one hand, it still feels like I've lost my loves and with them, all my zip and drive. On the other hand, if I am in charge of my imagination, this loss of loves is an imagined loss. This means I am not sinking as low as I usually do. I am "somewhat" sad instead of totally miserable. Although I am still floating in the abyss I have not free-fallen into it. The fact that I have not hit bottom , that I am hovering "somewhat" above the pit, dangling "slightly" above the black hole, accounts for why I am dazed. It is a new place for me.

I have moved away from the extremes.

Does this mean instead of ecstasy I will have to "settle" for enjoyment? And, if I do, is that so bad? It may be a more peaceful, calm, and even rewarding state. I may even be able to maintain it.

My past ecstasies have usually been followed by crashing downs. Up and down, heaven and hell, ecstasy and depression; I have lived in the realm of these "exciting" extremes. I've always pushed the envelop.

The question now emerges: why have I done this? Why have I

wanted to put myself in such and out-of-control state? Why do I want to burn in ecstasy and crash in shit? Is this a form of self-punishment at its best?

It could be that I needed these extremes, needed to push the envelop in order to discover who I was. And, I discovered it: I am my imagination! Period. I am the abandoner, not the abandoned; the rejector, not the rejectee; the captain, not the slave. I even create, in an exciting drama, the extremes of ecstasy and depression, in order to stimulate myself. I even create my women.

Sure, there may be an "outside reality" but I sure can't see it. I hardly understand the concept. "Outside reality?" What's that? I can't conceive of it. When people say, "Get real. Be realistic. There's a reality out there to contend with, etc." I hardly know what they're talking about. Plus, I resent them. Who are they to say these things? Why are they so pompous? In fact, why are they so ignorant? And why do they push their ignorance on me? Just because their imaginations are buried in a swamp and they have forgotten or never knew who they are is no reason to burden me with their high-refuse tonnage. Or maybe their actions demonstrate the nature of ignorance. In any case, I am my imagination. We'll leave it at that for today.

>   EXTREMES AND THE LIMITLESS
>   Why do people want and go to extremes?
>   In order to discover the limits.
>   Why do they want to discover the limits?
>   In order to discover the limitless.
>   Where is the limitless?
>   It is in you.
>   When you discover the limitless in your self
>   The extremes become boring.
>   You no longer need them.

I Love Trauma (I Hate It, Too!)

Crayton Rowe said: "Precocity comes from trauma, early trauma." I like that. It shows the positive aspect of trauma.

I have no one to turn to but myself. If so, what is there to improve? And why should I bother improving on anything?

But I like the road to improvement; I like the illusion of progressing towards a higher goal. It motivates me and gives me pleasure.

Pleasure? Why not aim higher? Why shouldn't I have ecstasy? Why take its incredible high away from me? Can mere "enjoyment" ever really be a substitute? Enjoyment is a good way to see the earth; but ecstasy is the only way to see God! Sure, I may get depressed during the down part of the cycle, but so what? The joy-driven, heaven-inspired goal is worth it.

Don't take my ecstasy away! I want it! I'll take it along with doses of depression. The "even state" of "enjoyment," like candy after a meal, is okay. But the main course has to be ecstasy!

Now that I realize precocity, and perhaps even talent, come from trauma, I'll have to admit that, painful as it often is, I like my trauma. I'm drawn to it, attracted to it. Perhaps I even love it! It is the source of my stimulation, joys, and sorrows. It shoots me into the ecstasy firmament but also dumps me into the fires of hell. So be it. Like Columbus, I'd rather explore; I'd rather discover unknown lands beyond the status quo than live out my days in the dull and deadening "realities" of mundane existence.

I love trauma! I hate it, too. But, at least its extremes of hot and cold keep me out of the graveyard.

> THE PRIVILEGE OF BURNING
> Fires need wood
> It rise to the sky
> It is also extinguished.
> Life is like fire
> If you live in flames
> And your breath is fire
> Ecstasy and pain are small prices to pay
> For the privilege of burning.

Weight Training

What is weight training?
It is to walk on, appreciating the beauty and exhilaration even

while carrying the heavy, painful burdens (of life) on your back.

If Beauty is Truth, are sadness, anger, frustration, and depression lies?

Don't postpone the permanent state of spiritual bliss.
Start it today!

The Sieve

When reading try not to remember what you've read. Rather, let the beauty of the words, their sound and style, simply flow through you. Remembering happens naturally; you don't have to work at it. Whatever is important will settle by itself and of its own accord into the pool of your unconscious.

This is called "getting the knack of hopelessness. It accepts impermanence and change by letting the higher forces do all the "work."as I let the God within do all the "work." One simply relaxes and become a vehicle. Unconscious acts like a sieve, catching all the necessary words, juicy phrases, and startling ideas.

"Hard" Is Fun!

"Fun" echoes through eternity.
The laughing Buddha
The laughing hyena of Malta
Chuckling Jesus
The dancing rabbi
Silly Moses. There he is, sitting on the ground playing with the children. He's making funny faces as he counts "One, two, three, four, five, six, seven, eight, nine. . . ten commandments."

Bodhisattva

I go to heaven every morning. In the evening, I return. Then I visit others with my gifts.

After transcending, the Bodhisattva returns to take others back to heaven with him.

Bodhisattva is my route. After transcending, I return to bring others the fruits of heaven through dance, guitar, song, the printed word, and my own "presence."

Is this hubris? Probably not. What other way is there to go? Evidently, Bodhisattva, not solo monk, is the going-public route for me.

My vehicle is through art forms and my presence.
In the morning I visit heaven.
In the evening, I return.
I distribute gifts to the denizens of the earth.

I used to think that once my trials and tribulations were over, once I had been through therapy, conquered all my fears and worries, and finally put my life together, that I would return, cured and perfected, to my former life. How scary to realize then, that I am not returning. That I will never return. That I cannot return even if I tried!

How scary to think and even realize that the old life is over—irrevocably.

I won't be "working" in the old way; I won't be doing yoga, playing guitar, running, writing, or studying in the old way; I won't be doing my miracle schedule in the old way; I won't be running my tours in the old way; I won't even be running my weekends and dance classes in the old way.

Nothing of the old way will remain except a few haunting returns and a memory.

What forward and the future will be, I do not know. But there is no going back. The gates are shut and shutting. Only a wisp of smoke remains.

THE LAND OF APPRECIATION
But now I have crossed the border
And entered the Land of Appreciation.
I am taking my first baby steps.
I see a vast, sixty-one year old landscape:
I see the child playing at the fountain
I see the high school violin
And the junior college year voyage to France

And women, women, women—they were called girls
And Greenwich Village travels through the arts
And the bumpy ride of marriage, family, concerts, and money worries.
Then came the present.
It started twenty years ago
With a folk dance step, weekends, tours. . . all accompanied by writing.
Of the present I cannot say
Too close.
But in it I have created the tools
To knock down the walls of anger and fear
And build the protoplasm and muscle structure of new legs
On which to walk, gratefully and slowly into
The Land of Appreciation.

"Trapped" in the Terrestrial

Practice the art of appreciation.

See radiance in the concrete.

See the power—a reflection of the Divine Power, implanted, stuck, and drilled into concrete me.

The transcendence is fastened, nailed, tied down, injected into me. It is me. I cannot escape.

Why would I want to?

I am locked in a box of power. My power. It is concrete and down to earth.

Is that why I feel tight and claustrophobic? Glad to be trapped—I think. But trapped, locked in, nevertheless.

Locked in the power of appreciation. Stuck in the box of concrete wonder.

How can one dream in a box?

How can one fly in concrete?

Perhaps that is the reason for my claustrophobia. My transcendence has been brought down to earth, riveted in the concrete and material world.

I fear I may be trading my dreams, visions, and flights of fantasy for this new power of appreciation. These flights took place in my room, the studio of my mind. How can I fly, imagine, or have spiritual and transcendent visions when I am anchored in the concrete, anchored in appreciation of my power? It feels so worldly, so planted in solid soil.

Am I not trapped in the terrestrial?

I think not. Rather, it feels like an expansion of the transcendent, a visitation of power, a direct planting of radiance into the soul of my earthly existence.

It is here for good.

I have climbed another rung of Jacob's ladder.

Get used to it.

Self-Appreciation? Fuck It!

I'm afraid of my power. Always have been. I'm afraid of my radiance. Always have been.

Interesting, eh? There is a reason for my fear, a good reason. God's power is great. His radiance, implanted in my soul, has the power to destroy me. Careful, careful. Kundalini rising is beautiful but, when misused, can obliterate cities, countries, and universes as well.

What does all this mean?

A step into the New Land of Appreciation is not as easy as it looks. Not everyone wants to live there even though they might say they do. Too scary. What if you actually saw the world in all its magnificent, radiance, and glory. You probably couldn't take it. Too much. It would destroy every preconceived notion, every vested attitude of misery and hopelessness. Who can stand such a change? Better to retreat into lesser modes of anxiety, depression, or vague worries about the future. The walls you create will protect you from that grand vision of glory, majesty, and magnificence of the radiance within.

This power within can burn away cancer cells. But it burns away brain cells as well, those cells of limited vision which see only inches in front of you. Limitless vision is just too scary for most. This includes me. Oh sure, I dream, think, and wish for such an apocalyptic vision. But when it comes, oh boy, watch out! Too much! I'll take a glimpse, a whiff of infinity. But please leave me out of a permanent long-term vision. How could I continue my small life with it? How could I worry about bank accounts, relationships, marriage, love life, hate life, death life, or life? How could I focus on my miseries which give my mind something do by filling up the empty moments passing through my head? Who wants those vacuums to be filled with radiance or glory? Not I. Hell, no! Give me Pathmark, ice cream, food supplements, bone damage, falling stocks, or warts on my hands.

I'll do almost anything to limit my vision.

Don't tell me people want to be happy. They just say that to make conversation. Of course, some of them might even believe it until the possibility emerges right in front of their face. Then they run like crazy into the wilderness, inventing clumps of sickness, planting forests of new diseases, overturning dirt piles covers with leaches, or sawing down trees of ancient dreams and turning them into stumps. Anything, I'll do anything to get rid of it! Take away this fucking radiance! I can't stand it! Get rid of it. What do you call him, anyway? God, Radiance, Power, Divine, Pipsqueak, Buddha, Chin-Chang, Kung Fu, Chi Kong, Henry, or Gladys? Well, whatever you call him just kick him out the door. I want to keep my mind small. I want to stay in a limited world. I'm safe within the walls of my fears and worries. My shouts of anger and rage at the ants crawling through my basement energize me.

Sure I feel claustrophobic with this radiance, power, and self-appreciation shit coming down on me. Who needs it? I enjoy hating myself. I enjoy hating others. Don't take these small pleasures away.

Loss of Motivation

Maybe it's just plain boring to sit around all day and appreciate myself. After all, once you see you own power and appreciate your past, present, and future self, then, well, what else is new?

Perhaps I'm looking for a new way to go back to work. A new attitude, and new approach, even a new reason. Anger and fear just won't work anymore. But what else do I know? What other sources of motivation am I familiar with? None I can think of for the moment.

PERFORMANCE

The route home is through my songs.

Last night's concert on the GROW Weekend simply proved it again.

Patricio on the violin, Marvin on the mandolin, George singing Cucurucucu with me, I with my guitar, gaida, and improvised coordinations. What a serendipity! Born from nothing, created out of nothing, the program rose to one of our great evenings of discovery and enchantment.

I won't describe it anymore. Too early for that. Let me simply say that my route home is through my songs. Songs give me the chance to stand in front of my audience and improvise. Sure enough, in the middle of the program, Phil asked me to play "something serious." I played Serenade my Malats. I played it beautifully, slowly, and well. Everybody loved it. It was probably just enough for that kind of evening although I can see in future evenings I could play a few more classical pieces. But the timing was in the middle. I was loose, warmed-up, and the audience was totally won over and with me.

I could also have said that our songs were also serious: seriously funny songs. Of course, I knew what Phil meant so I didn't have to answer him directly. Still, it is good to remember that all my songs are "serious," even the ones that are "seriously funny."

The route home is through my songs. It is my "public form" of journal writing. As I stand on stage before my audience, I talk to them just like I talk to my journal. I improvise and create my New Leaf program on the spot. Through mouth, tongue, throat, fingers, stomach, hands, liver, kidney, fingers, heart, soul, and other unseen inner organs. I create the universe on the spot.

Perhaps I have reached a juncture. I have taken a giant leap forward; I am jumping into the public arena with my full brain.

I Need an Audience

I need an audience.
Simple as that.
But now I recognize it on the deepest of levels.
That's what the Grow Weekend told me.

I need an audience for my songs, guitar, writing, improvisation, weekends, tours, and folk dance classes.

That is why without an audience I feel incomplete.

I am part monk, part audience-needer, part hermit, part cenobite, part soloist alone in my mind creating, part audience-needer.

I need both.

I always have.

Both make one.

So it is in relationships too. A relationship is an audience of one.

The audience is the other.

There are two of us

I and the other

Both of us together

Equal one.

My need-for-an-audience revelation puts everything I do in a new light.

It shows why I must publish. It shows why I must give concerts, reach out for customers, run weekends, and give folk dance classes; it shows why I must have people who understand and are in my corner; it shows why I must have friends who appreciate me.

The depth of this audience-need will change my direction. It is the ultimate shock wave from my Grow Weekend. The walls broke with the realization that I will start my concerts with songs.

Guitar

I could never have made these guitar playing discoveries—stomach tightening during shoulder relaxation, index finger, shoulder: how my muscles work with my mind—except by going deep, deep, deep within myself.

To my knowledge, no one knows about these guitar "techniques." Perhaps others have discovered this about themselves, perhaps not. I don't know. I've never read about them or heard about them from teachers.

To my knowledge, they are my own unique discoveries about myself.

These discoveries might all be brand new in the world of guitar.

The Columbus of Guitar

What does this new knowledge of my guitar self do for me?

It moves me from, "What's wrong with me? How come it takes me so many years to learn to play the fucking guitar?" to "Wow! What a discovery I have made! I'm like Columbus. I've found a new land!"

BUSINESS

Ad Agency

1. Write my own ads. My kind of ads. Crazy ads. Wild, wooly, and enthusiastic ads a la Smorgasbord.

2. Something new: start an ad agency! My own ad agency for my own stuff.

The primary purpose of this agency would be to express myself in public. It's secondary purpose would be to sell things. Imagine that, an ad agency whose secondary purpose is to sell things! But of course and why not? Sales are secondary. The have to be. Primary has to be self-expression. A further expansion and growth. An expression of the "results" of psychotherapy. A going public.

An ad agency. An Ad Agency in capital letters is the ultimate expression of going public through business.

What are the pluses of this approach?

1. First, ads and its hand-maiden, public relations, are something I've always hated with a passion. That means I have a passion for it. True, it is a passion expressed in hate. But nevertheless, the key word here is passion.

Passionate hatred means I have a tremendous attraction to the hated object. Such hatred, such attraction, can "easily" turn into love—passionate loved! (I once hated the stock market and look how I fell in love with it.)

2. Maybe I can start by using my writing and artistic skills to create my own brochures. Rather than hire Barbara, use her as a consultant, teacher, guide, and helper.

For this I have to learn more computer skills, more graphic, click art and etc. skills. I may even learn how to create my own web pages but that is far down the line.

3. Create wild and wooly ads with click art, graphics, writing, and computer skills.

On Becoming a Walking Ad Agency

This Ad Agency approach would also be expressed in my concert and folk dance bookings. These programs are sales programs; my appearances help promote my events.

I will, and should, become, a walking Ad Agency. It means going public in a larger way.

Loss of Motivation Continued

The idea of living without anger or fear has really got me down. It has totally sapped my motivation. Why bother doing anything if I'm not angry or afraid? Without these primary motivating factors, I cannot think of one reason.

Now, what do I mean by "anything?"

"Anything" here means anything to do with work. And what is work within this definition? Work for money. In other words, without anger or fear to motivate me, I see no longer see any reason to do forced labor. And forced labor is always based on fears of penury and humiliation. How penury? If I don't push my tours, weekends, and dance classes, people will soon stop coming. Without people paying, my finances will go down. Soon I'll have no more money, and, as a flat broke rebornee, I'll be out on the street looking in garbage cans for food and sleeping in alleys. And this without my guitar or computer to keep me warm.

But, suppose I didn't have to worry about money? Or suppose, I developed a minimalist life style where I could live off my "ha" savings. In other words, the question arises, what would I do in a life lived without anger or fear? This is precisely my question now.

What would I do? Probably exactly what I'm doing now. Almost. There would be some adjustments. I would have to cut back on tours. Why? First, no one is registering for the ones I have.

Aha, it's coming into focus. Depressed? Where have I heard that word before? It's somewhat easy to see why. The phone hasn't rung for over a month. I have almost zero interest or registration for my wonderful upcoming tours and New Year's Weekend. Business is totally dead. Every day the mailman brings only junk mail. No registration checks of love in the mail. I have been totally forgotten. And every day it seems to be getting deader.

Now I have been through the lows of these business cycles countless times. And each time it makes me feel as miserable and depressed as it does now.

Can this be changed? Am I fooling myself by saying the walls of anger have broken down? Maybe I'm still just as angry. But rather than turning my anger against women, I am now angry because no one is registering. Rejection and abandonment have reared their ugly heads again. Only this time it is business abandonment rather than woman abandonment.

But I am so sick of going through these cycles. Isn't there another way? Why can't I accept the downs and simply move on?

Well, if I ever expect to, I must first recognize that I am down, that I am down because I am mad, and I am mad because my fucking clients are not romancing me, not registering for my events, not sending me love checks in the mail.

How can I stay in business if I have no business?

Maybe I should not stay in business. Maybe I should give it all up, teach only folk dancing, and spend the rest of my time peacefully writing, reading, playing guitar, studying, doing yoga, and running. That in itself would be a wonderful life. Why must I burden myself with business? Why not cut all things back to a minimum so my mind is free to pursue the wonders on my miracle schedule. Yes, I have gone through the ups and downs of these business cycles countless times before. Only this time I'd like something to be different. I'd like to come out of this with a new attitude, and even a new life style.

Is there any way to escape from the return of these kinds of business worries? Do they naturally come with the territory? Must I give up business in order not to worry about business? Or must I give up worry in order not to worry?

I cannot change the fact that I am moving into the Land of

Appreciation. I cannot change the fact that the walls of anger and fear have crumbled. Nor would I want to. But I don't yet know how to live in this new place. Right now I'm walking on the beaches of quicksand, sinking into the quagmires of life in a strange country.

New Markets

Perhaps for the new life beyond the walls of anger and fear in the New Land of Appreciation I need to find a new market for my events.

Perhaps that is the direction of my search. I have gone public; I am in the new neighborhood of the new land; the old walls of anger and fear have fallen. How do I approach my new public in my new land? Well, first I have to find a new public; I have to find new markets.

INVENTIONS

Turnip O Toole Visits the Singing Tree

Rumblers crit by the wayside at Mama's Burn and Steam restaurant. Never have so many cyclic marmades or tewesbury critics turned sour.

Turnip O'Toole, the friendly slave, cannot believe what he's thinking: freedom might be a relief! Imagine saying that! O'Toole, who is prisoner of Penelope, prisoner of Great Dungeon of Doolittle, and former prisoner of Black Castle where forest cakes plummet from the sky, batting errant eyelids on the firmhead while circumventing proper burial rites for paupers, pawn brokers, and purveyors of delicatessen foods.

Freedom? O'Toole can't believe it. Instead of one marriage how about fourteen? Instead of one wife, how about twenty-three in succession. Simultaneous wifehood would be too much. Besides, O'Toole hates verticals. Horizontal matches his form slave style; he likes one-at-a-time freedoms cascading down his delicious lined throat.

But it is the freedom he most relishes, diving into life again, whole, and vivacious, and sound, with mind and body boiling up totally crazy juices! He feels reborn. Did he ever die? Was that trip to the dungeon with its silver and gold chains really a tour of hell? Or was it merely a backward look at heaven from the eye of a pig's ass? Hard to say.

In any case, O'Toole off to flying school again. Ripe cucumbers hang from the ceiling; carcases of cactuses gone to lunch no longer prick his style with the needle-warts of former days. Tree tops are singing. Stop them, ha! Not one policeman is in sight.

Singing trees are such nuisances in the old neighborhood. So are smiling leaves, gargling branches, and laughing twigs. But for the new neighborhood, they are joy incarnate!

Spontaneous Combustion Is Best

Suddenly, I know why I was panicked about dying before fulfilling my tasks on earth; why I was feeling down, claustrophobic, angry, inhibited, and stuck. When Clayton said—or he imply?—best to stay silent when Martha (change names, etc!!!!!!!!) is talking. Try to "hear" her experience; don't interrupt with your own, etc. I agreed that this was a good idea and that I would try it. But at that moment, running wild was temporarily struck down. Upon further reflection, although abstractly remaining silent might be a good idea for someone else, for me it is absolutely terrible. What kind of relationship is it if I can't say what I want when I want to? Who needs it? Just because Bernice is going to blow up and act crazy over what I have to say is no reason to shut up. Why should I inhibit the birth and expression of my best ideas simply to "understand, be sympathetic with, relate to, appreciate, and even love her experience?" Forget it. Fuck her experience! What about my experience? If she says something asinine, lacking, or even if she says something brilliant, why shouldn't I have the right, even duty, to interrupt her right in the middle of her sentence and say what I want? Sure, it's impolite and inconsiderate. Sure, she'll probably blow her top. But so what? The other way is to hold back, give up spontaneity, and say nothing. Even worse is to wait patiently and reasonably until she is through speaking, then, in measured and controlled fashion, say what I think. If I wait like that, not only will the bite and spark disappear from my words, but worse, I'll probably forget what I wanted to say in the first place. Seize the moment! Say what you have to say when you have to say it! Damn the consequences! Restraint may not be considered the "best, most reasonable, and considerate" way to go in polite society. But it certainly is the way I am going to go. My marriage is not hardly a polite society, anyway, and it most certainly is not reasonable and considerate.

Let others keep quite. But, as for me, I've kept quiet for too long. Been there, done that. It's time for some noise. If she's too weak, broken-hearted, sick, or is too much of a victim to take it, let her learn repentance, diligence, and restraint.

Here's a perfect example of how right I am. I couldn't think of the word "restraint." I stopped writing. I consciously tried to remember it. Nothing happened. Then, I decided to write down whatever comes to mind. I wrote "repentance, diligence." Suddenly, "restraint," the word I wanted, popped into my head.

Spontaneous combustion is best. Mine is the spontaneous instantaneous approach. Hopefully, my approach will be best for others, too. And I think, in the long run—even the short run, it is. Bernice may benefit from my ideas even though she hates hearing them. If she doesn't, at least I will. That makes one of us happy. (It's better than none.) Forcing myself to remain silent will only make me angry. In the long run, in some subtle or unsubtle fashion, I'll take it out on Bernice. Then no one will be happy.

Simply because spontaneous combustion sometimes causes immediate pain does not mean, it is not the best way to go. Who cares about pain, anyway? We give it too much credence and attention. Perhaps we should thank it instead of trying to avoid it. Pain is a pathway to knowledge, and a very quick one at that!

Selling out in A Flat

Ugh, I feel beaten down. I've sold out. I'm walking around sick with worms of nausea and self-loathing drilling into my back. Where is this coming from? What supine and gallant monsters swim through the Rhine River, carrying sausages and German hams at break neck speed, routing their rotting lumps of turnip stumps through backward Lithuanian mask tools and awkward Pripet Marsh plumping gear south of Minsk?

Sausages are coming! They carry plumes of partridge cheese and Feta feathers on their backs. Sold out? Indeed, I've pricked my side with pickled pomegranates while pins of steel mold my iron boots.

Give up anger? Let the walls fall? If I do, who will protect me? Who will man the furnaces of boiling bile? Who will drink the putrescent juices whose steel pins prick and percolate the bunions of latent homosexuals, homosevenuals, and even homoeightuals? Instead, why not let languages limp their egos in your hands.

Flowing biosphere with its ionic contabulants is here again. God bless bottom kissing! It grows beneath the tulip trees! Let the ants crawl! Let them imbibe their formitic doctrines. Can there ever be a better diet for vegetable eaters?

I'm closer to home again. Nevertheless, selling out shows its white-washed, haunted, disgusting face. I still see glimpses of the wimp-steel rod on the horizon, sad and lonely, lifting pills of Putroloath.

The Wind and the King

Once upon a time a beautiful Wind came to visit a castle.

The King came out to meet the Wind.

He loved her.

"Join me," said the Wind. "We can play and explore the wild universe together."

"Ah, I would love that," said the King. "But I live in a castle. What will happen to my subjects? Can they live without a king? Can I live without them?"

The Wind remained silent as she pondered.

Then the King asked, "Can't we build a new castle somewhere in the universe for my kingdom and you?"

Drivel in Morning Swisschard Form

Sam Snodgrass sat in his GROW hotel room ready, willing, and able to die for an idea. Truly, he was bursting at the seams. He didn't know what to do with his mind's energy. Something off-the-wall and crazy seemed about to happen, but he didn't know what.

In terms of social relations, his head met his shoulders just below the waist. Later his legs swivelled in their chairs, bursting each leg irons at each squall and caterwaul. Was it too much coffee, or lack of exercise? Was it a lark-like subspecies of subterranean scum sneaking up on him, getting ready to pounce on his gyroballs, rip his onions to shreds, shake up his carbuncles, and generally tank the molasses soft parts of his syrupy brain? Would such swirling maple-tree energy turn his syrup substance wash-mind machine into a hum dinger scrub-a-dub dub to perfume and perforate the rusty corners of his horn-fried mind?

Hard to say. What was going on? Who could know but a lamb basted in stew. But, no doubt about it, goings on were certainly going on!

As a cat screeched in his inner sanctum a great strawberry of herculean muscle-fruit power, proportioned with breasts of cantaloupe/banana size, saddled up to his attendant liver, patting his lactate patch just beneath his stomach enzyme. Soon a frittled lunch of baked herring fried its marmalade, the very Mama hen eggs which Marma laid.

Onions circled his world. What could the poor herring do? Not a thing, especially on an empty stomach.

"But I just feel so good!" yelped Mattie. "Sure I look down in the dumps; sure my appendices are waddling out of my mouth every time I throw up; sure I look like a mop about to flop as I sit in the corner chewing my tongue, spitting out cod fish, and basting my ovarian tubes in cod liver oil. Indeed they fetch a tidy sum of oil-and-gold money from the potty-and-potash chair mine; and this even though aluminum prices are going down and I can't take a good shit worth beans. Nevertheless, do not let my looks fool you. The inner dog is in fine shape. I'm just preparing myself for human status with humanungus heaps of barnaberries dressing in sugar, cream, molasses, herring bones, and tidy break-gas burst-water pine tree engines gurgling before they supine.

Such Joycean phrenologies cannot be but not wrong. But, as sad drench-o-tear coughs its lachrymose way up from behind the pillow case, Sam asks: can the licking from a dog's tongue really serve as a coffee substitute?

Burn and Sizzle

Turnip Strawberry, Dean of Lumbar Region, wouldn't take it any longer. "Burn, sizzle, and crash the old forms!" he shouted lancing his caterpillar thighs with deep spaghetti regrets. "The horn-ribbed cathedrals whose ceilings are spread apart with bridal gowns, can spire no more. Nor can they conspire or inspire. Down with medieval turnip-twisters! A pox on all your tulips! Never more will we cement dandelions to daisies nor glue pristine pine barrens to South Jersey coal mines!"

Turnip fumed in his labrador stew. His wind was up; so were his sails. Why should he consider organizing and running such a Yodeling Tour Of Switzerland? Did he want to hear mountains sing or brooks trickle into mouth-watering orgasms? Did he want to hear the whispering sound of suckling pigs sucking their sucker titted Ma, who, sequined in her white-water graduation gown was ready to dance at the First Pig Prom of '98?

Indeed, borders were turning into dust, and brains swelled at every guard rail. Not a free fall could be found, nor could he see a cloud lined between the mountains. Was an abyss sighted from the prow of his whale ship? Hard to say.

"Expect Nothing, Get Everything"

The winter king walks in bitter pursuit. Behind his tasseled earring sits a lump of lumpen proletariat, a sweet song dedicated to truth.

The upside of down markets can't be far from wrong. As the price of gold rises so do the spirits of John Turnbull, famous bull market stock speculator. Indeed, Turnbull is a man who ;earned how to turn his base longings into gold. A true alchemist. Starting off only with only a dried up, old, three-inch chunk of manure, he discovered, over a period of only two years, how to create a financial and philosophical profit both excrementally and incrementally.

How did he do it? How did a mere stalk of a man, a creature so low on the human totem heap, so deep-throated, dentalized, and diminished by his panicked fall into the abyss of time's unmanly warp, turn the basest of fertilizers into a pure gold?

And he did it all without seeds.

Indeed, this was a true planting of the metaphysical variety.

In Turnbull's biography, Life Among The Cows, Angus Bovine Huxley explains: "Turnbull's uncanny ability to fertilize vast arenas of nothingness, plant seeds in the Void, and to fill volumes of space with even more space, has placed him among the top fertilizer and stock market analysts. In the process, he has become one of the richest men in the world. His motto: "turn nothing into more nothing," has caught on throughout, not only the financial world, but the moral global market as well. Youth on planets, asteroids, and galaxies are forming John Turnbull Investment Clubs. One such club, the "Club V", located in Haircunt County on the asteroid Venus-Upon-Venal, is making quite a financial killing by selling space in vacant entrances. They plan to expand their operations to large intestines and have even opened up a branch to investigate futures in the esophagus market.

Turnbull, every moving forward, has other plans as well. He says, with full Turnbull confidence, if I can turn nothing into more nothing I believe that, as my skills develop, I will one day be able to turn something into something else. Eventually, with enough capital, time, and investment savvy, I'll be able to turn nothing into something! Thus, a zero investment would yield vast sums. Asking nothing of others would yield an incredible return. This is investment at its best!"

Turnbull's new philosophy, "Expect nothing; get everything." is now plastered on every John Turnbull Investment Club.

The second century Greek philosopher, Diogenes Egocentric asked: "What is the most difficult thing in the world?"

He answered: "To be your true self."

Then he asked: "What is even more difficult than that?"

He answered: "To be your true self in front of others."

Spinoza Never Ate Turkey

Bumping past the bambling route. Psychophants and sycophants of blabbering brook rambling no longer work here.

But is that a reason to give up snookers? Not at all. Even better, now is the time to rise up, grab the horn by the bit, twist the screw in every orange juice, and shake the rafters. Finally, an ubiquitous, uxorial kneeling program can be put in place. It is time to wrest the torn cartilage from the knee cap.

What is marriage but a knee cap gone to seed? Some call it a field lost in solitude where a plenitude of beer cans wrestle to pile up their seminal juices in broken pipes and battered houses with battened-down roof tops.

Can the flow ever be stopped? Why would a can opener opt for such wizened vicissitudes and broken Dutch dreams? Did Spinoza every stick his thumb in such a dam? Did he ever write and amplitude about such broken dikes and fingered lesbians?

I shall not question such pipple squeaks. Nor is it my job to grab the remnants of shardhood from an ample nightmare of horses riding through the mist.

Can you see the sun through the fog? Can you see the dark beer can riding on a cloud of hope? Can you see the lone star sitting on a pole, eating a turkey sandwich, and hoping to catch the next sun to Mars?

Vegetarians say Spinoza never ate turkey. Is this true? We'll see when I go down to breakfast.

A Rowing Session with Crayton

or Marriage Therapy In Sub-Cellular Form

Hey, what kind of gunkatio is this? I've got to swell my whoopie bits, swallow my lumps of wolverine prepocity as lacework gratuities disappear from my roof? Not on your life. Is such a shut-down prison marriage with carriage and mirage on the side worth fighting for? Not on your bacon bits! If I must close my prison sewer to leave startling cliff hangers dwelling in the bosom depths of my bowel movements, let vapid sewers flow by without a word, shut my pipes to let such a stuffed steamed clam open up, I must ask: is such a relation-ship worth saving? Or any ship, for that matter. Is "Clam up to save up!" a viable motto for a full-blooded Navahojunk schooner ship sailing the Black Sea coast in a paddy wagon? Not on your two-bit life!

But Master White Hair gave the word. Without one rabbit foot in his mouth, he told me to kick the talking habit. In its place, foster the listening one. I nodded in knowing fashion, politely bowing to superior $100-an-hour wisdom. But later, when I left the stinking

Manhattan piss-pot chamber, dragging my limp, wisp-of-the-willow, weak-kneed, limp wristed, whiff of a willow wyfe into the street, I realized, Master White Hair, rather than delivering a gem of forest wisdom to my doorstep may well have dumped a load of shit on my house instead.

Shut up? Me? Why? Simply to keep the peace and be understood? Simply to foaster, foist, and foster a re-lat-ion-ship that is worth piddledy peets on the marriage stock exchange? Talk about stocks going down! Talk about the penny market crashing, bears clawing high-priced trees, pruning tails ripe for picking whose do-little nobodies stream their panties with wet-warm noodle pudding! Shut up! Me? Not a good recipe for pound cake on Mount Relationship.

But hey, what the fuck, is it worth a try? If I don't take it too seriously, of course. Step on a twig and the forest will break, blow on a cinder and the woods will burn. It's true. But why tolerate it just because it's true? I thrive on illusion and falsehood. So-called truth, especially in lower shutting up form simply destroys my membranes. I can't stomach, fathom, or foam it. But I can certainly belly ache and put my diaphragm points up in the locker room.

But I feel it coming. In a few moments I m sure to piss on sanctity.

Will My Limousine Ever Arrive?

Wienerschnitzels have fled.
Carcass green is my color this morning.
Open up the berry and the ripe bottom falls out.
Discouraged and down, tight and angry, will my limousine ever arrive?
Certainly, perking carrot sticks perambulating carcoid waters cannot crack a dank-stick worth a dam.
Chilly here in dawn's inner sanctum. Tongues lolling, eyeballs twisting as the carpets roll green again. Is it vomit? Or the results of yesterday's Chinese stew? Can a stink, bred from a tight-assed group of psychotic carrot sticks ever turn a monk into an elephant, a tuber into a peapod, or a stinkoid into a rose? Can the smell of therapeutic oil and kerosene ever rattle Klein's bargain basement or scoop handfuls of Great Macys underwear off rag-picked shelves and turn them

into shipping clerks?

The micro king rises. Piddle steps mark his path. Klein-moving in such a manner can he ever reach heaven?

GOD

Is being abandoned by a woman the same as being abandoned by God?

Does it feel the same?

Can God actually abandon a man or woman?

Sure, He threw Adam and Eve out of the Garden of Eden. Why? Because they broke the rules.

Does God really reject those who break His rules? Does He actually abandon them?

Or, is it we who do the rejecting? Are we the ones abandoning God?

God has given man has free choice. Superficially, it appears that He expelled Adam and Even from the Garden of Eden; the surface reasons seem to be because they broke His rules. But suppose it was simply a case of Adam and Eve not wanting to take responsibility for their decision? Suppose they did not want to face the terrors of their own freedom? Suppose, instead of accepting responsibility, they decided to blame it all on God?

"He did it! He threw us out! We're just innocent victims. Oh sure, we decided to eat an apple. Hey, big deal. Why make such a fuss. Just because He said don't do it. Who's He, anyway? We'll do what we want! No one can push us around! If we want to eat apples, we'll eat apples. If we want to talk to serpents, we'll talk to serpents! We're in charge of our lives. We're free to decide. Whatever happens happens. Damn the consequences!"

Now that would be Adam and Eve taking responsibility. However, as biblical cowards, they decided to blame it all on God.

Now, back to our original question: Can God really abandon and reject man?

On the deepest level, it is impossible. Not only is God omnipotent, he is also omnipresent. That means He is everywhere, in everything and everyone. How can He go away? How can He reject anyone or anything when He is their very essence? He would be, in effect, rejecting Himself. True, God, being omnipotent, has the power even to reject Himself. But why would He do such a thing? To eat Chinese food?

God's rejection and abandonment of man is an impossibility. Only man can reject God. And he sure does, often with a vengeance. But that is his choice. It's part of the learning process, part of lifting the veil, part of the road past illusion and into oneness.

On Hating the Mosaic Law

Why do I hate the Mosaic Law so much?

Because "someone" from the outside is telling me what to do. "Someone" is demanding that I perform in a certain way. I am not consulted or even considered.

The entire Mosaic Law seems to come from the outside.

But suppose it came from the inside. Suppose these God-given Laws were made up by me instead of a so-called outside force that Moses named God.

If God is within, why shouldn't these Laws be within, too?

In other words, why shouldn't these Laws be my Laws?

I do make laws. My miracle schedule has its own laws. I follow its "rules." They come from the God within.

I suppose it is the arrogance of the Mosaic Laws that bother me too much. There is the presumption: "they" know God; "they" know what He wants; "they" are the arbiters of His rule; "they" say, you'd better do what He wants or else!

Well, who are "they" to tell me what to do? What presumption! What arrogance! Fuck them! I'll make up my own rules, my own Laws; I'll follow my own advice, consult with my own God. Our conferences within the walls of my brain will yield the appropriate rules, regulations, and Laws to guide my life. I don't want "their" rules. I thoroughly resent "they" and "them" trying to impose their so-called God invented rules on me.

Who are "they" to speak in God's name, anyway?

I'll discover my own God. I'll speak to Him directly and find out what He wants from me. I don't need Mosaic Laws to tell me what to do. However, they are good to consider as I discover my own.

First, recognize my hatred of these so-called Laws imposed on my from the outside.

We'll see where this leads.

Judaism

Since all is within, why not assume that the Mosaic Laws, the Torah, etc. are within, too. They are my vision.

According to Judaism, man is made in God's image.

Thus killing a man is an offense against God.

But the very notion that God can be offended is absurd.

Such "personalizing" of God is a Jewish contribution to enforce its ethics. Not a bad thing; the ethics are good. But, as far as using God to enforce them, absurd.

God creates man and the free theater in which he operates. Then He sits back and enjoys the show.

The Ten Commandments are Moses' invention. He credited them to God. He was partly right. All creation comes from God, including the Aserot Hadibrot. But they were filtered through the mind of Moses. Moses gets the credit. So does God. They were a team.

And, even if they don't realize it, everyone else in the world is on the same team.

The Mosaic Laws are excellent laws of human relationships. But, like all things, they are created by God through man. Sure, God gets credit for them. But He gets credit for everything else, too.

Moses is thus the prime human creative force behind Judaism, with Abraham as a distant foundation somewhere in the background.

It's not called the Book of Moses for nothing.

Moses is the supreme artist. There is artistry in his Laws. They are his instruments and the instruments through which the Jewish people, his orchestra, play Hebrew tunes. He created them; but they are instruments of God.

Moses is the Vladimir Horowitz of the Law. The artist, Horowitz, created and followed the laws of music. The artist, Moses, created and followed the laws of relationships.

Seeing Moses as an artist puts me right on top of him.

www.ingramcontent.com/pod-product-compliance
Lightning Source LLC
Chambersburg PA
CBHW060500090426
42735CB00011B/2052